Binary Arithmetic and Boolean Algebra

Angelo C. Gillie *Professor of Electrical Technology
and Chairman, Division of Career Programs
Niagara County Community College
New York*

McGRAW-HILL BOOK COMPANY

New York
St. Louis
San Francisco
London
Toronto
Sydney

Preface

This book is designed to provide a comprehensive treatment of computer arithmetic and Boolean algebra fundamentals. The material in this text has been taught to technical institute and community college students by the author over a period of several years. The text can be utilized in the training of computer personnel and technicians. It has been written for use in community and junior colleges, technical institutes, military service schools, and industrial in-plant training programs. The method of presentation enables the student to progress on his own with a minimum of supervision.

The material in this text falls within two broad categories. Chapters 1 to 4 are concerned with logic arithmetic and its relationships with the binary number system. The last seven chapters deal with Boolean algebra fundamentals and their applications to switching circuits. The basic concepts are developed in a manner that readily enables the student to apply them to any switching device. In this way, the material is just as valid for solid-state switches as it is for the electromechanical relay.

Chapter 1 presents a detailed analysis of the decimal and binary number systems. Included is the manner in which switches can represent numerical values in both these systems. Special emphasis is given to the conversion from one system to the other. Chapter 2 expands the study into an analysis of other number systems that have found use in modern computer work. Special coded binary systems in common use are also studied. Chapter 3 is devoted to the techniques for addition and sub-traction of binary numbers. Binary multiplication and division are developed in Chap. 4. Almost 600 problems are included in the first four chapters, thereby presenting the student with ample opportunity for practice in logic arithmetic.

Boolean algebra concepts are developed in Chap. 5. Chapter 6 shows the manner in which Venn diagrams and truth tables can be utilized in circuit simplification. The rules of duality and negation, and the manner in which they are used as circuit simplification tools, are examined in Chap. 6.

Chapter 7 presents an analysis of Boolean matrices. Their construction and applications in noncombinational switching circuits are developed with frequent use of illustrated examples. Karnaugh maps are studied in Chap. 8. The techniques for both read-in and read-out are carefully illustrated. Chapter 9 shows how Boolean algebra and Karnaugh maps can be utilized in designing switching circuits from an original set of statements. Illustrated examples are provided.

Circuit synthesis by several other methods are given consideration in Chaps. 10 and 11. Over 300 problems have been included in the last seven chapters. Answers to one-half of the more than 900 problems are provided in a separate answer booklet.

The author wishes to express his appreciation to the many people who have helped in the development of this text. Special thanks are extended to Chester A. Gehman and Forest C. Tyson, Jr., both of the Ward Technical Institute (a division of the University of Hartford), for their many suggestions and ideas. Special appreciation is owed to three students in the electrical technology program of the Niagara County Community College for the hours they spent in working out many of the problems in the text. They are R. Warren Marsh, John N. McLennan, and Kenneth C. Root.

Angelo C. Gillie

Contents

Chapter 1   **The Decimal and Binary Number Systems**   1

The Decimal System: Whole Quantities. The Decimal System: Fractional Quantities. The Decimal System: Combined Quantities. Representation of Decimal Numbers by Switches. The Binary System. Binary to Decimal Conversion by the Direct Method. Binary to Decimal Conversion by the Double-dabble Method. Conversion of Binary Fractions to Decimal Equivalents by the Vertical Column Method. Conversion of Decimal Integers to Binary by the Direct Method. Conversion of Decimal Integers to Binary by the Double-dabble Method. Conversion of Decimal Fractions to Binary Fractions.

Chapter 2   **Special Computer Number Systems and Codes**   16

The Trinary (Ternary) System. Conversion of Trinary Numbers into their Decimal and Binary Equivalents. Conversion of Binary and Decimal Numbers into their Trinary Equivalents. The Octal System: Conversion of Octal Integers to Decimal. Conversion of Decimal Integers to

Octal. Conversion of Fractions: Octal to Decimal. Conversions of Fractions: Decimal to Octal. Conversion of Binary to Octal. Conversion of Octal to Binary. The Binary-coded Decimal Notation System. The Excess-3 Code. The Reflected Binary (or Gray) Code. Conversion of Binary Numbers into the Gray Code. Conversion of Gray Code into Binary. The 7421 Code. The Biquinary Code.

Chapter 3   Binary Addition and Subtraction   33

Binary Addition: Integers. Binary Addition: Fractions. Binary Addition: Mixed Numbers. Direct Binary Subtraction: Integers. Direct Binary Subtraction: Fractions and Mixed Numbers. Decimal Subtraction by 10's Complement. Decimal Subtraction by 10's Complement with Negative Remainders. The 9's Complement. Decimal Subtraction by the 9's Complement. The 2's Complement of Binary Numbers. Binary Subtraction by the 2's Complement. The 1's Complement of Binary Numbers. Binary Subtraction by the 1's Complement.

Chapter 4   Binary Multiplication and Division
             and Binary Code Arithmetic   58

Binary Multiplication. Binary Division. Excess-3 Code Addition. Ternary Code Addition. Ternary Code Subtraction.

Chapter 5   Fundamental Topics of Boolean Algebra   70

Switching States and Notation. Circuit Representation by Switches. Series Circuit Relationships. Parallel Switch Circuit Relationships. Summary of Series and Parallel Logic. Series-parallel Circuits. The First Distributive Law. Application of the First Distributive Law. The Second Distributive Law. Application of the Second Distributive Law. The Use of Boolean Functions in Analyzing Switching Circuits. Logical Diagram Construction and Uses.

Chapter 6   Basic Switching Circuit
               Simplification Techniques   92

Venn Diagrams. The Universe Table. Truth Table Construction and Use. Criteria for Circuit Simplification. The Expanded Truth Table. The Concept of Duality. Circuit Simplification by the Double-dual Technique. Principles of Negation.

Chapter 7   Analysis and Simplification of
               Switching Circuits
               with Boolean Matrices   112

The Assignment of Node Numbers. The Closed-path Tracing Technique (Closure Analysis). The Wye-to-Delta Transformation Technique. The Use of Nodes in Matrix Construction. The Boolean Matrix Technique. Analysis of Multiterminal Circuits with Boolean Matrices.

Chapter 8   Analysis and Simplification of Switching
               Circuits with Karnaugh Maps   135

The Two-variable Karnaugh Map. Construction of Three-variable Karnaugh Maps. Construction of a Four-variable Karnaugh Map. The Five-variable Karnaugh Map. The Six-variable Karnaugh Map. Karnaugh Map Techniques for Series and Parallel Connections.

Chapter 9   Conversion of Original Circuit Requirements
               into a Simplified Switching Circuit   165

Phrasing the Logic into a Set of Statements and Assignment of Symbols. Determination of the Number of States. Specifications Analysis with an Input-Output Table. Construction of a Synthesis Map. Conversion of the Synthesis Map into the Boolean Function of the Final Circuit. Design of an Interlock System for a Power Supply. Design of the

Logic Circuit for an "In-line Numerical Read-out Display."
Design of a Switching Circuit by the Synthesis Map Technique. The Design of a Dispensing Machine.

Chapter 10   Circuit Synthesis by Use of Boolean Matrices
and Minimization of Switches   194

Circuit Design by Expansion of a Boolean Matrix. Spurious Terms. Minimization in Relay Circuits. Minimization of Diode Matrix Circuits. Minimization in Diode Circuits by the Logic Tree Technique.

Chapter 11   Circuit Synthesis by Use of Coding Systems
and the Odd Parity Check   208

Identification of Map Entries by Numbers. System States and State Diagrams. Determination of the Required Number of Controls. State Coding and Uses. Translation of a Coded State Diagram into Control Circuitry. The Gray Code and Uses for Control Circuit Design. The Odd Parity Check and Uses for Control Circuit Design.

Answers to Odd-numbered Problems   229

Index   245

CHAPTER 1

The Decimal and Binary
Number Systems

Introduction

The decimal number system is the common radix-10 number system used in everyday computation. Computer and logic circuits lend themselves more readily to a radix-2 (binary) number system. The reason for this lies in the simple fact that the switches used in logic and computer circuitry have two states or conditions, i.e., ON (1) and OFF (0).

The original information to be fed into the computer system is often in decimal notation. The first problem in many such cases is to convert these quantities into their binary equivalents. Several sections of this chapter are devoted to developing techniques for quick conversion of decimal into binary notation. The opposite problem may exist at the output of the computer. The computer output information is in binary notation, which in some cases must be translated into its decimal equivalent before it can be utilized. Techniques by which the binary-to-decimal conversion is accomplished are also developed here. For practice, a total of 60 problems have been interspersed throughout the chapter.

1·1 The Decimal System: Whole Quantities

The decimal number system is the most popular number system now in use. Therefore, it is the number system most readily understood by most people. The *radix* of the decimal system (the number of symbols used in the system) is 10. These symbols are:

$$0, 1, 2, 3, 4, 5, 6, 7, 8, 9$$

In order to permit the expression of more than 10 values in the decimal system, the concept of *positional* value has been introduced. The meaning of positional value is best analyzed with an example.

Example 1. Consider the quantity represented by 247:

$$247 = 2 \times 10^2 + 4 \times 10^1 + 7 \times 10^0$$

i.e.,

$$
\begin{array}{r}
2\,0\,0 \\
4\,0 \\
7 \\
\hline
2\,4\,7
\end{array}
$$

The first position to the left of the decimal point (occupied by the symbol 7 in the example) denotes the number of units or ones. The second position to the left of the decimal point (occupied by the symbol 4) denotes the number of tens. The third position to the left of the decimal point (occupied by the symbol 2) indicates the number of hundreds. Notice that in moving from the decimal point toward the left, each position is ten times greater than the position to its immdeiate right (7 ones, 4 tens, 2 hundreds, etc.).

The purpose of the symbol zero in the decimal system is to help designate positional value, as shown in the following example.

Example 2. Consider the quantity 2,470. Notice that the symbols 247 are used as in Example 1, except that each is moved one more place to the left. This results in a quantity ten times greater than that of Example 1, i.e.,

$$2{,}470 = 2 \times 10^3 + 4 \times 10^2 + 7 \times 10^1 + 0 \times 10^0$$

i.e.,

$$
\begin{array}{r}
2{,}0\,0\,0 \\
4\,0\,0 \\
7\,0 \\
0 \\
\hline
2{,}4\,7\,0
\end{array}
$$

Example 3. Consider the quantity 2,047. The same symbols used in Examples 1 and 2 (2, 4, and 7) are used again. Since the zero is in a different position, the quantity of the numerical expression is changed, i.e.,

$$2,047 = 2 \times 10^3 + 0 \times 10^2 + 4 \times 10^1 + 7 \times 10^0$$

and combining,

$$
\begin{array}{r}
2,0\,0\,0 \\
0\,0\,0 \\
4\,0 \\
7 \\
\hline
2,0\,4\,7
\end{array}
$$

Therefore it is seen that the positional values of the decimal symbols can be readily changed by use of the symbol zero.

1·2 The Decimal System: Fractional Quantities

Let us now consider the progression of positional values with quantities that are less than 1.

Example 1. Consider the quantity 0.247. Starting from the decimal point and decreasing by tenths, we obtain the following:

$$2 \times 10^{-1} + 4 \times 10^{-2} + 7 \times 10^{-3}$$

and combining,

$$
\begin{array}{r}
0.2\,0\,0 \\
0.0\,4\,0 \\
0.0\,0\,7 \\
\hline
0.2\,4\,7
\end{array}
$$

Therefore the positional values for fractional quantities in the decimal system decrease in steps of tenths.

1·3 The Decimal System: Combined Quantities

Figure 1·1 illustrates the positional values for the decimal numbering system for a combined quantity up to four places on both sides of the decimal point.

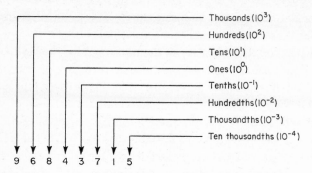

Fig. 1·1   Positional values of the decimal number system.

Expressing the quantity illustrated in Fig. 1·1, we obtain

$$9{,}684.3715 = 9 \times 10^3 + 6 \times 10^2 + 8 \times 10^1 + 4 \times 10^0 + 3 \times 10^{-1}$$
$$+ 7 \times 10^{-2} + 1 \times 10^{-3} + 5 \times 10^{-4}$$

which is

$$
\begin{array}{r}
9{,}0\,0\,0.0\,0\,0\,0 \\
6\,0\,0.0\,0\,0\,0 \\
8\,0.0\,0\,0\,0 \\
4.0\,0\,0\,0 \\
0.3\,0\,0\,0 \\
0.0\,7\,0\,0 \\
0.0\,0\,1\,0 \\
0.0\,0\,0\,5 \\
\hline
9{,}6\,8\,4.3\,7\,1\,5
\end{array}
$$

Notice the importance of zero in expressing this quantity. The entire quantity of a decimal number can be expressed by the following relationship:

$$K = (A^{10^0} + B^{10^1} + C^{10^2} + \cdots) + (a^{10^{-1}} + b^{10^{-2}} + c^{10^{-3}} + \cdots)$$

where A = symbol of units
$\quad\quad B$ = symbol of tens
$\quad\quad C$ = symbol of hundreds, etc.
$\quad\quad a$ = symbol of tenths
$\quad\quad b$ = symbol of hundredths
$\quad\quad c$ = symbol of thousandths, etc.
$\quad\quad K$ = total quantity

Note that the left bracket contains the whole quantities, and the right bracket the fractional quantities.

Using numerical quantities in computers. The decimal system is most widely used in nontechnical fields of endeavor but does not readily lend itself to computer operation. Since electronic computer circuits respond to the change from one condition to a second condition (such as zero volts and some predetermined magnitude of voltage), the ideal number system to use would be the one which has a base of 2. Restricting the states to two (instead of the ten symbols of the decimal system) is particularly useful in simplifying the required circuit, especially in terms of hardware. The binary (two-state number system) type of operation is easily represented in the current mode as well as by voltage. Furthermore, the binary conditions can conveniently be represented in a number of other ways, including:

1. The direction of magnetization within a magnetic tape or a magnetic core
2. The presence or absence of light as detected by light sensors

The binary number system, which is studied in the following section, naturally lends itself to computer work because it has a base of 2. The conversion of original decimal information into its binary equivalent at the input and the conversion of the binary output into its decimal equivalent introduce a design problem. An additional complexity of design is often incorporated that enables the operator to read into and out of the computer in decimal form while the system performs its functions in binary notation. The resultant simplicity of read-in and read-out warrants the added system complexity.

1·4   Representation of Decimal Numbers by Switches

Decimal numbers can be represented by switches in several ways. Figure 1·2 illustrates one possibility. Each switch has ten positions to coincide with the ten symbols of the radix-10 number system. The one symbol out of the ten possibilities that are present is indicated by the position at which the switch makes physical contact. Hence the switch at the far left in Fig. 1·2 registers "7."

Note that each symbol can have a positional value. The switch at the far right would be the units position, the middle switch would

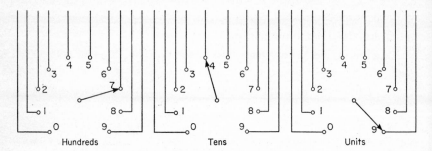

Fig. 1·2   Representation of the decimal number 749 by manual switches.

serve as the tens position, while the switch at the far left would serve as the hundreds position.

It should be noted that the use of the manual switches in Fig. 1·2 to designate radix-10 number quantities is for illustrative purposes only. In practical applications, every contact on each of the switches would be replaced with an electronic circuit that would perform the identification function of ON or OFF. In this manner, more rapid calculations would be possible.

Multivibrators could be used to replace the individual contacts on each of the hand switches. In such a case each manual switch would be replaced with 10 multivibrators. Each multivibrator in turn consists of two transistors. Therefore a total of 20 transistors and their associated components are required to represent the decimal numbers 0 to 9. The use of binary notation results in a considerable reduction in the number of transistors required. For example, four multivibrators entailing eight transistors represent 16 separate states for the first 16 binary numbers. Later sections deal with the manner in which such a reduction is made possible.

Note: In this text the use of the term *multivibrator* with no further specification is understood to mean the *bistable multivibrator*. The term *flip-flop* or *toggle* is sometimes used in place of multivibrator. The two other types of multivibrators (astable or monostable) are not to be considered in this discussion.

1·5   The Binary System

The binary system is a radix-2 system since only two symbols are used. The symbols 0 and 1 are the most popular. The positional values for both integers and fractional quantities of the binary numbering system are illustrated in Fig. 1·3.

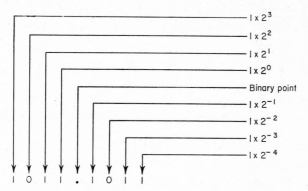

Fig. 1·3 Positional values of the binary system.

Each 1 or 0 of the binary number is called a *bit*. It might be of interest to point out that bit is a contraction of the words BInary biT. Therefore the quantity 1011.1011 is an eight-bit number.

Notice that starting from the binary point, positional values change by the powers of 2. When going to the left of the binary point, which represents whole numbers, each position indicates 2^{n-1}, where n is the number of places the bit is located to the left of the binary point. For fractional values, which are to the right of the decimal point, each position indicates 2^{m}, where m is the number of places the bit is located to the right of the binary point.

Because the binary system has only two symbols, it can be easily represented by any device that is capable of existing in two states. Figure 1·4 illustrates several of the common possibilities.

Notice how the four-bit number 1010 is represented by the multivibrator block diagrams. In each case, the right-side output is the "1" side and the left-side output is the "0" side. The side output selection is arbitrarily chosen by the designer; it could have been just the opposite.

The 1 output is 1 only when that side of the multivibrator is turned ON. When the 1 output is not conducting (turned OFF), the 0 output is ON and will be 1. This is also arbitrarily determined, as it could have been opposite to that shown. In many applications, the multivibrator

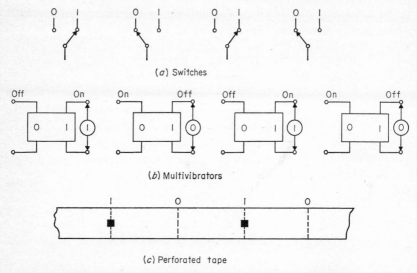

(a) Switches

(b) Multivibrators

(c) Perforated tape

Fig. 1·4   Representation of 1010 by several two-state devices.

output is considered 1 when its collector potential is maximum, which is the condition where that transistor is cut off.

Notice how the perforated tape can be utilized to indicate binary information. In the illustration, a hole is punched for the 1, and no hole indicates a 0. This could have been reversed (i.e., a hole could be punched for 0, and no hole would indicate 1).

1·6   Binary to Decimal Conversion by the Direct Method

The techniques associated with translating binary quantities into their decimal equivalents are very important because of their common use. Recognizing the positional values of 1 in the binary quantity to be analyzed is the key to translating it to its decimal equivalent by the direct method. The following example illustrates this technique.

Example 1. Convert 101101 to its decimal equivalent by the direct method.

Solution. Arranging the binary number into a vertical column along with the corresponding powers of 2 for each bit results in obtaining the quantities shown in the first two columns at the top of page 9:

$$1 = 1 \times 2^5 = 32$$
$$0 = 0 \times 2^4 = 0$$
$$1 = 1 \times 2^3 = 8$$
$$1 = 1 \times 2^2 = 4$$
$$0 = 0 \times 2^1 = 0$$
$$1 = 1 \times 2^0 = \underline{1}$$
$$45$$

The decimal equivalent of each bit, determined by its position in the original number, is shown in the third column. Therefore,

$$\text{Binary } 101101 = \text{decimal } 45$$

1·7 Binary to Decimal Conversion by the Double-dabble Method

A second technique for the conversion of a binary integer into its equivalent decimal is commonly called the double-dabble method. There are three basic steps to this technique:

1. Multiply the higher-order binary bit by 2. Add this product to the next highest order bit. Record this total.
2. Multiply the total obtained (in step 1) by 2. Add the new product to the next highest order bit. Record this sum.
3. Continue this process until all the bits have been worked. The final total is the decimal equivalent of the original binary quantity.

The double-dabble technique can be used for two or more integers.

Example 1. Convert the binary quantity 101101 to its decimal equivalent by use of the double-dabble method.

Solution. Following the procedure outlined above results in converting the binary quantity into its decimal equivalent in five steps. It should be noted that the number of steps involved in the conversion process is equal to one less than the number of bits in the original binary quantity.

Since the binary quantity 101101 has six bits, then its conversion by the double-dabble method requires five steps, as shown:

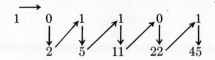

Taking it step by step,

Step 1. $(1 \times 2) + 0 = 2$
Step 2. $(2 \times 2) + 1 = 5$
Step 3. $(5 \times 2) + 1 = 11$
Step 4. $(11 \times 2) + 0 = 22$
Step 5. $(22 \times 2) + 1 = 45$

Therefore,

Binary 101101 = decimal 45

1·8 Conversion of Binary Fractions to Decimal Equivalents by the Vertical Column Method

A simple method for the conversion of binary fractions into their decimal equivalents is the vertical column technique. It should be noticed that the powers of 2 of each bit descend by the order of -1 with each position to the right of the decimal point. The following example illustrates this fact.

Example 1. Convert 0.101011 into its decimal equivalent by use of the vertical column method.

Solution. Constructing the vertical table, we obtain:

$$1 = 1 \times 2^{-1} = \tfrac{1}{2} \times (1) = 0.500000$$
$$0 = 0 \times 2^{-2} = \tfrac{1}{4} \times (0) = 0.000000$$
$$1 = 1 \times 2^{-3} = \tfrac{1}{8} \times (1) = 0.125000$$
$$0 = 0 \times 2^{-4} = \tfrac{1}{16} \times (0) = 0.000000$$
$$1 = 1 \times 2^{-5} = \tfrac{1}{32} \times (1) = 0.031250$$
$$1 = 1 \times 2^{-6} = \tfrac{1}{64} \times (1) = \underline{0.015625}$$
$$\text{Total} \quad 0.671875$$

Therefore,

Binary 0.101011 = decimal 0.671875

It is recommended that the student practice the conversion of binary quantities into their decimal equivalents until the process presents no difficulty. The following problems are included for this purpose.

PROBLEMS

Convert the following binary integers into their decimal equivalents:

1·1	111		1·2	100
1·3	1001		1·4	10100
1·5	11001		1·6	11110
1·7	10111		1·8	101001
1·9	100001		1·10	111000

Convert the following binary fractions into their decimal fraction equivalents:

1·11	0.11		1·12	0.011
1·13	0.101		1·14	0.1011
1·15	0.0110		1·16	0.0101
1·17	0.1111		1·18	0.0001
1·19	0.100111		1·20	0.111011

Convert the following binary quantities into their decimal equivalents:

1·21	110.110		1·22	101.101
1·23	100.001		1·24	111.111
1·25	1011.1001		1·26	1101.1011
1·27	1110.0111		1·28	101110.101
1·29	110011.11		1·30	1110100.101

1·9 Conversion of Decimal Integers to Binary by the Direct Method

The process of converting from binary quantities to decimal equivalents, as analyzed in the preceding section, is the type of numerical adaptation that might have to be made after the information is received at the output of a computer. Assuming the computer performed its logic in binary notation, the original input must be converted from decimal into its binary equivalent. This and the following section deal with several techniques which may be utilized for performing this conversion.

In the direct method, the original quantity is examined for the largest possible power of 2 that can be subtracted from it. This process is repeated with the remainder until there is no remainder. The final answer is obtained by adding all the quantities that were subtracted out. Consider the following example, which illustrates this technique.

Example 1. Convert decimal 38 into its binary equivalent by the direct method.

Solution

Step 1. The largest possible power of 2 in 38 is $1 \times 2^5 = 32$; hence

$$
\begin{array}{r}
3\,8 \\
-3\,2 = 1 \times 2^5 \\
\hline
6
\end{array}
$$

Step 2. The largest possible power of 2 in 6 is 1×2^2; therefore

$$
\begin{array}{r}
6 \\
-4 = 1 \times 2^2 \\
\hline
2
\end{array}
$$

Step 3. The largest possible power of 2 in 2 is 1×2^1; therefore

$$
\begin{array}{r}
2 \\
-2 = 1 \times 2^1 \\
\hline
0
\end{array}
$$

Step 4. Combining,

$$38 = 1 \times 2^5 + 0 \times 2^4 + 0 \times 2^3 + 1 \times 2^2 + 1 \times 2^1 + 0 \times 2^0$$

and checking,

$$\text{Decimal } 38 = \text{binary } 100110$$

1·10   Conversion of Decimal Integers to Binary by the Double-dabble Method

The double-dabble method for converting decimal to binary is the reverse of the double-dabble method for converting binary quantities into their decimal equivalents. The steps are as follows:

1. Divide the original decimal number by 2. Place the quotient directly below the dividend. Place the remainder to the right of the quotient.
2. Divide the first quotient by 2, placing the second quotient below the first quotient (which is the dividend for the second division process), and place the remainder to its right.
3. Repeat the process until the final quotient is zero.
4. The remainders, starting from the bottom, constitute the equivalent binary quantity.

This technique is illustrated in Example 1.

Example 1. Convert decimal 41 into its binary equivalent by use of the double-dabble technique.

Solution. Setting up the quotient and remainder columns and proceeding:

Quotients	Remainders
41	
20	1
10	0
5	0
2	1
1	0
0	1

Reading the remainders column, starting from the bottom,

$$\text{Decimal } 41 = \text{binary } 101001$$

1·11 Conversion of Decimal Fractions to Binary Fractions

The following rules are to be applied when converting a decimal fraction into its equivalent binary fraction:

1. Multiply the original decimal fraction by 2. The integer part of the product is removed and stored to the right of the product.
2. Multiply the new product, without its integer, by 2. Subtract out the integer (if there is one) and store it to the right of the product. If there is no integer, indicate this by storing a zero in the right-hand column.

3. Continue this process until the remaining fractional portion of the product is zero or the required number of binary places have been obtained.

4. The binary equivalent is equal to the integer parts. The binary point is at the top; therefore the binary quantity is obtained by reading down.

Example 1 illustrates this technique.

Example 1. Convert 0.7852 into its binary equivalent up to eight places.

Solution. Setting up the product and integer columns and then proceeding,

Products	Integers
0.7852	
1.5704	1
0.5704	
1.1408	1
0.1408	
0.2816	0
0.5632	0
1.1264	1
0.1264	
0.2528	0
0.5056	0
1.0112	1

Therefore,

$$\text{Decimal } 0.7852 = 0.11001001+$$

When the remainder is other than zero, the fraction is not terminated, and the result should indicate this with a plus sign at the right end.

PROBLEMS

Convert the following decimal integers into their equivalent binary quantities:

1·31	17	1·32	42
1·33	35	1·34	70
1·35	54	1·36	81
1·37	27	1·38	92
1·39	76	1·40	68

Convert the following decimal fractions into their equivalent binary quantities up to eight places:

1·41	0.159		**1·42**	0.425
1·43	0.3256		**1·44**	0.7531
1·45	0.5392		**1·46**	0.8432
1·47	0.9246		**1·48**	0.5020
1·49	0.6835		**1·50**	0.2948

Convert the following decimal quantities into their equivalent binary values:

1·51	2.986		**1·52**	12.462
1·53	15.755		**1·54**	28.282
1·55	34.395		**1·56**	34.3856
1·57	45.8136		**1·58**	54.2555
1·59	60.9753		**1·60**	82.1573

Special Computer
Number Systems and Codes

Introduction

This chapter is concerned with two additional basic number systems and several modified number codes. The radix-3 (trinary) and radix-8 (octal) systems are analyzed in the first half of this chapter. Techniques for all the important conversions are analyzed with worked-out examples. The special techniques involved in fraction conversion are studied in separate sections. The conversions of binary to octal and octal to binary are given special attention because of their frequent use.

The last half of this chapter deals with five of the special number codes that have been devised for computer applications. The nature of these codes and their conversions is studied.

A total of 220 problems are included in this chapter. Problems relating to each section of the chapter have been furnished. Working out the problems will better enable the reader to master the number systems and conversion techniques studied here.

2·1 The Trinary (Ternary) System

The trinary system, as implied by its name, is a three-radix system. The three symbols are $-$, 0, and $+$, where

$$- = -1$$
$$0 = 0$$
$$+ = +1$$

The positional values (reading from left to right) are 9, 3, and 1.

Table 2·1   The Trinary Number System with Decimal Equivalents

$$--- = (-1 \times 3^2) + (-1 \times 3) + (-1) = (-9) + (-3) + (-1) = -13$$
$$--0 = (-1 \times 3^2) + (-1 \times 3) + (0) = (-9) + (-3) + (0) = -12$$
$$--+ = (-1 \times 3^2) + (-1 \times 3) + (1) = -12 + 1 = -11$$
$$-0- = (-1 \times 3^2) + 0 + (-1) = -9 + (-1) = -10$$
$$-00 = (-1 \times 3^2) + 0 + 0 = -9$$
$$-0+ = (-1 \times 3^2) + 0 + 1 = -9 + 1 = -8$$
$$-+- = (-1 \times 3^2) + (1 \times 3) + (-1) = -9 + 3 - 1 = -7$$
$$-+0 = (-1 \times 3^2) + (1 \times 3) + 0 = -9 + 3 = -6$$
$$-++ = (-1 \times 3^2) + (1 \times 3) + 1 = -9 + 3 + 1 = -5$$
$$0-- = 0 + (-1 \times 3) + (-1) = -3 - 1 = -4$$
$$0-0 = 0 + (-1 \times 3) + 0 = -3$$
$$0-+ = 0 + (-1 \times 3) + 1 = -3 + 1 = -2$$
$$00- = 0 + 0 + (-1) = -1$$
$$000 = 0 + 0 + 0 = 0$$
$$00+ = 0 + 0 + 1 = 1$$
$$0+- = 0 + (1 \times 3) + (-1) = 3 - 1 = 2$$
$$0+0 = 0 + (1 \times 3) + 0 = 3$$
$$0++ = 0 + (1 \times 3) + (1) = 3 + 1 = 4$$
$$+-- = (1 \times 3^2) + (-1 \times 3) + (-1) = 9 - 3 - 1 = 5$$
$$+-0 = (1 \times 3^2) + (-1 \times 3) + 0 = 9 - 3 = 6$$
$$+-+ = (1 \times 3^2) + (-1 \times 3) + 1 = 9 - 3 + 1 = 7$$
$$+0- = (1 \times 3^2) + 0 + (-1) = 9 - 1 = 8$$
$$+00 = (1 \times 3^2) + 0 + 0 = 9$$
$$+0+ = (1 \times 3^2) + 0 + 1 = 9 + 1 = 10$$
$$++- = (1 \times 3^2) + (1 \times 3) + (-1) = 9 + 3 - 1 = 11$$
$$++0 = (1 \times 3^2) + (1 \times 3) + 0 = 9 + 3 = 12$$
$$+++ = (1 \times 3^2) + (1 \times 3) + 1 = 9 + 3 + 1 = 13$$

Table 2·1 lists the 27 possible quantities of the ternary system and their decimal equivalents. Notice that the decimal equivalents of the trinary numbers range from -13 to $+13$, which is a total of 27 values (including zero). The trinary number system has found limited use in computer applications.

2·2   Conversion of Trinary Numbers into Their Decimal and Binary Equivalents

Any trinary number can be converted into its decimal equivalent by the utilization of Table 2·1. Conversion of a trinary number into its binary equivalent is a relatively simple two-step process:

1. Convert the original trinary number into its equivalent decimal value by use of Table 2·1.
2. Convert the decimal equivalent obtained in step 1 into its binary equivalent.

The following example illustrates this technique.

Example 1. Convert trinary $0 + 0$ into its binary equivalent.

Solution

Step 1. Referring to Table 2·1, we find that trinary $0 + 0 =$ decimal 3.

Step 2. Converting from decimal to binary, we find that decimal $3 =$ binary 11.

2·3 Conversion of Binary and Decimal Numbers into Their Trinary Equivalents

To convert a decimal number into its trinary equivalent, Table 2·1 can again be utilized. Find the decimal number in the table, and then read the trinary equivalent found to its immediate left.

For converting from binary to trinary, a two-step procedure is suggested:

1. Convert the binary number into its decimal equivalent.
2. Locate the decimal equivalent determined in step 1 in Table 2·1. Read the trinary equivalent to its left.

Example 1. Convert binary 111 into its trinary equivalent.

Solution

Step 1. Binary $111 = (1 \times 2^2) + (1 \times 2) + (1 \times 2^0)$; therefore binary $111 =$ decimal 7.

Step 2. From Table 2·1: decimal $7 =$ trinary $+ - +$.

2·4 The Octal System: Conversion of Octal Integers to Decimal

As implied by the name, the octal system has a radix of 8. It has found several special uses in computers. The symbols used are 0, 1,

2, 3, 4, 5, 6, and 7. The positional values, starting from the octal point and moving to the left, increase in steps of powers of 8.

To convert an octal number to its decimal equivalent, the descending power of 8 (reading from left to right) must be taken into account.

Example 1. Convert octal 462 into its decimal equivalent.

Solution

$$\text{Octal } 462 = (4 \times 8^2) + (6 \times 8^1) + (2 \times 8^0)$$
$$= 256 + 48 + 2 = 306$$

Therefore,

$$\text{Octal } 462 = \text{decimal } 306$$

2·5 Conversion of Decimal Integers to Octal

The double-dabble method with special adaptations is used in converting decimal numbers into their octal equivalents. The steps to follow are:

1. Divide the decimal integer by 8. Record the remainder in a separate column.
2. Divide the new quotient by 8. Record the remainder in the same manner as in step 1.
3. Continue this process until the quotient of zero is obtained.
4. The octal equivalent is given by the remainders, reading from bottom to the top.

Example 1. Convert decimal 169 into its octal equivalent.

Solution. Setting up the table and following the procedure outlined above, we obtain:

Division		Quotient	Remainder
$169/8$	=	21	1
$21/8$	=	2	5
$2/8$	=	0	2

Therefore,

$$\text{Decimal } 169 = \text{octal } 251$$

Checking by converting octal 251 back into its decimal equivalent:

$$\text{Octal } 251 = (2 \times 8^2) + (5 \times 8^1) + 1$$
$$= 128 + 40 + 1 = 169$$

2·6　Conversion of Fractions: Octal to Decimal

The same technique prescribed for the conversion of binary fractions to decimal fractions can be utilized in converting octal fractions into their decimal equivalents. This fact is illustrated in the following example.

Example 1. Convert the octal fraction 0.531 into its decimal equivalent.

Solution

$$\text{Octal } 0.531 = (5 \times 8^{-1}) + (3 \times 8^{-2}) + (1 \times 8^{-3})$$
$$= \tfrac{5}{8} + \tfrac{3}{64} + \tfrac{1}{512}$$
$$= 0.625 + 0.0468 + 0.00195$$
$$= \text{decimal } 0.67375+$$

2·7　Conversion of Fractions: Decimal to Octal

To convert a decimal fraction into its octal equivalent, the following procedure can be utilized:

1. Multiply the original decimal fraction by 8. Record the integer portion of the product in a second column.
2. Multiply the fractional portion of the product by 8. Record the integer portion as in step 1.
3. Repeat this process until no fractional portion remains (in the case of terminating fractions) or until the desired number of places have been obtained (in the case of nonterminating fractions).
4. The octal equivalent is equal to the recorded integer portion, reading from the top down.

Example 1. Convert the decimal fraction 0.745 into its octal equivalent. Carry the translation to six places if it is a nonterminating fraction.

Solution. Using the preceding set of rules, the following result is obtained:

$$0.745 \times 8 = 5.960 \qquad 5$$
$$0.960 \times 8 = 7.680 \qquad 7$$
$$0.680 \times 8 = 5.440 \qquad 5$$
$$0.440 \times 8 = 3.520 \qquad 3$$
$$0.520 \times 8 = 4.160 \qquad 4$$
$$0.160 \times 8 = 1.280 \qquad 1$$

Therefore,

Decimal 0.745 = octal 0.575341

2·8 Conversion of Binary to Octal

Since the octal number system has several uses in computer work, the conversions of octal to binary and of binary to octal should be wel' 'nderstood. Binary numbers are often written in octal form when recorded by computers. Programming instructions are often written in octal notation. Furthermore, large decimal quantities are most easily translated into binary by first converting them into octal.

Following is a procedure for converting binary to octal:

1. Group the integers.
   a. Starting at the binary point and moving toward your left, group off the original binary into three-digit clusters.
   b. If the original binary number is not evenly divisible by 3, complete the last group on the left with the required number of zeros.
2. Group the binary fractions.
   a. Starting at the binary point and moving toward your right, group off the original binary fraction into three-digit clusters.
   b. If the binary fraction is not evenly divisible by 3, complete the last group on the right with the required number of zeros.
3. Read out.
   a. Read out each group of three in binary numbers.
   b. The combined read-out numbers will be the octal equivalent of the original binary numbers.

Example 1. Convert binary 1101001.11101 into its octal equivalent.

Solution. Grouping the original binary number and adding the necessary zeros as directed in the previous procedure, we obtain

$$001 \quad 101 \quad 001 \quad \cdot \quad 111 \quad 010$$

Reading out from binary to the octal equivalent, we obtain

Binary 001 101 001 · 111 010 = 151.72 octal

2·9 Conversion of Octal to Binary

Converting octal numbers into their binary equivalents is essentially the reverse of the procedure given in Sec. 2·8:

1. State each digit in the original octal number in a binary cluster of 3. This will be the expression of the octal number in binary clusters.
2. If the complete binary translation is desired, move the cluster together.

Example 1. Convert octal 1645 into its binary equivalent.

Solution. Stating each digit in the original octal number in a binary cluster of 3, we obtain

$$1645 = 001 \quad 110 \quad 100 \quad 101$$

and then combining the clusters,

Octal 1645 = binary 1110100101

PROBLEMS

Convert the following decimal quantities into their ternary equivalents:

2·1	4	2·2	−2
2·3	13	2·4	11
2·5	7	2·6	−9
2·7	−6	2·8	3
2·9	−13	2·10	0

Convert the following ternary numbers into their decimal equivalents:

2·11	− − −		2·12	0 − +
2·13	− 0 0		2·14	+ 0 0
2·15	+ 0 +		2·16	− − +
2·17	+ 0 −		2·18	− 0 −
2·19	− + +		2·20	+ − −

Convert the following ternary quantities into their binary equivalents:

2·21	+ + +		2·22	0 − +
2·23	0 − 0		2·24	− 0 −
2·25	+ + 0		2·26	0 0 +
2·27	+ − +		2·28	− − +
2·29	+ 0 0		2·30	+ + −

Convert the following binary quantities into their ternary equivalents:

2·31	010		2·32	100
2·33	011		2·34	111
2·35	001		2·36	1011
2·37	−1001		2·38	1101
2·39	−1101		2·40	0110

Convert the following octal integers into their decimal equivalents:

2·41	267		2·42	135
2·43	104		2·44	770
2·45	426		2·46	373
2·47	632		2·48	467
2·49	173		2·50	765

Convert the following decimal integers into their octal equivalents:

2·51	192		2·52	361
2·53	678		2·54	904
2·55	848		2·56	715
2·57	246		2·58	567
2·59	399		2·60	986

Convert the following octal fractions into their equivalent decimal fractions:

2·61	0.672		2·62	0.146
2·63	0.374		2·64	0.267
2·65	0.466		2·66	0.394
2·67	0.556		2·68	0.162
2·69	0.234		2·70	0.425

Convert the following decimal fractions into their equivalent octal fractions:

2·71	0.548		2·72	0.690
2·73	0.806		2·74	0.440
2·75	0.250		2·76	0.601
2·77	0.555		2·78	0.741
2·79	0.843		2·80	0.628

Convert the following binary quantities into their octal equivalents:

2·81	1001		2·82	11011
2·83	1010110		2·84	1100111
2·85	1001101		2·86	1110011
2·87	0.0111		2·88	0.011101
2·89	0.11101		2·90	0.110111
2·91	111.11011		2·92	1101.101101
2·93	111.11111		2·94	10111.10111
2·95	111101110.1110111		2·96	1011100110.1001011
2·97	1000100010.1001011		2·98	11111.111011
2·99	111111.111111		2·100	1111101.11110001

Convert the following octal quantities into their binary equivalents:

2·101	16		2·102	163
2·103	2450		2·104	2736
2·105	6457		2·106	3562
2·107	42065		2·108	12345
2·109	76541		2·110	64275
2·111	126.14		2·112	375.166
2·113	420.042		2·114	1275.144
2·115	1474.341		2·116	1316.1412
2·117	1517.1140		2·118	1753.7642
2·119	7452.2547		2·120	5314.7624

2·10   The Binary-coded Decimal Notation System

As stated in several of the earlier sections, the computer can be easily adapted to binary notation because it is designed around two-state devices. (Transistors, magnetic tapes, and diodes are common examples.) Since the original information to be fed into the computer is often in decimal notation, it must be converted into a binary form suitable for computer operation.

The binary-coded decimal notation system is one special way of expressing decimal quantities in binary form. In this system, each digit of the original decimal number is expressed directly as a binary group. The number of binary groups corresponds to the number of digits in the original decimal quantity.

Example 1. Express the decimal number 839 in the binary-coded decimal notation.

Solution. Expressing each digit in binary form results in the following:

$$8 = 1000$$
$$3 = 0011$$
$$9 = 1001$$

Then,

Decimal 839 = 1000   0011   1001   (in binary-coded decimal notation)

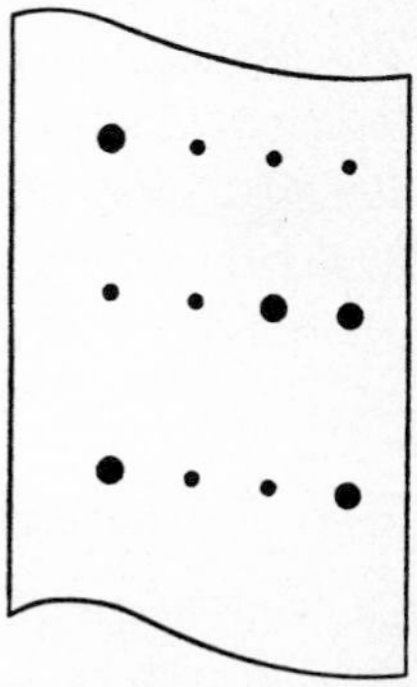

Fig. 2·1 Binary-coded decimal notation of decimal 839 on perforated tape.

The read-out of a perforated tape is a typical example of how the binary-coded decimal notation is used. Figure 2·1 illustrates the manner in which the binary bits are recorded on the tape. In this case, a hole indicates 1 and its value is determined by its position. The section of tape illustrated in Fig. 2·1 depicts the decimal number 839 in binary-coded decimal notation.

2·11   The Excess-3 Code

The excess-3 code is a special adaptation of the binary-coded decimal notation system. It is in popular use in computer work and therefore warrants consideration in this chapter. In the excess-3 code, each individual decimal digit is converted into its binary equivalent *plus three.* This is done for each digit in the original decimal number, as illustrated in the following example.

Example 1. Express the decimal quantity 839 in the excess-3 code.

Solution

Original	Decimal + 3	Binary Equivalent
8	$8 + 3 = 11$	1011
3	$3 + 3 = 6$	0110
9	$9 + 3 = 12$	1100

Therefore,

Decimal 839 = excess-3 code 1011   0110   1100

The use of the excess-3 code permits the utilization of greatly simplified logic circuits for the performance of arithmetic subtraction. It also has the advantage of having 1s in its representation of decimal 0 (decimal 0 = 0011 in the excess-3 code). Therefore the computer can more easily tell the difference between circuit failure and the presence of the absolute quantity of zero.

2·12   The Reflected Binary (or Gray) Code

The reflected binary or Gray code is also known as the cyclic code. In this system, only one bit changes as the decimal integers progress in value. Table 2·2 illustrates this relationship between the decimal

Table 2·2   Decimal to Gray-code Relationships

Decimal	Gray code	Pure binary
0	0000	0000
1	0001	0001
2	0011	0010
3	0010	0011
4	0110	0100
5	0111	0101
6	0101	0110
7	0100	0111
8	1100	1000
9	1101	1001

quantity, its Gray-code equivalent, and its pure binary equivalent. The Gray code is used in analog-to-digital conversion equipment and in certain control-circuit applications.

2·13 Conversion of Binary Numbers into the Gray Code

Following are the rules for converting a binary number into reflected binary (Gray-code equivalent):

1. Carry the highest-order digit of the binary as it stands. This is the first digit of the Gray code.
2. Add this highest-order digit and the next digit of the binary. This sum is the second digit of the Gray-coded number. Disregard the carry, if there is one.
3. Add the second digit of the binary and the third digit of the original binary. This sum is the third digit of the Gray-code number.
4. Continue this process until all the digits in the original binary have been involved.

Example 1. Convert 1011 into the Gray code:

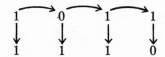

The Gray-code number:

First digit = first digit of the binary
Second digit = binary first digit + binary second digit
Third digit = binary second digit + binary third digit
Fourth digit = binary third digit + binary fourth digit

Therefore,

Binary 1011 = Gray code 1110

2·14 Conversion of Gray Code into Binary

To convert a Gray-code number into its equivalent binary, the following steps can be used:

1. The highest digit of the Gray code becomes the first digit of the binary.
2. The second binary number is equal to the sum of the second Gray-code digit and the first binary digit.
3. Continue this process until all the Gray-code digits have been involved in the process.

Example 1. Convert Gray-code 1010 into binary.

Solution

Binary digit 1 = Gray-code digit 1
Binary digit 2 = binary digit 1 + Gray-code digit 2
Binary digit 3 = binary digit 2 + Gray-code digit 3
Binary digit 4 = binary digit 3 + Gray-code digit 4

Therefore,

$$\text{Gray-code } 1010 = \text{binary } 1100$$

2·15   The 7421 Code

Recall that in the pure binary system, the positional value of the bits is as follows:

$$\begin{array}{cccc} 1 & 1 & 1 & 1 \end{array}$$
$$1(8) + 1(4) + 1(2) + 1(1)$$

Therefore, in this sense, the pure binary code can be called the 8421 code.

It is sometimes desirable to utilize a binary code in which all the decimal digits can be expressed by the use of two or fewer 1s. Using a binary system where the positional values of the digits are 7421 will meet this requirement.

Example 1. Express the decimal quantity 1,925 in the 7421 code.

Solution. Converting each decimal digit into the 7421 code,

$$0001 \quad 1010 \quad 0010 \quad 0101$$

Checking by converting back to the decimal,

$$0001 = 0(7) + 0(4) - 0(2) + 1(1) = 1$$
$$1010 = 1(7) + 0(4) + 1(2) + 0(1) = 9$$
$$0010 = 0(7) + 0(4) + 1(2) + 0(1) = 2$$
$$0101 = 0(7) + 1(4) + 0(2) + 1(1) = 5$$

Reading down,

    0001   1010   0010   0101   (7421 code) = 1,925 decimal

2·16   The Biquinary Code

Seven bits, two of which are 1s and the remaining five are 0s, are used to represent each decimal digit in the biquinary code. The obvious disadvantage of such a code is the increased number of bits in the representation of a decimal digit. The chief advantage of the biquinary code is the fact that there are exactly two 1s in the representation of any decimal digit. Therefore a computer error is easily detected by the simple fact that less than or more than two 1s appear in the digit output presentation. Sensing circuits can be designed around this fact.

The positional values for the biquinary code are:

        5   0   4   3   2   1   0

Notice that the bits are divided into two groups. Also notice that the value of the extreme right position in both groups is zero. The manner in which each decimal digit is expressed in the biquinary code is shown in Table 2·3.

Table 2·3   Conversion of Decimal Digits to the Biquinary Code

Decimal	Biquinary						
	5	0	4	3	2	1	0
0	0	1	0	0	0	0	1
1	0	1	0	0	0	1	0
2	0	1	0	0	1	0	0
3	0	1	0	1	0	0	0
4	0	1	1	0	0	0	0
5	1	0	0	0	0	0	1
6	1	0	0	0	0	1	0
7	1	0	0	0	1	0	0
8	1	0	0	1	0	0	0
9	1	0	1	0	0	0	0

Example 1. Express decimal 247 in the biquinary code.

Solution. Expressing each decimal digit,

$$
\begin{array}{ccccccc}
0 & 1 & 0 & 0 & 1 & 0 & 0 = 2 \\
0 & 1 & 1 & 0 & 0 & 0 & 0 = 4 \\
1 & 0 & 0 & 0 & 1 & 0 & 0 = 7
\end{array}
$$

PROBLEMS

Express the following decimal numbers in the binary-coded decimal notation:

2·121	249		2·122	937
2·123	140		2·124	673
2·125	485		2·126	396
2·127	573		2·128	1,247
2·129	1,418		2·130	1,927

Express the following binary-coded decimal values in their equivalent decimal numbers:

2·131	1010	0110	1010	2·132	1000	0100	0010
2·133	0100	1000	0100	2·134	1110	0010	1100
2·135	1111	0001	0110	2·136	1100	1110	0111
2·137	1011	1101	0111	2·138	1101	0111	0010
2·139	1000	1111	1011	2·140	0110	1001	0011

Express the following decimal numbers in the excess-3 code:

2·141	26		2·142	47
2·143	151		2·144	169
2·145	192		2·146	363
2·147	496		2·148	999
2·149	7,128		2·150	8,546

Convert the following excess-3–coded values into their decimal equivalents:

2·151	0111	0011	1100	2·152	1011	1100	0101
2·153	1100	1001	1000	2·154	1001	0110	0100

2·155	1010	1011	0011	2·156	0110	1100	0101
2·157	0101	1001	1010	2·158	1000	0110	1011
2·159	1001	1011	1100	2·160	0101	0011	0011

Convert the following binary quantities into their Gray-code values:

2·161	0110	1101	0001	2·162	1010	1001	0101
2·163	1000	1110	1011	2·164	1101	1011	1001
2·165	0011	0000	1110	2·166	1010	1111	0010
2·167	1100	0010	1111	2·168	1001	0110	0100
2·169	1000	1001	1100	2·170	0101	1100	1011

Convert the following Gray-code numbers into their binary equivalents:

2·171	0011	1001	0110	2·172	1010	0110	1010
2·173	1000	0100	1000	2·174	1101	0010	0111
2·175	0111	1100	1110	2·176	0110	0001	1111
2·177	1100	0010	1110	2·178	0100	1000	0100
2·179	1010	1010	0110	2·180	0010	1000	0100

Express the following decimals in the 7421 code:

2·181	64	2·182	52
2·183	251	2·184	691
2·185	291	2·186	643
2·187	469	2·188	8,217
2·189	9,992	2·190	6,458

Convert the following 7421-coded numbers into their equivalent decimals:

2·191	1001	1000	1010	2·192	0101	0101	1001
2·193	1010	1000	1000	2·194	0011	1001	0001
2·195	1001	0001	0000	2·196	1000	0110	1001
2·197	0101	1001	0101	2·198	1000	1010	0110
2·199	0010	1000	1000	2·200	1000	0011	1010

Express the following decimal values in the biquinary code:

| 2·201 | 52 | 2·202 | 94 |
| 2·203 | 293 | 2·204 | 348 |

2·205	384		2·206	132
2·207	243		2·208	1,892
2·209	3,514		2·210	4,324

Convert the following biquinary-coded numbers into their decimal equivalents:

2·211	01	00100		2·212	10	01000
2·213	10	10000		2·214	01	00001
2·215	10	00100		2·216	01	00010
2·217	10	10000		2·218	10	00001
2·219	01	01000		2·220	10	00010

Binary Addition and Subtraction

Introduction

This chapter begins with a three-section treatment of binary addition and the laws associated with this arithmetic procedure. Direct binary subtraction is then treated in two separate sections.

The concept of subtraction by utilization of complements is heavily stressed throughout the remainder of the chapter. Since subtraction by complements is performed in a manner that appears as addition, it permits the use of greatly simplified electronic circuits and is consequently very important in computer work.

Decimal subtraction by both the 10's and 9's complements is studied. Then binary subtraction by the 2's complement and then the 1's complement is developed in a direct and simple manner.

To better facilitate the mastery of these arithmetic processes, a total of 80 problems have been included.

3·1 Binary Addition: Integers

The process of adding in the binary system retains the mechanical features of decimal system addition. Exceeding the limit of a particular digit position necessitates a carry of 1 to the next higher digit position (which is immediately to its right) and the placement of 0 in the original position.

The four basic laws for binary addition can be stated in the following manner:

Law 1. The sum of 0 plus 0 is 0 with no carry, i.e.,

$$0$$
$$\underline{+0}$$
$$0$$

Law 2.   The sum of 0 plus 1 is 1 with no carry, i.e.,

$$0$$
$$\underline{+1}$$
$$1$$

Law 3. The sum of 1 plus 0 is 1 with no carry, i.e.,

$$1$$
$$\underline{+0}$$
$$1$$

Law 4. The sum of 1 plus 1 is 0 with a carry of 1, i.e.,

$$1$$
$$\underline{+1}$$
$$0 \text{ with a carry of 1}$$

Notice that a carry is involved only when 1 is added to 1. The manner in which a carry is handled is illustrated in the following addition example.

Example 1. Find the sum of $1001 + 0101$.

Solution. Arranging the numbers in columns,

```
        1       carry from column A
    1 0 0 1
  +0 1 0 1
  ─────────
    1 1 1 0
    D C B A
```

Following is a description of the addition process, column by column.

Column A. The sum of $1 + 1$ is determined from law 4: $1 + 1 = 0$ with a carry of 1. The carry of 1 is added to the top of the B column.

Column B. The first sum to be determined in column *B* is the carry 1 plus the top bit 0. Hence $1 + 0 = 1$ by law 3. This sum is now added to the bottom bit in column *B*, that is, $1 + 0 = 1$ (again in accordance with law 3).

Column C. With no carry involved, the sum of this column simply involves $0 + 1 = 1$, which is in accordance with law 2.

Column D. This column involves $1 + 0$, whose sum is 1 (law 3).

The final sum is 1110. Checking this by converting it into its decimal equivalent, we obtain the following:

$$\text{Top row binary } 1001 = (1 \times 2^3) + (0 \times 2^2) + (0 \times 2^1) + 1$$
$$= 8 + 0 + 0 + 1 = 9$$
$$\text{Bottom row binary } 0101 = (0 \times 2^3) + (1 \times 2^2) + (0 \times 2) + 1$$
$$= 0 + 4 + 0 + 1 = 5$$
$$\text{Answer } 1110 \text{ in decimal} = (1 \times 2^3) + (1 \times 2^2) + (1 \times 2) + 0$$
$$= 8 + 4 + 2 = 14$$

Adding in decimal notation,

$$\begin{array}{r} 9 \\ + \ 5 \\ \hline 14 \end{array}$$

Therefore, binary 1110 = decimal 14, and it is verified that the binary addition is correct.

Example 2. Find the sum of 1101 and 0101.

Solution. Arranging the binary quantities in columns,

$$\begin{array}{cccc} 1 \ 1 & 1 & & \text{carrys} \\ 1 \ 1 & 0 & 1 & \\ 0 \ 1 & 0 & 1 & \\ \hline 1 \ 0 \ 0 & 1 & 0 & \\ E \ D \ C & B & A & \end{array}$$

Then we proceed with the addition by columns. Column *A* involves law 4. The sum is 0 with a carry of 1. The carry of 1 is placed at the top of column *B*. Column *B* involves $1 + 0 + 0 = 1$ with no carry (law 3). Column *C* is $1 + 1 = 0$ with a carry of 1 (law 4). The carry of

1 is placed at the top of column D. In column D, $1 + 1 = 0$ with a carry of 1 *plus* 0 (the original bottom bit in column D). The answer brought down to the bottom of column D is 0, and the carry of 1 is taken to the left (labeled column E). Since there are no other bits in column E, this carry is taken down to the answer row as though it were the addition of $1 + 0 = 1$. Therefore,

$$1101 + 0101 = 10010$$

3·2 Binary Addition: Fractions

Binary fractions are added in accordance with the same rules. The first step in the addition process takes place in the position farthest to the right of the binary point. Example 1 illustrates the process of adding binary fractions.

Example 1. Find the sum of 0.1011 and 0.1101

Solution

$$
\begin{array}{r}
0.1\ 0\ 1\ 1 \\
+0.1\ 1\ 0\ 1 \\
\hline
1.1\ 0\ 0\ 0 \\
E\ D\ C\ B\ A
\end{array}
$$

The positions are again lettered for ease of reference.

Position A

   $1 + 1 = 0$ with a carry of 1

Position B

   $1 + 0 = 1$, then adding the carry of 1:
   $1 + 1 = 0$, with a new carry of 1

Position C

   $0 + 1 = 1$, then adding the carry of 1:
   $1 + 1 = 0$, with a new carry of 1

Position D

> $1 + 1 = 0$ with a carry of 1
> Then $0 + 1$ (carry from position C) $= 1$, with the carry of 1 from the initial addition in position D. Therefore the carry of 1 is taken to position E.

Position E

> $0 + 0 = 0$
> Then $0 + 1$ (carry from position D) $= 1$

3·3 Binary Addition: Mixed Numbers

The same rules and procedures also apply to the addition of binary mixed numbers, as illustrated in Example 1.

Example 1. Find the sum of 111011.1001 and 110101.0111.

Solution

$$
\begin{array}{l}
1\ 11\ 01\ 1.1\ 0\ 0\ 1 \\
1\ 10\ 10\ 1.0\ 1\ 1\ 1 \\
\hline
1\ 1\ 10\ 00\ 1.0\ 0\ 0\ 0 \\
K\ J\ I\ H\ G\ F\ E\ D\ C\ B\ A
\end{array}
$$

Column A

> $1 + 1 = 0 + 1$ carry

Column B

> $0 + 1 = 1$
> Then $1 + 1$ carry $(A) = 0 + 1$ carry

Column C

> $0 + 1 = 1$
> Then $1 + 1$ carry $(B) = 0 + 1$ carry

Column D

> $1 + 0 = 1$
> Then $1 + 1$ carry $(C) = 0 + 1$ carry

Column E

$1 + 1 = 0 + 1$ carry
$0 + 1$ carry $(D) = 1 + 1$ carry

Column F

$1 + 0 = 1$
Then $1 + 1$ carry $(E) = 0 + 1$ carry

Column G

$0 + 1 = 1$
Then $1 + 1$ carry $(F) = 0 + 1$ carry

Column H

$1 + 0 = 1$
Then $1 + 1$ carry $(G) = 0 + 1$ carry

Column I

$1 + 1 = 0 + 1$ carry
Then $0 + 1$ carry $(H) = 1 + 1$ carry

Column J

$1 + 1 = 0 + 1$ carry
$0 + 1$ carry $(I) = 1 + 1$ carry

Column K

The 1 carried from column *J*

PROBLEMS

Find the sum of the following binary quantities:

3·1
```
  1 0 1 0
+ 1 0 0 0
```

3·2
```
  1 1 1 0
+ 1 0 0 1
```

3·3
```
  1 1 1 0 1 1
+ 1 0 1 0 0 0
```

3·4
```
  0 1 1 1 1 0
+ 1 0 0 1 0 1
```

3·5	1 1 0 0 0 1 1 1 0 0 +1 0 1 0 1 0 0 1 1 0	3·6	1 1 1 0 0 0 1 1 0 0 +0 1 1 0 0 1 1 1 0 0
3·7	1 1 0 1 1 0 1 1 0 0 +1 1 1 0 1 1 1 0 0 1	3·8	1 1 1 1 1 0 0 0 0 0 +1 1 1 0 0 1 1 1 0 0
3·9	0 0 1 0 0 1 0 0 1 1 +0 1 1 0 0 0 1 0 1 0	3·10	0 0 0 1 1 1 0 0 0 0 +1 0 1 1 0 1 1 0 0 0
3·11	1 1 1 0 0 0 1 1 1 1 +0 1 0 0 1 0 0 1 1 1	3·12	1 1 0 1 1 0 1 1 0 0 +1 0 0 1 1 1 0 1 0 1
3·13	0 0 0 0 0 1 1 1 1 1 +0 0 0 1 1 0 0 0 1 1	3·14	0 0 1 0 0 1 0 0 1 1 +0 0 0 1 0 0 0 1 1 0
3·15	0 0 0 1 1 1 0 0 1 1 +1 0 0 1 1 0 0 0 1 1	3·16	0 0 1 1 1.0 0 0 1 1 +0 1 0 1 0.1 1 0 0 1
3·17	0 0 1 1 0.0 0 1 1 1 +0 0 1 1 1.0 0 1 1 0	3·18	1 0 0 1 1 1 0.1 1 1 +0 0 1 1 0 1 1.0 1 1
3·19	1 1 0 0 1 0 0.1 0 0 +1 1 0 1 0 0 0.1 1 0	3·20	0 0 0 0.1 1 1 0 0 0 +0 0 0 1.0 1 0 1 1 1

3·4 Direct Binary Subtraction: Integers

Direct binary subtraction is the simplest type of subtraction in the binary system. It is rarely used in digital computers, however, since the circuitry required for direct addition and direct subtraction in the same circuit is very complicated. Subtraction by the complement method, discussed in the next two sections, is most frequently used in digital computer applications.

The four basic rules for direct binary subtraction are:

Law 1

$$0 - 0 = 0 \text{ (with no borrow)}$$

Law 2

$$1 - 1 = 0 \text{ (with no borrow)}$$

Law 3

$1 - 0 = 1$ (with no borrow)

Law 4

$0 - 1 = 1$ (with a borrow of 1) or $10 - 1 = 1$
Let us clarify these rules by several examples.

Example 1. Subtract 1010 from 1111.

Solution

$$
\begin{array}{r}
1\ 1\ 1\ 1 \quad \text{minuend} \\
-1\ 0\ 1\ 0 \\
\hline
0\ 1\ 0\ 1 \\
D\ C\ B\ A
\end{array}
$$

Examining the process by columns results in:

Column A

$1 - 0 = 1$ (with no borrow): law 3

Column B

$1 - 1 = 0$ (with no borrow): law 2

Column C

$1 - 0 = 1$ (with no borrow): law 3

Column D

$1 - 1 = 0$ (with no borrow): law 2

The subtraction is checked by converting the minuend, subtrahend, and remainder into decimals:

$$
\begin{aligned}
\text{Binary } 1111 &= (1 \times 2^3) + (1 \times 2^2) + (1 \times 2^1) + (1 \times 2^0) \\
&= 8 + 4 + 2 + 1 = \text{decimal } 15
\end{aligned}
$$

$$
\begin{aligned}
\text{Binary } 1010 &= (1 \times 2^3) + (0 \times 2^2)\,1 \times 2' + (0 \times 2^0) \\
&= 8 + 0 + 2 + 0 = \text{decimal } 10
\end{aligned}
$$
$$
\begin{aligned}
\text{Binary } 0101 &= (0 \times 2^3) + (1 \times 2^2) + (0 \times 2') + (1 \times 2^0) \\
&= 0 + 4 + 0 + 1 = \text{decimal } 5
\end{aligned}
$$

and then subtracting in decimal notation:

$$
\begin{array}{r}
1\,5 \\
-1\,0 \\
\hline
5
\end{array}
$$

Since binary 0101 = decimal 5, the subtraction process is correct.

Example 1 illustrates the most simple type of direct binary subtraction because no borrow was involved. Let us consider an example in which borrowing is required.

Example 2. Subtract 011011 from 110101.

Solution

0	10	10	0	10		minuend changes after borrowing
1	1	0	1	0	1	minuend original
−0	1	1	0	1	1	subtrahend
	1	1	0	1	0	
F	*E*	*D*	*C*	*B*	*A*	

Explaining the subtraction process column by column:

Column A

$1 - 1 = 0$ (with no borrow): law 2

Column B

$0 - 1 = 1$ (with a borrow of 1): law 4
Notice that the minuend is changed from 0 to 10.

Column C

$0 - 0 = 0$ (with no borrow): law 1
Notice that the minuend is changed from 1 to 0 because of the borrow required for column *B*.

Column D

$0 - 1 = 1$ (with a borrow of 1): law 4
Notice that the minuend is changed from 0 to 10.

Column E

0 − 1 = 1 (with a borrow of 1): law 4

Notice that the minuend is changed from 0, which resulted from the column *C* borrow, to 10 by borrowing from column *F*.

Column F

0 − 0 = 0 (with no borrow): law 1

3·5   Direct Binary Subtraction: Fractions and Mixed Numbers

The same rules apply in the direct subtraction of binary fractions and binary mixed numbers, as illustrated in the following example.

Example. Subtract 011.001 from 110.011.

Solution

```
    0   10  10              minuend changes
    1   1   0  .  0  1  1   original minuend
   −0   1   1  .  0  0  1   subtrahend
   ─────────────────────
    0   1   1  .  0  1  0
    F   E   D     C  B  A
```

Explaining the subtraction process column by column:

Column A

1 − 1 = 0 (with no borrow): law 2

Column B

1 − 0 = 1 (with no borrow): law 3

Column C

0 − 0 = 0 (with no borrow): law 1

Column D

0 − 1 = 1 (with a borrow of 1): law 4

Notice that the minuend is changed from 0 to 10 by borrowing 1 from column *E*.

Column E

0 − 1 (with a borrow of 1): law 4
The original minuend was changed from 1 to 0 by the borrowing required by column *D*. Now this 0 must be changed to 10 by borrowing from column *E*.

Column F

0 − 0 = 0 (with no borrow): law 1
Notice that the original minuend 1 was changed to 0 by the borrowing required by column *E*.
See the following problem section for additional practice work on direct binary subtraction.

PROBLEMS

Subtract the following binary quantities by use of the direct method:

3·21
```
  1 0 1 0
 −1 0 0 0
```

3·22
```
  1 1 0 0
 −0 1 1 0
```

3·23
```
  1 1 1 1
 −0 0 1 1
```

3·24
```
  0 1 0 1
 −0 1 0 0
```

3·25
```
  1 1 1 0
 −1 0 1 0
```

3·26
```
  1 1 0 0 0.1 1 1 0 0
 −1 0 0 1 0.1 0 0 1 0
```

3·27
```
  1 1 1 0 0 0 1 1 0 0
 −0 1 1 0 0 1 1 1 0 1
```

3·28
```
  1 1 1 0 1 1 1 0 0 1
 −1 1 0 1 1 0 1 1 0 0
```

3·29
```
  1 1 1 1 1 0 0 0 0 0
 −1 1 0 0 0 1 0 0 1 1
```

3·30
```
  0 1 1 0 0 0 1 0 1 0
 −0 0 1 0 0 1 0 0 1 1
```

3·31
```
  1 1 1 0 0 0 1 1 1 1
 −0 1 0 0 1 0 0 1 1 1
```

3·32
```
  1 1 0 1 1 0 1 1 0 0
 −1 0 0 1 1 1 0 1 0 1
```

3·33
```
  0 0 0 1 1 0 0 0 1 1
 −0 0 0 0 0 1 1 1 1 1
```

3·34
```
  0 0 1 0 0 1 0 0 1 1
 −0 0 0 1 0 0 0 1 1 0
```

3·35   1 0 0 1 1 0 0 0 1 1   3·36   1 1 1 0 0.0 0 1 1 0
      −0 0 0 1 1 1 0 0 0 1   −0 1 0 1 1.1 1 0 0 1

3·37   1 0 0 1 1 1 0.1 1 1   3·38   1 1 1 1 0.0 0 0 0 1
      −0 0 1 1 0 1 1.0 1 1   −1 0 0 1 1.1 1 0 0 1

3·39   1 0 1 1 1.1 1 0 1 1   3·40   1 1 1 1 1.1 1 1 1 1
      −1 0 0 0 1.1 1 1 1 1   −0 1 0 1 0.1 0 1 0 1

3·6   Decimal Subtraction by 10's Complements

As mentioned in the preceding section, the performance of both addition and direct subtraction requires a very complicated circuit. On the other hand, a circuit whose only requirement is to perform addition is considerably more simple. Ideally, a circuit should be as simple as the addition circuit but capable of performing both addition and subtraction. This ideal situation is approached by performing subtraction by a special technique, i.e., addition of numerical complements. *This section deals with the manner in which the complementary technique can be utilized in the decimal system.* The following section analyzes the complementary approach to the binary system.

The 10's complement. The 10's complement of any number can be found by

$$C_{10} = 10^a - N$$

where C_{10} = 10's complement of the number N
      N = number whose complement is to be found
      a = number of digits to be carried out (in computers this is the number of digits the computer can register)

The following example illustrates how the 10's complement of a number can be computed.

Example 1. Determine the 10's complement of 450. Assume that a total of eight digits can be handled.

Solution. The basic equation for computing the 10's complement is

$$C_{10} = 10^a - N$$

where
$$a = 8$$
$$N = 450$$

Substituting values,

$$C_{10} = 10^8 - 450$$

which is

$$
\begin{array}{r}
1\ 0\ 0\ 0\ 0\ 0\ 0\ 0\ 0 \\
-\ \underline{4\ 5\ 0} \\
9\ 9\ 9\ 9\ 9\ 5\ 5\ 0
\end{array}
$$

Therefore,

$$C_{10} \text{ of } 450 = 99999550$$

The manner in which subtraction can be performed by the addition of complements is as follows:

1. Determine the 10's complement of the subtrahend.
2. Find the sum of the minuend and the 10's complement of the subtrahend.
3. If the sum (which is really the remainder of the subtraction) has a digit remainder (as shown in Example 2), the remainder is positive and the process is completed.
4. If there is no digit remainder (as shown in Example 1, Sec. 3.7), then:
   a. Determine the 10's complement of the remainder.
   b. Attach a negative sign to this remainder, which is now the final answer.

Example 2. Subtract 240 from 380 by use of the 10's complement method. Assume that 10 digits can be handled.

Solution. Find the 10's complement of 240.

$$
\begin{array}{r}
C_{10} = 10^{10} - 240 \\
1\ 0\ 0\ 0\ 0\ 0\ 0\ 0\ 0\ 0\ 0 \\
-\ \underline{2\ 4\ 0} \\
9\ 9\ 9\ 9\ 9\ 9\ 9\ 7\ 6\ 0
\end{array}
$$

In order to facilitate the addition process, the desired number of 0s are tacked in front of the minuend (380). Now adding to obtain the remainder,

$$
\begin{array}{rl}
0\ 0\ 0\ 0\ 0\ 0\ 0\ 3\ 8\ 0 & \text{minuend} \\
+\ \underline{9\ 9\ 9\ 9\ 9\ 9\ 9\ 7\ 6\ 0} & \text{subtrahend} \\
1\ 0\ 0\ 0\ 0\ 0\ 0\ 0\ 1\ 4\ 0 & \text{remainder}
\end{array}
$$

Notice the digit 1 in the eleventh position. This indicates that the sum (the remainder of the subtraction process) is positive. Since the sum is positive, the completion of this step is the final result. Therefore the remainder is 140.

3.7 Decimal Subtraction by 10's Complement with Negative Remainders

Let us now consider an example in which the remainder is negative. Any subtraction in which the minuend is larger than the subtrahend will produce this result, and an additional step is required to obtain the solution.

Example 1. Subtract 185 from 120 by utilization of the 10's complement. Assume that 10 digits can be handled.

Solution

Finding the 10's complement of 185,

$$
\begin{array}{r}
1\,0\,0\,0\,0\,0\,0\,0\,0\,0\,0 \\
-\ \ 0\,0\,0\,0\,0\,0\,0\,1\,8\,5 \\
\hline
9\,9\,9\,9\,9\,9\,9\,8\,1\,5 = C_{10} \text{ of } 185
\end{array}
$$

Now adding by complements,

$$
\begin{array}{r}
0\,0\,0\,0\,0\,0\,0\,1\,2\,0 \\
+\ 9\,9\,9\,9\,9\,9\,9\,8\,1\,5 \\
\hline
9\,9\,9\,9\,9\,9\,9\,9\,3\,5 \\
\text{no digit remainder}
\end{array}
$$

Notice that there is no digit remainder. Therefore step 4 of the preceding set of rules must be incorporated. Recomplementing,

$$
\begin{array}{r}
10^{10} = 1\,0\,0\,0\,0\,0\,0\,0\,0\,0\,0 \\
-9\,9\,9\,9\,9\,9\,9\,9\,3\,5 \\
\hline
-0\,0\,0\,0\,0\,0\,0\,0\,6\,5
\end{array}
$$

Therefore the recomplemented remainder is -65; i.e., subtracting 185 from 120 results in a remainder of -65.

3·8 The 9's Complement

The 9's complement of any number can be found by

$$C_9 = (10^a - 1) - N$$

where C_9 = 9's complement of the number N
N = number whose complement is to be found
a = number of digits to be carried out in the complementing process.

Example 1. Determine the 9's complement of 270. Assume that 10 digits can be handled by the computer.

Solution

$$C_9 = (10^{10} - 1) - 270$$

Step 1

$$
\begin{array}{r}
1\,0\,0\,0\,0\,0\,0\,0\,0\,0 \\
-\qquad\qquad\quad 1 \\
\hline
9\,9\,9\,9\,9\,9\,9\,9\,9
\end{array}
$$

Step 2

$$C_9 = 9999999999 - 270$$

$$
\begin{array}{r}
9\,9\,9\,9\,9\,9\,9\,9\,9\,9 \\
-\qquad\qquad 2\,7\,0 \\
\hline
9\,9\,9\,9\,9\,9\,9\,7\,2\,9
\end{array}
$$

Therefore,

$$C_9 \text{ of } 270 = 9999999729$$

3·9 Decimal Subtraction by the 9's Complement

The rules for subtraction by the 9's complement are identical to those for the 10's complement, as illustrated by the following two examples. One additional process, called the *end-around carry*, is introduced.

Example 1. Subtract 520 from 740 by utilization of the 9's complement method. Assume 10 digits can be handled by the computer.

Solution

Step 1. Find the 9's complement of 520.

$$C_9 = (10^{10} - 1) - 520$$

$$
\begin{array}{r}
1\,0\,0\,0\,0\,0\,0\,0\,0\,0\,0 \\
-1 \\
\hline
9\,9\,9\,9\,9\,9\,9\,9\,9\,9
\end{array}
$$

Then

$$
\begin{array}{r}
9\,9\,9\,9\,9\,9\,9\,9\,9\,9 \\
-5\,2\,0 \\
\hline
9\,9\,9\,9\,9\,9\,9\,4\,7\,9 = C_9 \text{ of } 520
\end{array}
$$

Step 2. Add by complements.

$$
\begin{array}{r}
0\,0\,0\,0\,0\,0\,0\,7\,4\,0 \\
+\ 9\,9\,9\,9\,9\,9\,9\,4\,7\,9 \\
\hline
1\,0\,0\,0\,0\,0\,0\,0\,2\,1\,9
\end{array}
$$

⌐ digit remainder

Step 3. The remainder of 0000000219 is called the *uncorrected remainder*. The digit remainder of 1 (the eleventh position) must be added to the uncorrected remainder. This is called the end-around carry process Hence,

$$
\begin{array}{r}
0\,0\,0\,0\,0\,0\,0\,2\,1\,9 \\
+1 \quad \text{digit remainder} \\
\hline
0\,0\,0\,0\,0\,0\,0\,2\,2\,0 \quad \text{corrected remainder}
\end{array}
$$

Let us next illustrate the procedure for subtracting by the 9's complement method when there is no digit remainder for the end-around carry process. In such a case, the end-around carry involves 0.

Example 2. Subtract 394 from 260 by utilization of the 9's complement method. Assume the use of 10 digits.

Solution

Step 1. Find the 9's complement of 394 (the subtrahend).

$$
\begin{array}{r}
9\,9\,9\,9\,9\,9\,9\,9\,9\,9 \\
-3\,9\,4 \\
\hline
9\,9\,9\,9\,9\,9\,9\,6\,0\,5 \;=\; C_9 \text{ of } 394
\end{array}
$$

Step 2. Add the 9's complement of the subtrahend to the minuend (260).

$$
\begin{array}{r}
0\,0\,0\,0\,0\,0\,0\,2\,6\,0 \\
+\;\; 9\,9\,9\,9\,9\,9\,9\,6\,0\,5 \\
\hline
0\,9\,9\,9\,9\,9\,9\,9\,8\,6\,5 \\
\uparrow
\end{array}
$$

zero digit remainder

The zero digit remainder indicates that the remainder is negative and must be recomplemented. The end-around carry does not change the remainder in this case, i.e.,

$$
\begin{array}{r}
0\,9\,9\,9\,9\,9\,9\,9\,8\,6\,5 \\
+0 \\
\hline
9\,9\,9\,9\,9\,9\,9\,8\,6\,5
\end{array}
$$

Step 4. Since the remainder is negative, it is to be recomplemented, as stated earlier:

$$
\begin{array}{r}
9\,9\,9\,9\,9\,9\,9\,9\,9\,9 \\
-9\,9\,9\,9\,9\,9\,9\,8\,6\,5 \\
\hline
0\,0\,0\,0\,0\,0\,0\,1\,3\,4
\end{array}
$$

Therefore, the final remainder is −134.

Rules for subtracting by the 9's complement

1. Find the 9's complement of the subtrahend.
2. Add the 9's complement of the subtrahend and the minuend.
3. Perform the end-around carry. If the carry is performed with a 1, the process is then completed. If the carry is performed with a 0, however, go on to step 4.
4. When the end-around carry is with a 0, recomplement the remainder. This recomplemented remainder with a minus sign is the final remainder.

PROBLEMS

Subtract the following decimal quantities, using the 10's complement method:

3·41	8,5 0 0		**3·42**	4,7 8 0
	−4,2 5 0			−3,6 9 0
3·43	9,3 6 1		**3·44**	5,7 1 6
	−7,9 5 2			−2,3 4 7
3·45	3,9 5 7			
	−2,5 9 0			

Subtract the following decimal quantities, using the 9's complement method:

3·46	5,8 0 0		**3·47**	8,7 4 2
	−2,4 0 5			−6,3 9 1
3·48	2,5 7 3		**3·49**	3,3 0 0
	−3,6 5 2			−4,7 0 0
3·50	7,7 2 2			
	−8,3 4 1			

3·10   The 2's Complement of Binary Numbers

Binary subtraction by complements follows the same basic principles as decimal subtraction by complements. The 2's complement in binary coincides with the 10's complement in the decimal system. The 2's complement of a binary number is determined by the following relationship:

$$C_2 = 2^a - N$$

where C_2 = 2's complement of the binary number under consideration
  a = number of digits to be handled in the process (generally 10)
  N = binary number whose 2's complement is to be computed

Example. Find the 2's complement of binary 10101101. Assume that 10 digits can be used by the computer.

Solution. Stating the previous equation and substituting values,

$$C_2 = 2^{10} - 10101101$$

$$
\begin{array}{r}
2^{10} = 1\,0\,0\,0\,0\,0\,0\,0\,0\,0\,0 \\
-0\,0\,1\,0\,1\,0\,1\,1\,0\,1 \\
\hline
1\,1\,0\,1\,0\,1\,0\,0\,1\,1
\end{array}
$$

Note that the complementing process involves direct binary subtraction, as analyzed in Secs. 3·4 and 3·5.

3·11 Binary Subtraction by the 2's Complement

The rules for subtracting by use of the 2's complement are identical to those used in the 10's complementing process examined in the preceding section. Example 1 illustrates this for cases in which the remainder is positive, while Example 2 depicts a subtraction where a negative remainder results.

Example 1. Subtract 0001110110 from 1101001011 by use of the 2's complement. Ten digits are to be used.

Solution

Step 1. Find the 2's complement of the subtrahend.

$$
\begin{array}{r}
2^{10} = 1\,0\,0\,0\,0\,0\,0\,0\,0\,0\,0 \\
-0\,0\,0\,1\,1\,1\,0\,1\,1\,0 \\
\hline
1\,1\,1\,0\,0\,0\,1\,0\,1\,0 = C_2
\end{array}
$$

Step 2. Add the 2's complement of the subtrahend to the minuend using the rules of binary addition stated in the first three sections of this chapter.

$$
\begin{array}{r}
1\,1\,0\,1\,0\,0\,1\,0\,1\,1 \\
+\ 1\,1\,1\,0\,0\,0\,1\,0\,1\,0 \\
\hline
1\,1\,0\,1\,1\,0\,1\,0\,1\,0\,1
\end{array}
$$

↑
digit remainder

Since the digit remainder is 1, the existing remainder is positive. Therefore, 1011010101 is the remainder.

Checking the results by converting the binary quantities into their decimal equivalents and subtracting,

Binary 1101001011 = decimal 843
Binary 0001110110 = decimal 118
Binary 1011010101 = decimal 725

And subtracting directly in decimal,

$$
\begin{array}{r}
8\ 4\ 3 \\
-1\ 1\ 8 \\
\hline
7\ 2\ 5
\end{array}
$$

Therefore the original remainder obtained by 2's complementing in binary form is verified as being correct.

Let us next consider a subtraction by the 2's complement technique where the remainder is negative.

Example 2. Subtract 11011 from 10010 by utilization of the 2's complementing technique. Assume the use of 10 digits.

Solution

Step 1. Find the 2's complement of the subtrahend.

$$
\begin{array}{r}
2^{10} = 1\ 0\ 0\ 0\ 0\ 0\ 0\ 0\ 0\ 0\ 0 \\
-0\ 0\ 0\ 0\ 0\ 1\ 1\ 0\ 1\ 1 \\
\hline
1\ 1\ 1\ 1\ 1\ 0\ 0\ 1\ 0\ 1 = C_2
\end{array}
$$

Step 2. Add the 2's complement of the subtrahend to the minuend.

$$
\begin{array}{r}
0\ 0\ 0\ 0\ 0\ 1\ 0\ 0\ 1\ 0 \\
+\ \ 1\ 1\ 1\ 1\ 1\ 0\ 0\ 1\ 0\ 1 \\
\hline
0\ \ 1\ 1\ 1\ 1\ 1\ 1\ 0\ 1\ 1\ 1
\end{array}
$$

↑
zero digit remainder

Since the digit remainder is zero, the existing remainder must be recomplemented.

Step 3. Recomplement the remainder 1111110111.

$$2^{10} = \begin{array}{r} 1\,0\,0\,0\,0\,0\,0\,0\,0\,0 \\ -1\,1\,1\,1\,1\,1\,0\,1\,1\,1 \\ \hline 0\,0\,0\,0\,0\,0\,1\,0\,0\,1 \end{array}$$

Therefore the remainder is -1001.

Checking in decimal,

$$\begin{array}{r} 1\,1\,0\,1\,1 = 2\,7 \\ -1\,0\,0\,1\,0 = 1\,8 \\ \hline -\ \ 1\,0\,0\,1 = -9 \end{array}$$

and $18 - 27 = -9$

3·12 The 1's Complement of Binary Numbers

Subtraction by utilization of the 1's complement is most common. The 1's complement of any binary number may be found by the following equation:

$$C_1 = (2^a - 1) - N$$

where $C_1 = $ 1's complement of the number

$a = $ number of digits to be handled by the computer

$N = $ binary number whose 1's complement is to be found

In the case where the computer will handle 10 digits (which is typical):

$$C_1 = (2^{10} - 1) - N$$

Note that

$$2^{10} = \begin{array}{r} 1\,0\,0\,0\,0\,0\,0\,0\,0\,0 \\ -\,0\,0\,0\,0\,0\,0\,0\,0\,0\,1 \\ \hline 1\,1\,1\,1\,1\,1\,1\,1\,1\,1 \end{array}$$

Therefore,

$$C_1 = 1111111111 - N$$

Notice that each digit of the binary number N is subtracted from 1. Recalling the rules for direct subtraction,

$$\begin{array}{r} 1 - 0 = 1 \\ 1 - 1 = 0 \end{array}$$

Examination of these two rules (where 0 is subtracted from 1 and where 1 is subtracted from 1) indicates that subtracting the digit from 1 actually changes the original digit. In effect, then, *the 1's complement of any number can be obtained simply by changing all the 1s to 0s and all the 0s to 1s.*

Example. Find the 1's complement of 1010101101.

   Solution. Changing all 1s to 0s and all 0s to 1s,

$$C_1 = 0101010010$$

Computers can easily perform the 1's complement type of conversion by the use of inverter circuits. Recall that the inverter "flips" the signal from 0 input to 1 input or from 1 input to 0 output.

3·13   Binary Subtraction by the 1's Complement

   Subtraction by the 1's complement technique is performed by the following steps (notice the similarity to the 9's complementing method for decimal numbers):

1. Determine the 1's complement of the subtrahend.
2. Add the 1's complement of the subtrahend to the minuend.
3. Perform the end-around carry. If a 1 is involved in this process, the final remainder has been obtained. If a 0 is involved, proceed to step 4.
4. When the end-around carry is with a 0, recomplement the remainder. This recomplemented remainder with a minus sign in front of it is the final answer.

   Let us illustrate the process of subtraction by the 1's complement with two examples. The first example illustrates the case where the remainder is positive, while Example 2 presents a problem which has a negative remainder.

Example 1. Subtract 0011101101 from 0101000000.

Solution

Step 1

$$C_1 \text{ of } 0011101101 = 1100010010$$

Step 2. Adding,

```
    0 1 0 1 0 0 0 0 0 0
+   1 1 0 0 0 1 0 0 1 0
    1 0 0 0 1 0 1 0 0 1 0
    ↑
```
1 digit remainder

Step 3. Performing the end-around carry,

```
    0 0 0 1 0 1 0 0 1 0
+                     1
    0 0 0 1 0 1 0 0 1 1
```

Since the end-around carry is 1, the final result is obtained.

Example 2. Subtract 1010010010 from 0100101000.

Solution

Step 1

$$C_1 \text{ of } 1010010010 = 0101101101$$

Step 2. Adding,

```
    0 1 0 0 1 0 1 0 0 0
    0 1 0 1 1 0 1 1 0 1
  0   1 0 1 0 0 1 0 1 0 1
      ↑
```
zero digit remainder

Step 3. Since the end-around carry involves a zero, the remainder must be recomplemented. Taking on the negative sign, this results in the following:

$$-0101101010$$

Immediately following is a group of problems which offer practice in binary subtraction by the 2's and 1's complements.

PROBLEMS

Subtract the following binary quantities, using the 2's complement technique:

3·51   1 1 0 1 0 1
      −1 0 1 0 0 1

3·52   1 0 0 1 0 1
      −0 1 1 0 0 0

3·53   1 1 1 0 0 1 1 0 0 0
      −1 0 1 0 1 0 0 1 1 0

3·54   1 1 0 0 0 1 1 1 0 0
      −0 1 1 0 0 1 1 1 0 0

3·55   1 0 1 1 0 1 1 0 0 0
      −0 0 0 1 1 1 1 1 0 0

Subtract the following binary quantities, using the 1's complement technique:

3·56   1 0 1 0
      −1 0 0 0

3·57   1 1 0 0
      −0 1 1 0

3·58   1 1 1 1
      −0 0 1 1

3·59   0 1 0 1
      −0 1 0 0

3·60   1 1 1 0
      −1 0 1 0

3·61   1 1 0 0 0.1 1 1 0 0
      −1 0 0 1 0.1 0 0 1 0

3·62   1 1 1 0 0 0 1 1 0 0
      −0 1 1 0 0 1 1 1 0 1

3·63   1 1 1 0 1 1 1 0 0 1
      −1 1 0 1 1 0 1 1 0 0

3·64   1 1 1 1 1 0 0 0 0 0
      −1 1 0 0 0 1 0 0 1 1

3·65   0 1 1 0 0 0 1 0 1 0
      −0 1 1 0 0 1 0 0 1 1

3·66   1 1 1 1 1.1 1 1 1
      −0 1 0 1 0.1 0 1 0

3·67   1 0 0 0 1.1 1 1 1 1
      −1 0 1 1 1.1 1 0 1 1

3·68   1 1 1 1 0.0 0 0 0 1
      −1 0 0 1 1.1 1 0 0 1

3·69   0 0 1 1 0 1 1.0 1 1
      −1 0 0 1 1 1 0.1 1 1

3·70 1 1 1 0 0.0 0 1 1 0
   −0 1 0 1 1.1 1 0 0 1

3·71 1 0 1 1 0 1.1 1 0
   −0 1 1 0 0 0.1 1 1

3·72 0 0 0 1 1 1 0 0 0 1 1
   −1 0 0 1 1 0 0 0 1 1 1

3·73 0 0 0 1 0 0 0 1 1 0
   −0 1 1 0 0 1 0 0 1 1

3·74 1 1 1 1 0 0 0 0 1 1
   −1 1 1 1 1 1 0 0 0 0

3·75 1 1 0 1 1 0 1 1 0 0
   −1 0 0 1 1 1 0 1 0 1

3·76 0 1 0 0 1 0 0 1 1 1
   −1 1 1 0 0 0 1 1 1 1

3·77 1 1 1 1 0 0 1 0 0 1
   −1 0 0 1 1 1 0 0 1 1

3·78 1 0 0 0 0 1 0 1 0 0
   −1 1 0 0 1 1 0 0 1 1

3·79 0 1 1 1 0 1 1 0 1 0
   −0 1 0 1 0 1 0 1 0 0

3·80 1 0 1 1 0 0 1 1 1 0
   −1 1 0 1 1 1 0 0 1 1

Binary Multiplication and Division and Binary Code Arithmetic

Introduction

The first two sections in this chapter are concerned with the principles of multiplying and dividing in the binary number system. The most common aspects of these processes are developed and are illustrated with worked-out examples.

Addition in the excess-3 coded system is dealt with in a separate section. Addition and subtraction in the ternary-coded system are also assigned separate sections. Each section in this chapter is followed by a set of exercise problems for practice purposes. A total of 120 problems are included.

4·1 Binary Multiplication

Multiplication with binary quantities follows essentially the same procedures as multiplication with decimal numbers. The rules for binary multiplication are as follows (see the illustrated example for identification of notation):

1. Set the multiplicand over the multiplier.
2. Multiply the multiplicand by the binary digit located at the extreme right of the multiplier. There are only two possibilities for any partial product.
   a. If the multiplier digit being used is 0, the partial product is 0 (as in the first partial product of the illustrated example).
   b. If the multiplier digit being used is 1, the partial product is

58

equal to the entire multiplicand (as shown in the second partial product of the illustrated example).

3. The process is repeated for each digit in the multiplier. The partial product is displaced one place to the left with each multiplier digit (see illustrated example). If should be noted that the displacement to the left by one position for each digit in the multiplier is always done in ordinary decimal multiplication.

4. The sum of the partial products is the final product of the binary multiplication. It should be noted that the four basic laws of binary addition are utilized in obtaining the sum of the partial products.

Illustrated Example of Binary Multiplication Notation

$$
\begin{array}{ll}
1\ 1\ 0\ 1 & \text{multiplicand} \\
\underline{\quad 1\ 0} & \text{multiplier} \\
0\ 0\ 0\ 0 & \text{first partial product} \\
\underline{1\ 1\ 0\ 1\ } & \text{second partial product} \\
1\ 1\ 0\ 1\ 0 & \text{product (sum of the partial products)}
\end{array}
$$

Example 1. Compute the product of 1101 and 1011.

Solution. Setting up the binary quantities for multiplication,

$$
\begin{array}{lr}
1\ 1\ 0\ 1 & \\
\times\ 1\ 0\ 1\ 1 & \\
\hline
1\ 1\ 0\ 1 & A \\
1\ 1\ 0\ 1 & B \\
0\ 0\ 0\ 0 & C \\
1\ 1\ 0\ 1 & D \\
\hline
1\ 0\ 0\ 0\ 1\ 1\ 1\ 1 & E
\end{array}
$$

Analyzing the multiplication by each partial product:

Partial Product A. Partial product A is the product of 1101×1, which is 1101.

Partial Product B. Partial product B is the product of 1101×1. Being the second partial product, the result is placed one position further to the left than the first partial product.

Partial Product C. This is the product of 1101 × 0, which equals 0000. The group of four zeros is located one position further to the left than the second partial product. Notice that this is two positions to the left of the first partial product.

Partial Product D. This is the product of 1101 × 1, which is equal to 1101. It is placed one position further to the left than the preceding partial product.

The Sum of the Partial Products (E). Starting from the extreme right, the partial products are added in accordance with the four laws studied in Sec. 3·1.

Check. Let us check the accuracy of the preceding binary multiplication by comparing the product with the product obtained by use of decimal notation.

$$\text{Multiplicand binary } 1101 = (1 \times 2^3) + (1 \times 2^2)$$
$$+ (0 \times 2) + 1 = 8 + 4 + 0 + 1 = 13$$
$$\text{Multiplier binary } 1011 = (1 \times 2^3) + (0 \times 2^2)$$
$$+ (1 \times 2) + 1 = 8 + 0 + 2 + 1 = 11$$
$$\text{Product binary } 10001111 = (1 \times 2^7) + (1 \times 2^3) + (1 \times 2^2)$$
$$+ (1 \times 2) + 1 = 128 + 8 + 4 + 2 + 1 = 143$$

Multiplying in decimal notation,

$$
\begin{array}{r}
1\,3 \\
1\,1 \\
\hline
1\,3 \\
1\,3 \\
\hline
1\,4\,3
\end{array}
$$

And

$$\text{Binary } 10001111 = \text{decimal } 143$$

Therefore, the binary multiplication is correct.

PROBLEMS

Find the products of the following by using binary multiplication:

4·1	11 × 01	4·2	11 × 11
4·3	101 × 11	4·4	101 × 10

4·5	101 × 01		4·6	111 × 01
4·7	111 × 10		4·8	111 × 11
4·9	110 × 10		4·10	110 × 01
4·11	110 × 11		4·12	1011 × 11
4·13	1011 × 01		4·14	1011 × 10
4·15	1101 × 101		4·16	1101 × 100
4·17	1101 × 011		4·18	1101 × 111
4·19	1010 × 111		4·20	1010 × 101
4·21	1010 × 100		4·22	1010 × 010
4·23	1001 × 010		4·24	1001 × 011
4·25	1001 × 100		4·26	1001 × 111
4·27	1100 × 111		4·28	1110 × 111
4·29	1111 × 111		4·30	1111 × 011

4·2 Binary Division

The general rules for decimal division are applicable in binary division. Example 1 illustrates a simple binary division with the corresponding notation.

Example 1. Determine the quotient of 1011 divided by 101.

Solution

```
                1 0   quotient
divisor   1 0 1 | 1 0 1 0   dividend
                1 0 1     partial quotient-divisor product
                    0     digit carried down
```

Following are the rules for binary division (refer to Example 1 for the notation):

1. Set the divisor and dividend into the conventional division position (as shown in Example 1).
2. Determine the number of places in the dividend required by the first division of the divisor into the quotient. Place the 1 of the quotient over the correct digit in the dividend.
3. Multiply the digit placed in the quotient by the divisor. Since the first digit of the quotient is 1, the product obtained by this multi-

plication is equal to the divisor. Place this partial quotient-divisor product directly below the correct dividend digits.

4. Subtract the partial quotient-divisor product from the dividend. Bring the next digit down from the dividend. If there is no remainder or carry-down, the division is complete.

5. If there is a remainder, repeat the division process until all the digits in the dividend have been used.

Let us consider several division examples that involve other complications.

Example 2. Find the quotient of 11110 divided by 11.

Solution. Setting up the example results in

$$
\begin{array}{r}
A\ B\ C\ D \\
1\ 0\ 1\ 0 \\
11\,\overline{)\,11\ 1\ 1\ 0} \\
\underline{1\ 1} \\
0\ 1\ 1 \\
\underline{1\ 1} \\
0\ 0 \\
\underline{0\ 0} \\
0
\end{array}
$$

Quotient A. 11 divided into 11 equals 1. Therefore 1 is placed in the quotient. Then, $1 \times 11 = 11$, which is placed in the partial quotient-divisor product. Then subtracting, $11 - 11 = 0$.

Quotient B. The first step is to carry down 1, the next digit in the dividend. The divisor 11 will not go into 01. Therefore 0 is placed in the quotient immediately to the right of the 1 determined for quotient A.

Quotient C. Carry down the next digit 1 from the dividend, which results in the number 011. The divisor (11) will go into 011 with a quotient of 1. This quotient of 1 is placed in position C. Multiplying, $11 \times 1 = 11$, and this is placed beneath 011. Subtracting, a remainder of 0 is obtained.

Quotient D. Since there is one more digit in the dividend, there must be one more division process. Carrying down the last digit (0) results in a remainder of 00. The divisor 11 will not go into 00; therefore the quotient in the D position is 0. Then multiplying, $0 \times 11 = 0$, which is placed underneath the 00. Subtracting leaves a remainder of 0.

The process of dividing 11110 by 11 is complete.

Check. Let us check the division by performing it in decimal notation.

$$\text{Binary divisor } 11 = \text{decimal } 3$$
$$\text{Binary dividend } 11110 = \text{decimal } 30$$
$$\text{Binary quotient } 1010 = \text{decimal } 10$$

$$
\begin{array}{r}
1\,0 \\
3\,\overline{)\,3\,0} \\
\underline{3} \\
0\,0 \\
\underline{0\,0} \\
0
\end{array}
$$

Therefore the preceding binary division is correct.

Example 3. Find the quotient of 10011 divided by 101.

Solution

$$
\begin{array}{r}
1\,1 \\
101\,\overline{)\,1\,0\,0\,1\,1} \\
\underline{1\,0\,1} \\
1\,0\,0\,1 \\
\underline{1\,0\,1} \\
1\,0\,0 \quad \textit{Answer: } 11 \; \tfrac{100}{101}
\end{array}
$$

Notice the problem encountered in this example. The divisor 101 will not go into the first three digits (100) of the dividend. Therefore 101 has to be divided into 1001, the first four digits of the dividend. The first digit in the quotient is four places in from the left because of this relationship. Also notice that a remainder is left, and it is treated in the same manner it would be in ordinary decimal division.

Again checking by reworking the problem in decimal notation,

$$\text{Binary divisor } 101 = \text{decimal } 5$$
$$\text{Binary dividend } 10011 = \text{decimal } 19$$
$$\text{Binary quotient } 11 = \text{decimal } 3$$
$$\text{Binary remainder } ^{100}\!/_{101} = \text{decimal } ^4\!/_5$$

The decimal division results in

$$
\begin{array}{r}
3 \\
5\,\overline{\big)\,1\,9} \\
1\,5 \\
\hline
4
\end{array}
\qquad Answer: 3 \ ^4\!/_5
$$

Therefore the binary division is correct. Notice that the binary subtraction laws as well as the binary multiplication laws must be observed in the performance of binary division. Following are several problems for practicing the arithmetic process.

PROBLEMS

Perform the following binary divisions:

4·31 $^{100}/_{10}$	4·32 $^{1000}/_{100}$	4·33 $^{110}/_{110}$
4·34 $^{1100}/_{110}$	4·35 $^{1100}/_{100}$	4·36 $^{1011}/_{101}$
4·37 $^{1111}/_{011}$	4·38 $^{10100}/_{101}$	4·39 $^{10010}/_{011}$
4·40 $^{11010}/_{1101}$	4·41 $^{11010}/_{1111}$	4·42 $^{11010}/_{1010}$
4·43 $^{11001}/_{1010}$	4·44 $^{11001}/_{1101}$	4·45 $^{11001}/_{1001}$
4·46 $^{11100}/_{1111}$	4·47 $^{11100}/_{1110}$	4·48 $^{11100}/_{1001}$
4·49 $^{11100}/_{1000}$	4·50 $^{11100}/_{1101}$	4·51 $^{11101}/_{1101}$
4·52 $^{11101}/_{1011}$	4·53 $^{11101}/_{1001}$	4·54 $^{11101}/_{1000}$
4·55 $^{11110}/_{1000}$	4·56 $^{11110}/_{1001}$	4·57 $^{11100}/_{1011}$
4·58 $^{11110}/_{1101}$	4·59 $^{11111}/_{1111}$	4·60 $^{11111}/_{1001}$

4·3   Excess-3 Code Addition

The process of addition in the excess-3 code is not as simple as in the decimal and straight binary systems. Since each original number is changed to 3 more than its first value, the sum of two such numbers has an excess of 6. Following are the rules to observe when adding excess-3 code numbers whose sum is less than 10:

1. Perform straight binary addition.
2. Subtract 3 in binary. The remainder will be the excess-3 code equivalent.

Example 1. Find the sum of $2 + 3$ in excess-3 code.

Solution. First express each number in its excess-3 code equivalent:

$$
\begin{array}{rl}
2 = & 0101 \\
3 = & 0110 \\
+ & \underline{} \\
& 1011
\end{array}
$$

As stated in the preceding paragraph, the sum (1011) has an excess of 6. Therefore, let us next subtract the binary 3 (0011) from this sum.

$$
\begin{array}{rl}
1011 & \text{original sum} \\
-0011 & \text{binary 3} \\
\hline
1000 & \text{corrected sum}
\end{array}
$$

Hence 1000 = decimal 8, the excess-3 code equivalent of 5.

To add two numbers in excess-3 code whose sum is 10 or greater, several other rules must be observed. Let us first perform such an addition before summarizing the steps.

Example 2. Find the sum of $8 + 4$ in excess-3 code.

Solution. First express each number in its excess-3 code equivalent:

$$
\begin{array}{rl}
8 = & 1011 \\
4 = & \underline{0111} \\
& 10010
\end{array}
$$

carry

The 1 to the extreme left is a carry and is written as the beginning of the next higher order, i.e.,

$$0001 \quad 0010$$

Then add binary 3 (0011) *to each order*, which results in the final sum.

$$
\begin{array}{cc}
0001 & 0010 \\
+0011 & 0011 \\
\hline
0100 & 0101 \\
\end{array}
$$

In other words,

$$0100 \quad 0101 = 45$$

Summarizing the addition process for cases in which the sum is 10 or more:

1. State each number in its excess-3 code equivalent.
2. Add in binary form.
3. Place the carry in the next higher order.
4. Add binary 3 to each order. This is the excess-3 code sum.

Checking the results of Example 2,

$$
\begin{array}{c}
8 \\
4 \\
\hline
12 \quad \text{in decimal}
\end{array}
$$

Adding 3 to each digit,

$$
\begin{array}{cc}
1 & 2 \\
3 & 3 \\
\hline
4 & 5 \\
\end{array}
$$

Note that each order in the binary corresponds to a digit in the decimal.

PROBLEMS

Perform the following additions in the excess-3 code:

4·61 2 + 5	4·62 2 + 6
4·63 3 + 2	4·64 1 + 4
4·65 3 + 3	4·66 4 + 7

4·67	5 + 8		**4·68**	6 + 7
4·69	9 + 3		**4·70**	8 + 9
4·71	4 + 8		**4·72**	4 + 6
4·73	5 + 6		**4·74**	6 + 8
4·75	7 + 7		**4·76**	5 + 7
4·77	7 + 9		**4·78**	9 + 6
4·79	8 + 7		**4·80**	9 + 9

4·4 Ternary Code Addition

Ternary addition can be performed by following these three rules:

1. The addition of two pluses equals a minus with a plus carry.
2. The addition of unlike signs equals a zero with no carry.
3. The addition of two minuses equals a plus with a minus carry.

Let us illustrate the application of these rules with an example.

Example 1. Convert the following numbers into ternary, and then find their sum: +7 and −2.

Solution. First convert the numbers into their ternary equivalents:

$$+7 = +-+$$
$$-2 = \underline{0-+}$$

Starting from the right-hand side and observing the rules stated in the preceding paragraph:

1. + plus + = − with a + carry.
2. + carry plus − = zero with no carry
   Then 0 plus − = − with no remainder
3. + plus 0 = +.

Checking by converting the ternary remainder into its decimal equivalent,

$$+-- = +(9) + (-3) + (-1) = +5$$

PROBLEMS

Perform the following additions in ternary notation:

4·81	$+2 + 2$		4·82	$-2 + 3$
4·83	$+5 + 4$		4·84	$-6 + 2$
4·85	$+7 - 2$		4·86	$+11 - 9$
4·87	$-11 + 6$		4·88	$+12 - 5$
4·89	$+8 - 11$		4·90	$+7 - 13$
4·91	$+1 + 1$		4·92	$+4 + 4$
4·93	$-4 + 7$		4·94	$+12 - 7$
4·95	$-11 + 9$		4·96	$-4 + 8$
4·97	$-11 + 3$		4·98	$-11 + 5$
4·99	$-4 + 9$		4·100	$+11 - 9$

4·5 Ternary Code Subtraction

Subtraction in the ternary code is a relatively simple process. First, the subtrahend is complemented. Then the complement of the subtrahend is added to the minuend. When a ternary number is complemented, the following rules are applied:

1. Change $+$ to $-$.
2. Change $-$ to $+$.
3. Leave the 0s unchanged.

Example. Subtract 6 from 12 in ternary.

Solution. First express each number in its ternary equivalent:

$$12 = ++0$$
$$6 = +-0$$

Complement the subtrahend, and then add: the complement of $+-0$ is $-+0$; then

$$\begin{array}{r} ++0 \\ -+0 \\ \hline +-0 \end{array}$$

Check by converting back into the decimal equivalent:

$$+-0 = (+9) + (-3) + (0) = +6$$

PROBLEMS

Convert the following quantities into their ternary equivalents and then subtract:

4·101	7 from 10		4·102	6 from 11
4·103	8 from 12		4·104	2 from 5
4·105	−5 from 2		4·106	−4 from 2
4·107	2 from 7		4·108	3 from 9
4·109	4 from 12		4·110	−3 from −12
4·111	6 from 11		4·112	7 from 10
4·113	4 from 6		4·114	1 from 4
4·115	−8 from 3		4·116	−6 from 5
4·117	3 from 8		4·118	4 from 7
4·119	5 from 11		4·120	−11 from −9

CHAPTER 5

Fundamental Topics
of Boolean Algebra

Introduction

The basic Boolean algebraic laws are analyzed in this chapter. This study proceeds from the basic Boolean relationships applicable to the series-circuit type of switching combinations to a development of the basic parallel-circuit laws. The series-parallel type of switching circuit is then introduced. The first and second distributive laws are developed and applied. In this way, the utility of these Boolean laws becomes easy to understand.

Early in the chapter, special emphasis is placed on three ways of representing switching circuits:

1. With switch symbols in an electric circuit
2. With a Boolean equation
3. With logic diagrams

The continuous use of this approach throughout the chapter helps to focus the reader's attention on relationships among these three representations of a switching combination.

A total of 60 problems are included in the chapter to provide the student with practice work.

5·1 Switching States and Notation

Boolean algebra, as used in conjunction with electronics, is concerned with two-state devices such as relays, mechanical switches, diodes, vacuum tubes, and transistors. Boolean algebra enables the user to simplify the circuit in a rapid, smooth manner. The two basic states of these devices are short—open, ON–OFF, etc. In many applications,

1 = ON or shorted or minimum resistance
0 = OFF or open or maximum resistance

The exact inverse relationship could be used if so desired by the designer. Using this notion, the following statement can be made:

If device Y is ON, it is transmitting and $Y = 1$.

Continuing with this type of analysis,

If the device Z is OFF, it is not transmitting and $Z = 0$.

When two or more devices are to be operated simultaneously by the same activation (signal), they are assigned the same letter notation. Three devices that are turned ON by the same signal, for example, can be represented in the manner shown in Fig. 5·1.

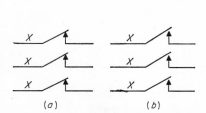

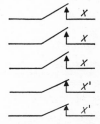

Fig. 5·1 Three devices turned ON or OFF by the same signal.

Fig. 5·2 Devices which act inversely.

There also exists a possibility that one or more devices can function inversely with one or more other devices when energized by the same signal. Figure 5·2 illustrates such a combination. It is seen that one group of devices which work together is assigned the same letter (X in Fig. 5·2). The group of devices which act inversely with the first group is assigned the same letter with a prime (X' in this case). Therefore X' means *not* X. Refer again to Fig. 5·2; when the signal is turned ON, the conditions of all the devices will be opposite to that shown (that is, X' will be 0 and X will be 1). *The conditions of the switches are customarily shown at the time when no signal is applied to the circuit, which is called the normal state of the circuit.* Therefore, in Fig. 5·2:

Condition OFF (normal): $X = 0$; $X' = 1$
Condition ON (activated): $X = 1$; $X' = 0$

The use of X' illustrates the *negation* of X. The principle of negation can be used in statements, such as:

Original statement: It is not raining.
Same statement with negation notation: It is (raining)'.

In terms of circuitry, negation indicates the inverse operation of two circuits or systems when excited by the same input signal. Therefore, if the first circuit is given the symbol X, its negation circuit would be assigned the symbol X'. It can be seen that X is the negation of X' and that X' is the negation of X. A circuit that is normally open (0) is the negation of a circuit that is normally closed (1); hence,

$$0' = 1 \ (\text{not OFF} = \text{ON})$$
$$1' = 0 \ (\text{not ON} = \text{OFF})$$

A double negation is equal to an affirmative, i.e.,

$$0'' = 0 \ (\text{not-not OFF} = \text{OFF})$$

and

$$1'' = 1 \ (\text{not-not ON} = \text{ON})$$

Therefore,

$$X'' = X, \text{ etc.}$$

5·2   Circuit Representation by Switches

A generalized method for the representation of the device as a switch, regardless of the type, is shown in Fig. 5·3. This type of representation can be used to designate transistor and diode switches as well as relays.

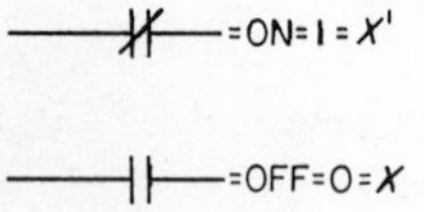

Notice that capital letters are used for both switch conditions. Switches that are ON when the circuit is not activated (the normal state) are given a primed letter symbol (such as X' in Fig. 5·3). Switches that are open when the circuit is not activated are given a letter symbol without the prime. *All the switches which are interconnected in such a way that they open or close together in response to a common*

Fig. 5·3 Notation for ON-OFF conditions.

signal are given the same letter symbol. The prime notation, or its absence, indicates whether these common switches are working directly or inversely.

5·3 Series Circuit Relationships

Figure 5·4 illustrates two switches connected in series and also the logical symbol for this switch circuit. Using the notation presented in the preceding section, we see that switches A and B in Fig. 5·4 are open when the circuit is in its normal state (not activated). This means that an energizing signal for switch A and a different energizing signal for switch B are required to close *both* switches.

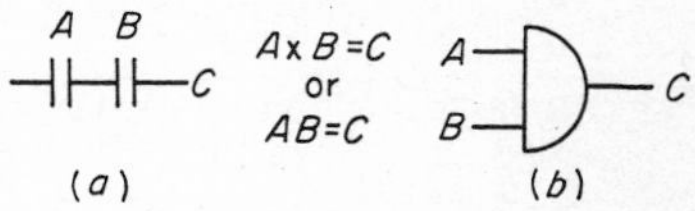

Fig. 5·4 Series circuit notation: (a) switch symbols, (b) logical diagram.

Notice that the series circuit can transmit information only when both switches (A and B) are closed. The symbol x is here used to designate a series circuit. Notice that the series switch circuit behaves in the same way as the statement *both* or *and.* In Boolean algebra notation, the series circuit of Fig. 5·4 is represented by $A \times B$ or simply AB. The

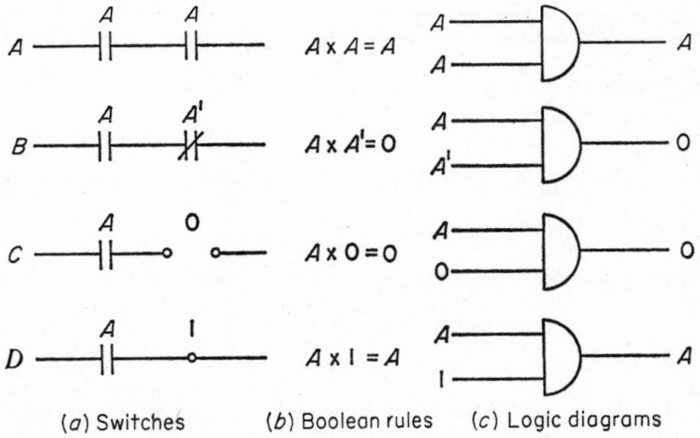

(*a*) Switches	(*b*) Boolean rules	(*c*) Logic diagrams

Fig. 5·5 Boolean multiplication rules.

operation of the series switch circuit is called *logical multiplication* and is also called the basic AND circuit. It is essential to recognize that logical multiplication is not identical to ordinary multiplication.

A number of rules for logical multiplication can be developed by examination of the series circuit possibilities, as shown in Fig. 5·5.

Figure 5·5a is the same diagram as Fig. 5·4 except that both switches are assigned the same letter (A) because they are activated together by the same signal. Since they both close upon receipt of the same signal and are open together in the absence of that signal, they are not in negation (no prime symbol for either is used). The circuit will transmit the signal only when both switches are transmitting (closed). In equation form,

$$A \times A = A$$

When both switches are transmitting,

$$1 \times 1 = 1$$

And when both switches are open,

$$0 \times 0 = 0$$

Refer to Fig. 5·5b. Switch A is the negation of switch A'. Being a series circuit, the switch negation ensures no signal transmission at any time (one of the two switches will always be open). In other words, the circuit of Fig. 5·5b will always act as an open circuit. In equation form,

$$A \times A' = 0$$

Let us substitute values and check this rule. Let $A = 1$, then $A' = 0$:

$$1 \times 0 = 0$$

Let $A = 0$, then $A' = 1$:

$$0 \times 1 = 0$$

Figure 5·5c illustrates a switch (A) in series with an open circuit (0). This combination always behaves as an open circuit, regardless of the state of switch A; that is,

$$A \times 0 = 0$$

Let $A = 1$:

$$1 \times 0 = 0$$

Let $A = 0$:

$$0 \times 0 = 0$$

In Fig. 5·5d, a switch (A) is in series with a closed circuit (1). This combination will always behave as if the switch were in the circuit by itself. That is, if the switch is closed, the circuit will transmit; and if the switch is open, the circuit will not transmit. In equation form,

$$A \times 1 = A$$

Let $A = 1$:

$$1 \times 1 = 1$$

Let $A = 0$:

$$0 \times 1 = 0$$

PROBLEMS

For Probs. 5·1 to 5·10:

1. State the Boolean function of each switch circuit.
2. Draw the logical diagram for each.
3. Simplify as much as possible.
4. Write the Boolean function and draw the logical diagram of the simplified circuit.

5·1

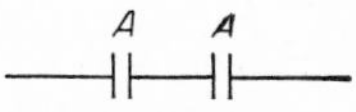

Fig. 5·6

5·2

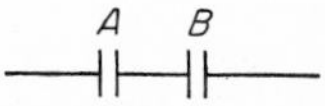

Fig. 5·7

5·3

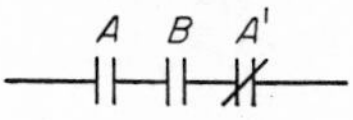

Fig. 5·8

5·4

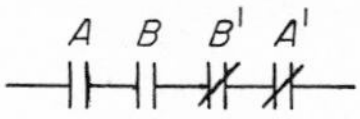

Fig. 5·9

5·5

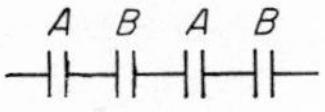

Fig. 5·10

5·6

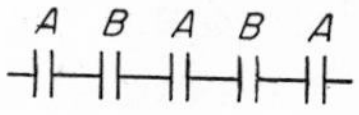

Fig. 5·11

5·7

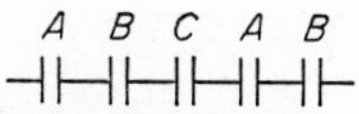

Fig. 5·12

5·8

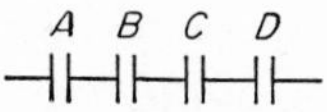

Fig. 5·13

5·9 A B C D A'

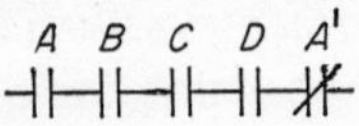

Fig. 5·14

5·10 A' B' C' D'

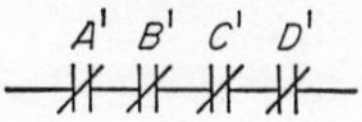

Fig. 5·15

In Probs. 5·11 to 5·20:

1. Draw the switch circuit and logical diagram that represent the given Boolean function.
2. Simplify the Boolean function.
3. Draw the simplified switch circuit and logical diagram.

5·11	AAA	5·12	ABA
5·13	$ABBA$	5·14	$ABA'B$
5·15	$A'B$	5·16	$ABCDBC$
5·17	$ABCDEBD$	5·18	$A'A'B'B'$
5·19	$ABCD$	5·20	$ABCBCAD$

5·4 Parallel Switch Circuit Relationships

Figure 5·16a illustrates a circuit in which two switches are connected in parallel, and diagram c illustrates the logical diagram for this combination. In Fig. 5·16, both switches are open when the circuit is

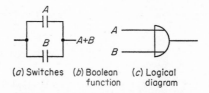

(a) Switches (b) Boolean (c) Logical
              function   diagram

Fig. 5·16 A simple parallel switch circuit.

deenergized (the normal state). Upon application of a signal, both switches will close and an output will be obtained. Notice, however, that an output is obtained if *either* or *both* of the switches are closed (1). The symbol used for designating parallel switch combinations is "$+$," and the process may be called *logical addition*. The parallel switch circuit is called the OR circuit. It should be emphasized that logical addition is not related to arithmetic addition.

The rules for Boolean addition are best discussed in conjunction with the circuit possibilities. Refer to Fig. 5·17. In Fig. 5·17a, since both

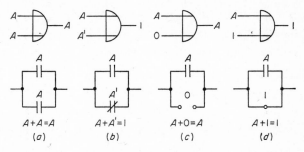

Fig. 5·17   Simple parallel possibilities (logical and switch diagrams).

switches work together directly, an output is obtained only when both switches are closed. In equation form,

$$A + A = A$$

Let $A = 1$:

$$1 + 1 = 1$$

Let $A = 0$:

$$0 + 0 = 0$$

In Fig. 5·17b: Switch A' is in negation with switch A. There will always be an output since one of the switches will be closed. In equation form,

$$A + A' = 1$$

Let $A = 1$, then $A' = 0$:

$$1 + 0 = 1$$

Let $A = 0$, then $A' = 1$:

$$0 + 1 = 1$$

Figure 5·17c illustrates a switch (A) in parallel with an open circuit (0). This circuit will transmit only if the switch is closed. In equation form,

$$A + 0 = A$$

When $A = 1$:

$$1 + 0 = 1$$

When $A = 0$:

$$0 + 0 = 0$$

The circuit of Fig. 5·17d consists of a switch (A) in parallel with a short circuit (1). Since a transmission path always exists, the circuit always transmits, regardless of the state of the switch. In equation form,

$$A + 1 = 1$$

Let $A = 1$:

$$1 + 1 = 1$$

Let $A = 0$:

$$0 + 1 = 1$$

5·5 Summary of Series and Parallel Logic

Following is a summary of the logic for simple series and parallel switch circuits.

Series circuits

$$
\begin{array}{ll}
0 \times 0 = 0 & (1) \\
1 \times 0 = 0 & (2) \\
1 \times 1 = 1 & (3) \\
A \times 0 = 0 & (4) \\
A \times 1 = A & (5) \\
A \times A = A & (6) \\
A \times A' = 0 & (7)
\end{array}
$$

In the series circuit logic presented above, notice the order of presentation. The first three relationships are in terms of 0 and 1, and can be expressed in terms of open and closed. In the fourth and fifth equations, one of the two series switches is labeled A while the second switch is a condition of 0 in Equation (4) and 1 in Equation (5). In Equation (6), both switches are in the same state, as indicated by the use of the same letter A. The switches are in negation in Equation (7). It is suggested that the student draw the logical diagrams for the preceding series rules.

Parallel circuit logic. The logic for simple parallel switch circuits can be conveniently expressed by the following seven equations.

These equations are developed in the same manner as the series relationships:

$$1 + 1 = 1 \qquad (8)$$
$$1 + 0 = 1 \qquad (9)$$
$$0 + 0 = 0 \qquad (10)$$
$$A + 1 = 1 \qquad (11)$$
$$A + 0 = A \qquad (12)$$
$$A + A = A \qquad (13)$$
$$A + A' = 1 \qquad (14)$$

It is suggested that the student draw the logical diagram for each of the preceding parallel rules.

PROBLEMS

In Probs. 5·21 to 5·30:

1. State the Boolean function of the circuit.
2. Draw the logical diagram of the original circuit.
3. Simplify the circuit.
4. State the Boolean function of the simplified circuit.
5. Draw the logical diagram of the simplified circuit.

5·21

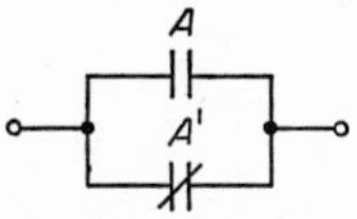

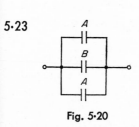

Fig. 5·18

5·22

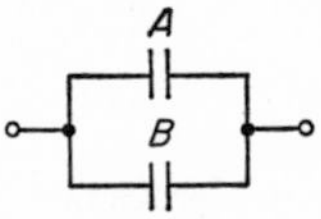

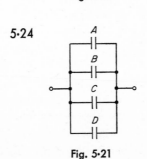

Fig. 5·19

5·23

Fig. 5·20

5·24

Fig. 5·21

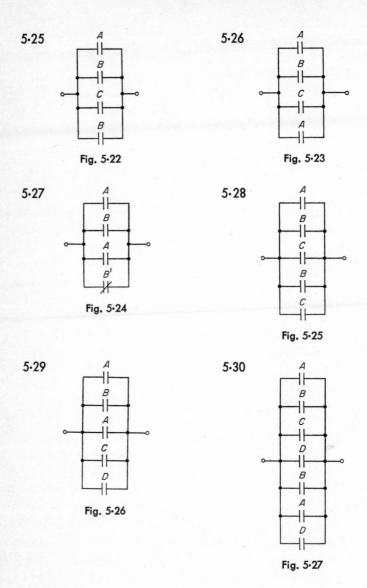

5·25   Fig. 5·22

5·26   Fig. 5·23

5·27   Fig. 5·24

5·28   Fig. 5·25

5·29   Fig. 5·26

5·30   Fig. 5·27

In Probs. 5·31 to 5·40:

1. Simplify the original Boolean function.
2. Draw the original circuit and its logical diagram.
3. Draw the simplified circuit and its logical diagram.

5·31 $A + B + B$ 5·32 $A + A' + B$

5·33 $A + A + B + C$ 5·34 $A + B + C + D + B$

5·35 $A + B + B + C + B + A$ 5·36 $A + B + A + B + C + C$

5·37 $A + B + C + D$

5·38 $A + B + C + B + D + C + E + D$

5·39 $A + A + B + B + C + D + E + B$

5·40 $A + B + C + D + E + F + C + D$

5·6   Series-Parallel Circuits

A simple series switch (AND) circuit and a simple parallel switch (OR) circuit are what can be called *first-order logic circuits*. More complicated two-terminal switching circuits, which are essentially series-parallel combinations, result in higher-order logic (second, third, fourth, fifth, etc.). In the simplification of the circuit function, the series rules are applied to the AND combinations and the parallel rules to the OR combinations. Specific examples of this mode of attack are given in a following section.

There are two Boolean rules, called the *distributive laws*, which are very helpful in the simplification of certain types of series-parallel circuits. The approach for circuits having more than two terminals is analyzed in later sections.

5·7   The First Distributive Law

Let us consider the first distributive law. Refer to Fig. 5·28 for the initial circuit which is to be simplified by the application of this law. Notice that both legs of the circuit contain a switch A. When signal A is not applied, both switch A's are open and, in accordance with a basic series Boolean law, both legs are open regardless of the condition of switches B and C (that is, the output of both AND circuits is zero). Upon receipt of signal A, both switch A's close; switch B is then in series with a closed circuit, and switch C is also in series with a closed circuit. The presence of switch A in both branches of the parallel circuit results in switch A's always affecting both legs (or both AND circuits) in the same manner. Since this is the case, the two switch A's can be replaced with a single switch A, which will be in series with the remainder of the parallel combination, as illustrated in Fig. 5·29.

The relationship described in the preceding paragraph and illustrated in Figs. 5·28 and 5·29 is called the *first distributive law*. This law may be stated in the following Boolean form:

$$AB + AC = A(B + C)$$

The circuit of Fig. 5·29 is generally considered more desirable than that of Fig. 5·28 since fewer switch contacts are required to perform

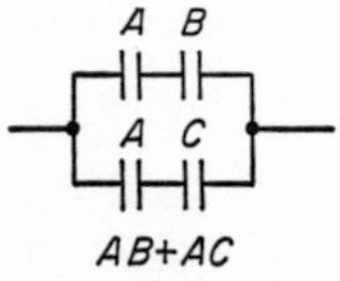

A B
A C
AB+AC

Fig. 5·28 A series-parallel switch circuit.

B
A
C
A (B+C)

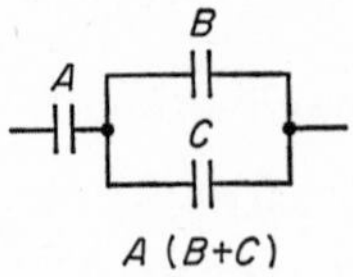

Fig. 5·29 Equivalent circuit of Fig. 5·28.

the same logic (three instead of four). The first distributive law is very useful in the simplification of Boolean functions, as is indicated in many of the problems that follow.

5·8 Application of the First Distributive Law

The first distributive law is also applicable in those cases in which several similar switches are located in each parallel leg of the circuit. In Fig. 5·30*a*, switches *A* and *B* are in both legs of the original circuit

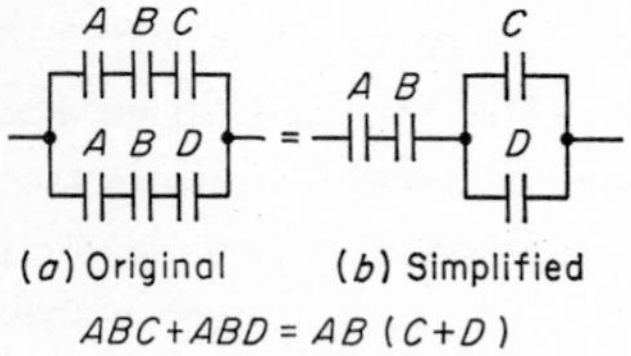
A B C
A B D
A B
C
D
(a) Original
(b) Simplified
ABC+ABD = AB (C+D)

Fig. 5·30

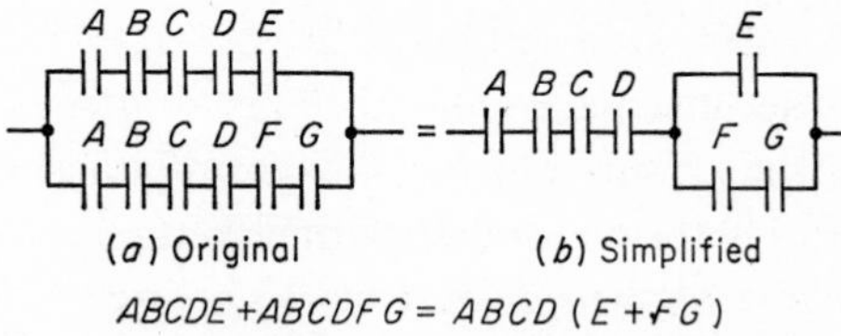
A B C D E
A B C D F G
A B C D
E
F G
(a) Original
(b) Simplified
ABCDE+ABCDFG = ABCD (E+FG)

Fig. 5·31 Application of the first distributive law for eleven contacts.

and therefore may be placed in series with both legs instead, as shown in Fig. 5·30*b*. Notice that this reduces the number of switch contacts from six in the original circuit to four in the simplified equivalent circuit.

The first distributive law is applicable for any number of series-connected switches in each leg. Figure 5·31 illustrates the application of this law in reducing a circuit with eleven contacts to seven contacts.

5·9   The Second Distributive Law

Refer to Fig. 5·32. The equation for this circuit is

$$(A + B)(A + C)$$

Since the same letter is used for two of the switches (A), it may be assumed that they are "ganged" together. Therefore they may be

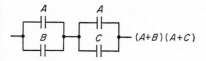

Fig. 5·32   A parallel network in series with a second parallel network.

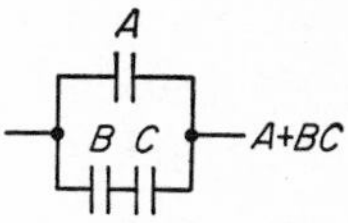

Fig. 5·33   Equivalent circuit of Fig. 7·32.

combined, and the circuit of Fig. 5·32 is simplified to that of Fig. 5·33. The equation for the circuit of Fig. 5·33 is

$$A + (BC)$$

Let us examine the circuits of Figs. 5·32 and 5·33 to see why they are equivalent. In Fig. 5·32, the two A switches work together as dictated by the same signal, and they are both closed or open. When the A switches are open, switches B and C are effectively in series, and the series laws are applied. When the A switches are closed, the circuit will transmit regardless of the conditions of switches B and C. Since the A switches work together and each is in parallel with another switch, they may be replaced with one switch in parallel with the other two switches. Both circuits (Figs. 5·32 and 5·33) appear identical to the input signal and are therefore equivalent circuits.

This can be also verified by determining the algebraic solution of the switching circuit of Fig. 5·32.

$$
\begin{aligned}
(A + B)(A + C) &= AA + AC + BA + BC \quad \text{(sum of products)} \\
&= A + AC + BA + BC \quad \text{(rule 6)} \\
&= A(1 + C + B) + BC \quad \text{(first distributive law)} \\
&= A(1) + BC \quad \text{(rule 11)} \\
&= A + BC \quad \text{(rule 5)}
\end{aligned}
$$

Therefore it is again proved that Figs. 5·32 and 5·33 are equivalent. In equation form,

$$(A + B)(A + C) = A + BC$$

This equation is called the *second distributive law* and is very useful in the reduction of complicated Boolean functions.

5·10 Application of the Second Distributive Law

The second distributive law can be applied to any circuit where each of a group of parallel combinations in series has an identical branch. Consider the circuit of Fig. 5·34. In Fig. 5·34*a*, the series combination

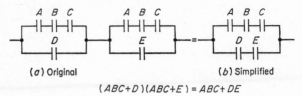

A B C
D
A B C
E
=
A B C
D E
(a) Original
(b) Simplified
(ABC+D)(ABC+E) = ABC+DE

Fig. 5·34 Application of the second distributive law.

of ABC is an identical branch in both parallel networks. Therefore the two parallel networks can be combined, one branch being ABC and the second branch being the series of the two remaining legs of the original circuit, DE.

Figure 5·35 is another example of how the second distributive law may be utilized. In Fig. 5·35*a*, the top legs of each parallel network are

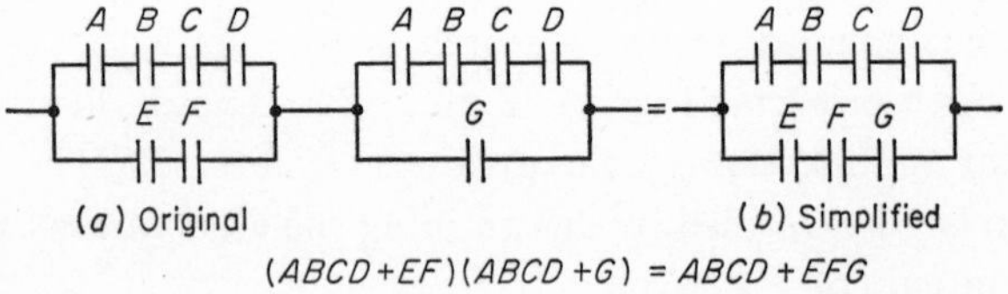

A B C D
E F
A B C D
G
=
A B C D
E F G
(a) Original
(b) Simplified
(ABCD+EF)(ABCD+G) = ABCD+EFG

Fig. 5·35 Another application of the second distributive law.

identical, and the two parallel networks can be combined in accordance with the second distributive law. The two lower legs are combined as a composite series arrangement. The simplified circuit is illustrated in Fig. 5·35*b*.

5·11 The Use of Boolean Functions in Analyzing Switching Circuits

Every Boolean function contains a number of different letters (called variables) and a number of individual entries (called literals). For example,

$$A(A + A + A)(A + B)$$

This function contains two variables (A and B) and six literals. Every function must contain at least as many literals as variables. In terms of a relay, each variable acts as a switch and each literal functions as a pair of contacts on one of the switches. When the switch is a diode, however, each variable acts as a "gang" of diodes, and each literal is one of the diodes in the ganged arrangement. One of the purposes of utilizing Boolean algebra is to minimize the number of contacts or diodes required to perform the same operation. Therefore, the equations are simplified to minimize the number of literals. The Boolean function of a circuit is used to determine the conditions under which the circuit will transmit.

Table 5·1   Boolean Laws and Language

Laws

$A + 0 = A$ (15)	$A \times 1 = A$ (24)
$A + 1 = 1$ (16)	$A \times 0 = 0$ (25)
$A + A = A$ (17)	$AA = A$ (26)
$A + A' = 1$ (18)	$AA' = 0$ (27)
$A + B = B + A$ (19)	$AB = BA$ (28)
$A(B + C) = AB + AC$ (20)	$A + BC = (A + B)(A + C)$ (29)
$A + AB = A$ (21)	$A(A + B) = A$ (30)
$A + A'B = A + B$ (22)	$A(A' + B) = AB$ (31)
$(A + B + C)' = A'B'C'$ (23)	$(ABC)' = A' + B' + C'$ (32)

Language

ON $= 1$
OFF $= 0$
Both A and B $= AB$
Either A or B or both $= A + B$
Not $A = A'$
Not-not $A = A'' =$ not $A' = A$

The Boolean function of an original circuit may be lengthy and might contain a number of unnecessary duplications of switches. By the application of the laws of Boolean algebra, the original function is reduced to the minimum number of required switches. Many of the rules for the simplification process have been introduced in the preceding pages. All the rules and laws to be utilized in this text are listed in Table 5·1 for convenient reference.

5·12 Logical Diagram Construction and Uses

With more complex circuits, the drawing of a logical diagram can result in simplifying the circuit in a more direct manner. Following is a suggested method for converting a Boolean equation into a logical diagram:

1. Identify the type of overall circuit, and draw the simplest operation. (It has to be an AND circuit or an OR circuit.)
2. Combine so that AND circuits do not supply other AND circuits and OR circuits do not supply other OR circuits. This results in economy of hardware.

This follows from observing the overall makeup of a Boolean equation. The literals that are ANDed together are associated in a single group (since they form a series circuit within the overall circuit) and the outputs of the ANDed groups are ORed together in the equation (and they form a parallel circuit within the overall circuit).

Example 1

$$AB + CD + EFG = y$$

There are three AND circuits (AB, CD, EFG) that are ORed together.

Example 2

$$(A + B + D)(E + F + H) = x$$

There are two OR circuits $(A + B + D, E + F + H)$ that are ANDed together.

3. Whenever possible, specify secondary inputs, thereby minimizing possible errors in expanding. Suggestions for the assignment of symbols are given in a following paragraph.
4. Use grouping marks (brackets, etc.) where it results in circuit clarification, such as when:
   a. An OR output is one of the inputs for an AND circuit

Example

$$(A + C)BD = x$$

b. The output of several OR circuits are inputs for an AND circuit

Example

$$(A + B + C + D)(E + F + G) = x$$

Orders of logic. Basic AND circuits and OR circuits constitute *first-order logic* circuits. *Second-order logic* is developed in a circuit where an AND circuit supplies an OR circuit or vice versa.

Example. Consider the circuit whose function is

$$CE + A + B + D = x$$

Solution. The overall circuit is an OR circuit, with the CE AND circuit output (called z) as one of the inputs. Proceeding with the drawing, we obtain Fig. 5·36.

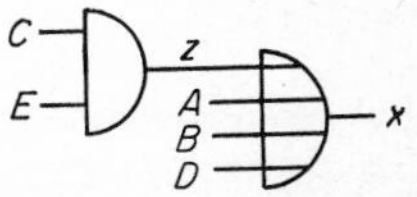

Third-order logic circuits are more complex, such as two OR circuits supplying an AND circuit or two AND circuits supplying an OR circuit.

Fig. 5·36 Logical diagram for $CE + A + B + D = x$.

Example. A circuit has the Boolean function $AB + DC = x$. Draw the logical diagram for this function.

Solution

Step 1. AB and DC are AND circuits, and their outputs are labeled y and z.

Step 2. The overall circuit is an OR circuit having the outputs of two AND circuits as its inputs (y and z). Proceeding with the drawing, we obtain Fig. 5·37.

Fourth-order logic circuits consist of one of the following diagram possibilities:

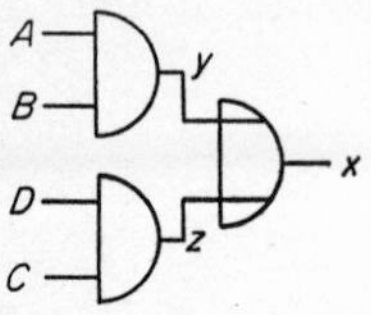

Fig. 5·37 Logical diagram for AB + $AC = x$.

1. AND → OR → AND → OR
2. OR → AND → OR → AND

The *fifth-order logic* possibilities are:

1. AND → OR → AND → OR → AND
2. OR → AND → OR → AND → OR

Let us now consider a complex circuit and how to develop its logical diagram.

Example. A circuit has the following Boolean function:

$$(AB + C)(DE + FG) = h$$

Draw the logical diagram.

Solution

Step 1. This is an overall AND circuit. Let the output of $AB + C = x$, and the output of $DE + FG = y$. Then

$$xy = h$$

Step 2. This furnishes us with the beginning of the logical diagram, as shown by the AND circuit of Fig. 5·38.

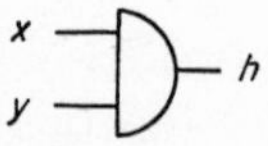

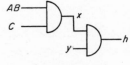

Fig. 5·38 Step 1 in the development of the logical construction $xy = h$.

Fig. 5·39 Expanding the x input $(AB + C)y = h$.

Step 3. We shall next identify x and y. x is the output of an overall OR circuit which has two inputs: the AND circuit AB and input C. The logical diagram is now expanded, as shown in Fig. 5·39.

Step 4. Identifying y as the output of an overall OR circuit, it is seen that it has two inputs. Each of these inputs is a dual-input AND circuit. Expanding, we have the diagram of Fig. 5·40.

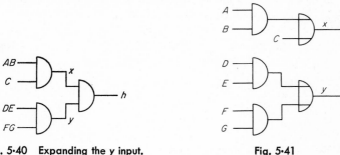

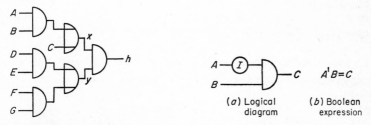

Fig. 5·40 Expanding the y input.   **Fig. 5·41**

Step 5. Now expanding the remaining AND circuits associated with each OR gate (Fig. 5·41) results in the completed logical diagram of Fig. 5·42.

Fig. 5·42 Complete logical diagram for (AB + C)(DE + FG) = h.   **Fig. 5·43**

Symbols. Let us determine how to distinguish the use of capital and small letters in the logical diagrams and equations. The output of a flip-flop is designated with a capital letter. Since the flip-flop has two possible outputs, they can be identified by the normal condition of each output. That is, the output which is 1 in its normal state is assigned an unprimed letter, such as A; the output which is 0 in its normal state is assigned the same letter, but primed, such as A'. Any switch (diode, etc.) can be designated in the same manner. When there is a series of flip-flops, subscript numbers are used to denote the order (A_1, A_2, etc.).

Gate outputs are commonly assigned small letters. For example, refer to the logical diagram of Fig. 5·36: The output of the CE AND gate is labeled z; the output of the $z + A + B + D$ OR gate is labeled x. Also, inverter outputs are always primed, as in Fig. 5·43.

PROBLEMS

Draw the logical diagrams of the Boolean expressions in Probs. 5·41 to 5·50:

5·41 $x'y + xy' + x'y' = z$
5·42 $xyz + x'yz + xy'z + xyz' = w$
5·43 $wxyz + w'xyz + wx'yz + w'x'yz = a$
5·44 $(x + y)(CD) + z = f$
5·45 $(x' + y + z)(x + y'z) = a$
5·46 $F(GHI + J) + K(L + M) = a$
5·47 $(x'y')(xz + wv) = a$
5·48 $x + (y' + z')(A + B) = f$
5·49 $[(w + x + y)A + B]CD = z$
5·50 $N[(D + E + F)(G + H) + J + K(L + M)] = a$

In the switching circuits of Probs. 5·51 to 5·60, write the original Boolean equation and then draw the logical diagram:

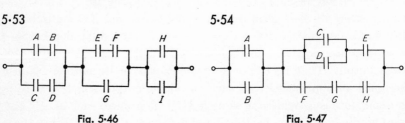

5·51

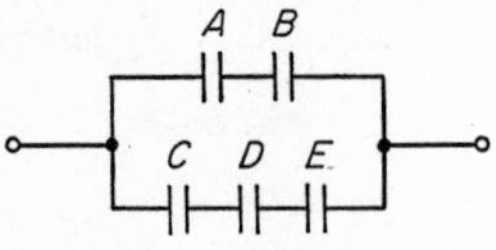

Fig. 5·44

5·52

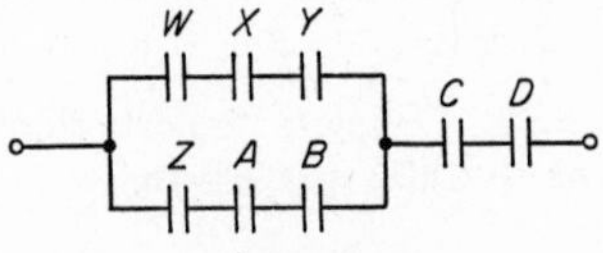

Fig. 5·45

5·53

Fig. 5·46

5·54

Fig. 5·47

5·55

5·56

5·57

5·58

5·59

5·60

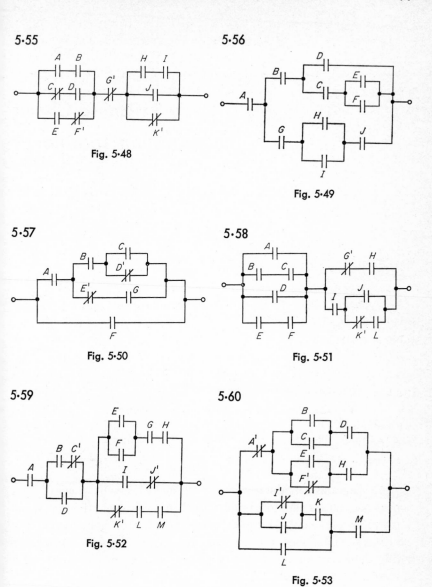

Fig. 5·48

Fig. 5·49

Fig. 5·50

Fig. 5·51

Fig. 5·52

Fig. 5·53

CHAPTER 6

Basic Switching Circuit
Simplification Techniques

Introduction

Venn diagrams and some of their uses are treated in the first section of this chapter. Then the universe table is introduced, and the manner in which a truth table is constructed as an outgrowth of the universe table is treated in detail with worked-out examples.

The latter half of this chapter deals with duality and negation. Particular emphasis is given to the great value of the double-dual technique for the simplification of many switch circuits. In all, 60 problems, which afford practice in all the techniques developed in this chapter, are included.

6·1 Venn Diagrams

Venn diagrams are illustrations which make a law or group of laws appear possible. It should be understood that the Venn diagram is not a rigorous mathematical proof of the function or law, but simply indicates the possibilities. Each variable may be represented as a circle within the diagram up to a limit of three variables, and the intersection possibilities are illustrated.

For example, consider the Venn diagram of Fig. 6·1. The variable A is represented by the circle. The entire rectangle (including A) is equal to 1. Since the circle represents A, the remainder of the rectangle is A', and

$$A + A' = 1$$

Consider the Venn diagrams in Fig. 6·2. Notice that the AND possibilities are represented by the common area of the variables included in the specific AND function. In Fig. 6·2a, the shaded portion is the common area of circles A and B, and only those circles. Diagram b

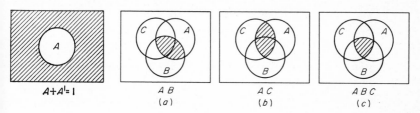

Fig. 6·1

Fig. 6·2 Venn diagram representation of AND possibilities.

represents the same relationship between circles A and C. When three variables are included in the AND function, only the common area of the three circles is shaded, as shown in Fig. 6·2c.

The OR function is represented by the complete shading-in of the circles which represent the involved variables. In Fig. 6·3a, which

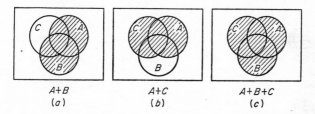

Fig. 6·3   Venn diagram representation of OR possibilities.

illustrates the function $A + B$, the A and B circles are completely shaded. This indicates that transmission will occur if A is present, or if B is present, or if both A and B are present. Notice that a portion of circle C is shaded. This can be interpreted to mean that transmission will occur with the presence of C only if it is accompanied by B or A or by A and B. Signal C itself has nothing to do with the transmission (as indicated by the fact that the portion of circle C which is not intersected by any other circle is left unshaded). The same analysis may be applied to Fig. 6·3b. In diagram c, which represents the function $A + B + C$, transmission will result if A or B or C, or any two of these (A and B, A and C, or B and C), or all three are energized. All these possibilities can be seen in the Venn diagram.

In summary, the following statements can be made for the interpretation of Venn diagrams:

1. The NOT possibility is represented by the area outside the circle(s) in the Venn enclosure.
2. The AND possibilities are represented by the common area formed by the intersection points of the circles representing the involved variables.
3. The OR possibilities are represented by the areas of the circles which represent the variables of the function.

Venn diagrams can be utilized in examining the possibilities of certain circuits. As an example, let us show by Venn diagrams that

$$(A + B)(A + C) = A + BC$$

Step 1. Draw the Venn diagrams for $(A + B)$ and for $(A + C)$. Note that horizontal lines are used for $(A + B)$ and vertical lines for $(A + C)$ to better distinguish the two in Fig. 6·5(a). The selection of this particular method is purely arbitrary.

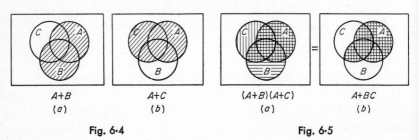

$A+B$	$A+C$	$(A+B)(A+C)$	$A+BC$
(a)	(b)	(a)	(b)

Fig. 6·4   Fig. 6·5

Step 2. Draw the Venn diagram for $(A + B)(A + C)$. Recall that the common area joined by the points of intersection of the two functions represents the desired product. The common areas formed by the points of intersection are indicated by the crosshatched area in Fig. 6·5a. This is then redrawn for additional clarity (Fig. 6·5b) and can be read as $A + BC$. Therefore the relationship $(A + B)(A + C) = A + BC$ can be illustrated by Venn diagrams.

The possibilities of any function's containing three or fewer variables can be illustrated by Venn diagrams. When more than three variables are involved, the Venn diagram technique tends to become cumbersome.

PROBLEMS

Illustrate the following relationships by Venn diagrams:

6·1	$A + A' = 1$
6·2	$AA = A$
6·3	$AA' = 0$
6·4	$A + AB = A$
6·5	$A(B + C) = AB + AC$
6·6	$A + A'B = A + B$
6·7	$A(A' + B) = AB$
6·8	$A(A + B) = A$
6·9	$A \times 1 = A$
6·10	$ABC + ABC = ABC$

6·2 The Universe Table

After the minimum circuit Boolean function has been derived by the application of the various laws stated in Table 5·1, the circuit may be analyzed for all possible input conditions by use of a special chart. The chart can list all the variables horizontally and all the possible 0 and 1 combinations vertically. In this way, 1 and 0 are substituted for each variable so that all possible combinations are included. Such a chart may be called a *universe table*.

The number of all possible combinations for the states of 1 and 0 is determined by

$$C = S^n = 2^n$$

where C = number of possible combinations

n = number of variables being considered

S = number of possible states (which is two, since 1 and 0 are the only possible states being considered)

As an example, two variables have $(2)^2 = 4$ possible combinations; three variables have $(2)^3 = 8$ possible combinations. The universe tables for two, three, and four variables are shown in Table 6·1. Universe tables can be made for any number of variables.

Table 6·1   Universe Tables for Two, Three, and Four Variables

Possibilities								
$2^n = 2^2 = 4$		$2^n = 2^3 = 8$			$2^n = 2^4 = 16$			
A	B	A	B	C	A	B	C	D
0	0	0	0	0	0	0	0	0
0	1	0	0	1	0	0	0	1
1	0	0	1	0	0	0	1	0
1	1	1	0	0	0	1	0	0
		0	1	1	1	0	0	0
		1	1	0	0	0	1	1
		1	0	1	0	1	1	0
		1	1	1	1	1	0	0
					0	1	0	1
					1	0	0	1
					1	0	1	0
					1	0	1	1
					0	1	1	1
					1	1	1	0
					1	1	0	1
					1	1	1	1

6·3   Truth Table Construction and Use

When the function of a given circuit and its universe table are known, the transmission of the circuit can be readily predicted. In Table 6·2, the first three columns are the universe table for three variables, and column 4 is the truth or transmission table for the circuit function $A(B + C)$, and only $A(B + C)$. Substitution of the states of 1 and 0 in all the possible combinations (as given in the universe table) into the Boolean function of the specific circuit results in a prediction of the circuit's transmission or hindrance. It should be noted that *the universe table is the same for any circuit having three variables, but the truth table is determined by the exact Boolean function of the particular arrangement under analysis.*

Let us verify the first distributive law by setting up the truth tables for Figs. 5·28 and 5·29. Refer to Table 6·2. Notice that each composite table includes a three-variable universe table and the function of the specific circuit. Since both of these circuits have three variables, their universe tables are identical. The fourth column is the truth table of the particular circuit arrangement, which is the worked-out circuit function for the switch conditions for the horizontal row in question. In this way, it can be determined when the circuit is transmitting.

Table 6·2   Truth Table Proof for the First Distributive Law

For Fig. 5·29					For Fig. 5·28				
A	B	C	$A(B+C)$	= output	A	B	C	$(AB)+(AC)$	= output
0	0	0	0(0 + 0)	= 0	0	0	0	(00) + (00)	= 0
0	0	1	0(0 + 1)	= 0	0	0	1	(00) + (01)	= 0
0	1	0	0(1 + 0)	= 0	0	1	0	(01) + (00)	= 0
0	1	1	0(1 + 1)	= 0	0	1	1	(01) + (01)	= 0
1	0	0	1(0 + 0)	= 0	1	0	0	(10) + (10)	= 0
1	0	1	1(0 + 1)	= 1	1	0	1	(10) + (11)	= 1
1	1	0	1(1 + 0)	= 1	1	1	0	(11) + (10)	= 1
1	1	1	1(1 + 1)	= 1	1	1	1	(11) + (11)	= 1

In both Fig. 5·28 and 5·29, the output is zero when:

1. Switch A is open
2. Switch A is closed and switches B and C are both open

Therefore the truth tables for Figs. 5·28 and 5·29 verify the first distributive law, which is stated as identity (20) in Table 5·1.

Table 6·3   Truth Table Proof for the Second Distributive Law

For Fig. 5·32					For Fig. 5·33				
A	B	C	$(A+B)(A+C)$	= output	A	B	C	$A+(BC)$	= output
0	0	0	(0 + 0)(0 + 0)	= 0	0	0	0	0 + (00)	= 0
0	0	1	(0 + 0)(0 + 1)	= 0	0	0	1	0 + (01)	= 0
0	1	0	(0 + 1)(0 + 0)	= 0	0	1	0	0 + (10)	= 0
0	1	1	(0 + 1)(0 + 1)	= 1	0	1	1	0 + (11)	= 1
1	0	0	(1 + 0)(1 + 0)	= 1	1	0	0	1 + (00)	= 1
1	0	1	(1 + 0)(1 + 1)	= 1	1	0	1	1 + (01)	= 1
1	1	0	(1 + 1)(1 + 0)	= 1	1	1	0	1 + (10)	= 1
1	1	1	(1 + 1)(1 + 1)	= 1	1	1	1	1 + (11)	= 1

Table 6·3 illustrates the truth tables for Figs. 5·32 and 5·33, the equivalent networks for the second distributive law. These truth tables verify that the networks of Figs. 5·32 and 5·33 have an output with identical signal conditions. The output is zero in both of these circuits when:

1. All switches are open
2. Switch A is open and either B or C is open

And the output is 1 when:

1. Switch A is open and both switches B and C are closed
2. Switch A is closed, regardless of the condition of switches B and C

Since the two truth tables are equivalent, the circuits of Figs. 5·32 and 5·33 are equivalent, and the second distributive law is verified, which is identity (29) of Table 5·1.

6·4 Criteria for Circuit Simplification

One of the chief purposes of Boolean algebra is to reduce a switching circuit to its simplest equivalent in the interest of determining the minimum number of switches required. Following is a five-step procedure for the simplification of switching arrangements.

1. Draw the logical diagram of the original switching circuit.
2. Derive the Boolean expression of the circuit.
3. Using the laws of Boolean algebra, as listed in Table 5·1, reduce the expression to its minimum form. Draw a simplified circuit diagram anytime during this process when it proves helpful.
4. Convert the minimum Boolean function into its equivalent logical diagram.
5. Using the universe–truth table technique analyzed in the preceding section, verify that the simplified circuit is the equivalent of the original circuit.

Verifying the equivalency of the two circuits (original and simplified) by the universe–truth table method of analysis can become time-consuming for more complicated arrangements.

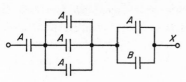

Fig. 6·6   Original circuit for Example 1.

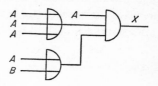

Fig. 6·7

Example 1. Convert Fig. 6·6 into its simplest equivalent.

Solution

Step 1. Draw the logical diagram (Fig. 6·7).

Step 2. Derive the equation for the original circuit. Using the series and parallel relationships, the equation is found to be

$$A(A + A + A)(A + B) = x$$

Step 3. Simplify the equation. Notice that:

$$A + A + A = A$$

[three switches ganged together in parallel act as one switch—identity (17)]. Substituting back into the original equation,

$$A(A)(A + B) = x$$

and

$$A(A) = A$$

[since two switches ganged together in series act as one switch—identity (26)].

Substituting back into the equation,

$$A(A + B)$$

and

$$A(A + B) = A = x \qquad \text{[identity (30)]}$$

This is the most simplified version of the original function.

Step 4. Convert the simplified equation into its equivalent circuit.

Step 5. Check truth table. A truth table is set up for both the original circuit and its simplified equivalent. Both circuits should

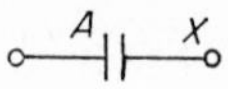

$$\circ \!-\!\!\overset{A}{\|}\!\!-\!\!\overset{X}{\circ}$$

Fig. 6·8   Simplified equivalent circuit of Fig. 6·6.

transmit under the same conditions and not transmit under all other conditions. (See Table 6·4.)

Table 6·4   Truth Table Check for Figs. 6·6 and 6·8

		Original		Simplified
A	B	$A(A + A + A)(A + B)$	= output	A = output
0	0	$0(0 + 0 + 0)(0 + 0)$	= 0	0 = 0
0	1	$0(0 + 0 + 0)(0 + 1)$	= 0	0 = 0
1	0	$1(1 + 1 + 1)(1 + 0)$	= 1	1 = 1
1	1	$1(1 + 1 + 1)(1 + 1)$	= 1	1 = 1

Example 2. Reduce the logical diagram of Fig. 6·9 to its simplest equivalent circuit.

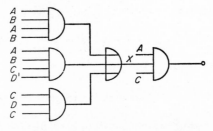

Fig. 6·9   Logical diagram for Example 2.

Solution

Step 1. The Boolean function of the circuit is

$$[(ABAB) + (ABCD') + (CDC)]AC$$

Step 2. In this step, the Boolean function is reduced to its minimum form. Notice that

$$ABAB = AB$$

and

$$CDC = CD$$

[two switches in series which respond similarly to the same signal act as one switch—identity (26)]. This simplifies the function to

$$(AB + ABCD' + CD)AC$$

and the logical diagram reduction is shown in Fig. 6·10.

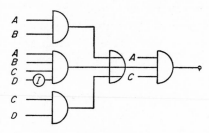

Fig. 6·10 Logical diagram reduction 1.   **Fig. 6·11**

By identity (20),

$$[AB(1 + CD') + CD]AC = x$$

and since $1 + CD' = 1$ [by identity (16)], then

$$(AB + CD)AC = x$$

The second reduction of the logical diagram is shown in Fig. 6·11. Expanding, in accordance with identity (20),

$$ACAB + ACCD = x$$

and using identity (26),

$$ABC + ACD = x$$

By identity (26) again,

$$AC(B + D) = x$$

The final reduction of the logical diagram is shown in Fig. 6·12. The final reduced switching circuit is given in Fig. 6·13.

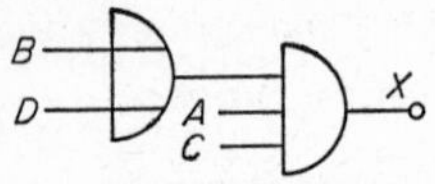

Fig. 6·12

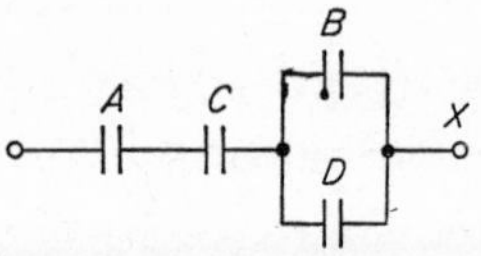

Fig. 6·13 Final reduced switching circuit.

In the preceding Examples 1 and 2, a gradual, step-by-step reduction of the original Boolean function with frequent redrawings of the reduced logical diagrams made it possible to determine the simplest equivalent circuit of the original network. There were 13 switch contacts in the original circuit of Example 2, while only four are needed for its simplest equivalent circuit.

The truth table analysis may be used to verify the results.

6·5 The Expanded Truth Table

When the Boolean function is of the more complicated series-parallel variety, the truth table is best constructed in steps. Each step is used for one of the operations (AND, OR, NOT). Following is an example of a step-by-step truth table.

Example. Prove that $A + BC = (A + B)(A + C)$ by the truth-table analysis. Notice that in Table 6·5 rows 1, 2, and 3 make up the uni-

Table 6·5 Step-by-step Truth Table

				Row			
1	2	3	4	5	6	7	8
A	B	C	BC	$A + BC$	$A + B$	$A + C$	$(A + B)(A + C)$
0	0	0	0	0	0	0	0
0	0	1	0	0	0	1	0
0	1	0	0	0	1	0	0
1	0	0	0	1	1	1	1
0	1	1	1	1	1	1	1
1	1	0	0	1	1	1	1
1	0	1	0	1	1	1	1
1	1	1	1	1	1	1	1

verse table. Row 4 is used for the BC operation, row 5 for $A + BC$, row 6 for $A + B$, row 7 for the $A + C$ operation, and row 8 for the $(A + B)(A + C)$ operation. Rows 5 and 8 must coincide if the stated identity in this example is correct. In observing rows 5 and 8, it is seen that they do coincide.

6·6   The Concept of Duality

The dual of a function is the opposite characteristic of that function. If a function indicates transmission, for example, its dual would indicate hindrance. The dual of a function may be determined by applying the following procedure to the original function:

1. Change all 0s to 1.
2. Change all 1s to 0.
3. Change all +'s to ×.
4. Change all ×'s to +.

It should be stated that every Boolean algebra law can be converted into another law by the application of the duality process. In referring to Table 5·1, it can be seen that identities (15) and (24), (16) and (25), (17) and (26), etc., are duals. Therefore identities (24) to (32) can be determined by finding the duals of identities (15) to (23).

The principle of duality can be utilized to examine the hindrance characteristics of a circuit. Perhaps a more widespread application of duality is in the simplification of circuits, as analyzed in the following section.

6·7   Circuit Simplification by the Double-dual Technique

After simplification of a circuit, it may not be certain whether the simplest circuit has been derived. Also, many functions may be difficult to simplify in their original form. In such cases, the double-dual technique may be profitably utilized. Recall that the function of a circuit specifies when it will transmit. The dual of that circuit function will specify when it will not transmit. The dual of the dual will again specify when the circuit will transmit, and the function will usually be in a simpler form than the original function.

The procedure for the double-dual technique is as follows:

1. Determine the Boolean function of the original circuit.
2. Determine the dual of this function.
3. Simplify the dual by the application of Boolean laws.
4. Determine the dual of step 3.
5. Simplify the result of step 4 by the application of Boolean laws.

The resulting function of step 5 will be the simplified equivalent of step 1.

Example. Reduce the circuit represented by the logical diagram of Fig. 6·14 to its simplest equivalent by use of the double-dual technique.

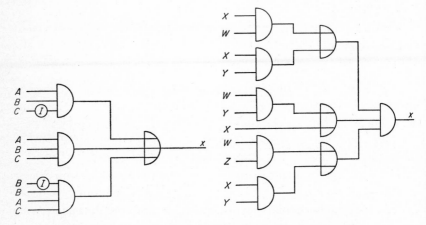

Fig. 6·14   Original logical circuit for the double-dual example.

Solution

Step 1. Determine the function of the original circuit depicted by the logical diagram.

$$f_{(x)} = (WX + XY)(WY + X)(WZ + XY)$$

and partially simplifying,

$$f_{(x)} = X(W + Y)(WY + X)(WZ + XY)$$

Step 2. Determine the dual of $f_{(x)}$.

$$dx = X + WY + (W + Y)X + (W + Z)(X + Y)$$

Step 3. Simplify dx.

$$
\begin{aligned}
dx &= X + WY + XW + YX + (W + Z)(X + Y) \\
&= X(1 + W) + Y(W + X) + WX + WY + ZX + ZY \\
&= X + WY + XW + YZ + WX + WY + ZX + ZY \\
&= X + Y(W + Z) + WY + ZY \\
&= X + Y(W + Z) + Y(W + Z) = X + Y(W + Z)
\end{aligned}
$$

Step 4. Determine the dual of dx.

$$dd(x) = X(Y + WZ)$$

6·8 Principles of Negation

Negation indicates the inverse relationship between two switches or circuits. The negation of a normally open series circuit is a normally closed parallel circuit, as shown in Fig. 6·15. The negation of a normally

$(AB)' = A' + B'$ (Identity 32)

$(A + B)' = A'B'$ (Identity 23)

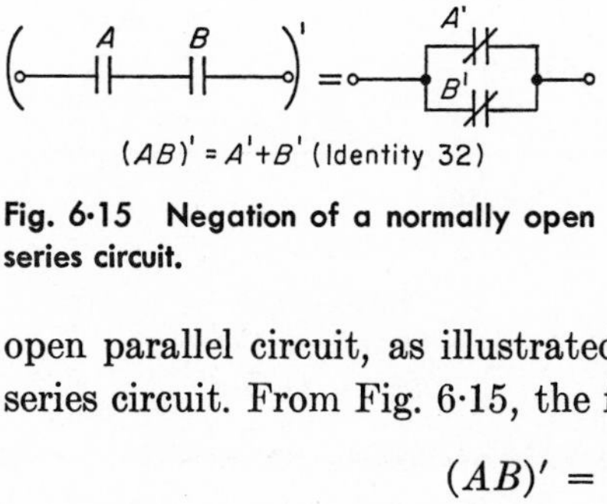

Fig. 6·15 Negation of a normally open series circuit.

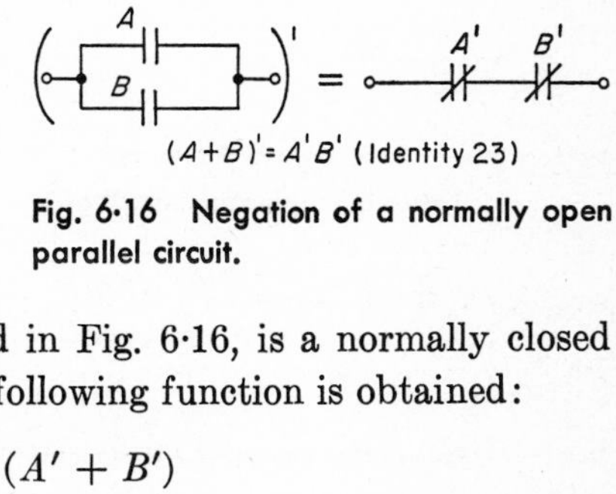

Fig. 6·16 Negation of a normally open parallel circuit.

open parallel circuit, as illustrated in Fig. 6·16, is a normally closed series circuit. From Fig. 6·15, the following function is obtained:

$$(AB)' = (A' + B')$$

Let us verify this relationship by use of a truth table (Table 6·6). The

Table 6·6 Verification That $(AB)' = (A' + B')$

A	B	Output $(AB)'$	A'	B'	Output $(A' + B')$
0	0	$(00)' = (0)' = 1$	1	1	$0' + 0' = 1 + 1 = 1$
0	1	$(01)' = (0)' = 1$	1	0	$0' + 1' = 1 + 0 = 1$
1	0	$(10)' = (0)' = 1$	0	1	$1' + 0' = 0 + 1 = 1$
1	1	$(11)' = (1)' = 0$	0	0	$1' + 1' = 0 + 0 = 0$

first two columns make up the universe table, while column 3 is the truth table. When A and B are both 0, the output would normally be 0, and therefore its negation is 1. When A or B are 0, the output is normally 0 and its negation is 1. When A and B are both 1, the output is normally 1 and its negation is 0.

The last three columns of Table 6.6 analyze the function $(A' + B')$ for all possible conditions of A and B. Notice that in columns 4 and 5, A' and B' are always the negation of A and B in columns 1 and 2. In the parallel circuit designated by $(A' + B')$ there is an output of 1 when both switches are closed or when one of the switches is closed. By comparing columns 3 and 4 of this table, it is seen that the output of both circuits is identical and therefore,

$$(AB)' = (A' + B')$$

Figure 6·16 can also be verified by a truth table analysis. In Table 6·7, notice that A' and B' are negations of A and B for all conditions. Columns 3 and 6 verify that the two functions are equal, i.e.,

$$(A + B)' = A'B'$$

Table 6·7   Verification That $(A + B)' = A'B'$

A	B	Output $(A + B)'$	A'	B'	Output $(A'B')$
0	0	$(0 + 0)' = 0' = 1$	1	1	$0'0' = 11 = 1$
0	1	$(0 + 1)' = 1' = 0$	1	0	$0'1' = 10 = 0$
1	0	$(1 + 0)' = 1' = 0$	0	1	$1'0' = 01 = 0$
1	1	$(1 + 1)' = 1' = 0$	0	0	$1'1' = 00 = 0$

The basic rules of negation of any Boolean function are:

1. Negate every element in the function.
2. Change $+$ to $\times$, and $\times$ to $+$.
3. A double negation reverts the function back to the affirmative.
4. All parentheses and/or brackets must remain in their initial positions.

Example 1. Negate the function $A + AB$ and verify with a truth table.

Solution

Step 1. Negate every element in the function.

$$A' + A'B'$$

Step 2. Change $+$ to $\times$; $\times$ to $+$.

$$A' \times A' + B'$$

Step 3. Therefore,

$$(A + AB)' = A'(A' + B') = A' \qquad \text{[by identity (21)]}$$

Step 4. Verify by use of a truth table (Table 6·8). Notice that the output of column 3 is the inverse of column 6 output, which proves

$$(A + AB)' = A'$$

Table 6·8 $(A + AB)' = A'$

A	B	Output $= (A + AB)'$	A'	B'	Output $= A'$
0	0	$0 + (00) = 0$	1	1	1
0	1	$0 + (01) = 0$	1	0	1
1	0	$1 + (10) = 1$	0	1	0
1	1	$1 + (11) = 1$	0	0	0

Example 2. Negate the function $A(B + C)$.

1. Rule 1: $A'(B' + C')$
2. Rule 2: $A' + (B'C')$
3. Verify the following identity by a truth-table analysis:

$$[A(B + C)] = A' + (B'C')$$

Examination of columns 3 and 6 of Table 6·9 verifies that the identity is true.

Table 6·9 $A(B + C) = A' + (B'C')$

A	B	C	Output $A(B + C)$	A'	B'	C'	Output $A' + (B'C')$
0	0	0	$0(0 + 0) = 0$	1	1	1	$1 + (11) = 1$
0	0	1	$0(0 + 1) = 0$	1	1	0	$1 + (10) = 1$
0	1	0	$0(1 + 0) = 0$	1	0	1	$1 + (01) = 1$
0	1	1	$0(1 + 1) = 0$	1	0	0	$1 + (00) = 1$
1	0	0	$1(0 + 0) = 0$	0	1	1	$0 + (11) = 1$
1	0	1	$1(0 + 1) = 1$	0	1	0	$0 + (10) = 0$
1	1	0	$1(1 + 0) = 1$	0	0	1	$0 + (01) = 0$
1	1	1	$1(1 + 1) = 1$	0	0	0	$0 + (00) = 0$

It will be noticed that the process of negating a function is effectively finding the equivalent inverse circuit of that function. The negation of a series circuit function results in the function of its equivalent inverse parallel circuit, and the negation of a parallel circuit function produces the function of its equivalent inverse series circuit. Double negation results in the return to the original function, or the affirmative.

Example 3. Double-negate the function $A + B$.

Step 1. First negation.

$A'B'$ (both elements are primed and $+$ is changed to $\times$)

Step 2. Second negation.

$A'' + B''$ (both elements are primed and $\times$ ix changed to $+$)

A'' means that A is NOT-NOT A, which means that it is A. B'' is NOT-NOT B, which means that it is B. Therefore,

$$A'' + B'' = A + B$$

This identity may be verified by the truth-table analysis.

PROBLEMS

In Probs. 6·11 to 6·25:

1. State the function of the original circuit.
2. Simplify.
3. Draw the simplified switching circuit and its logical diagram.

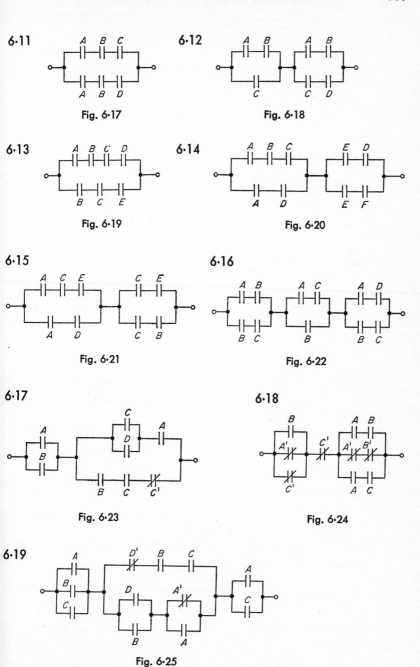

6·11

Fig. 6·17

6·12

Fig. 6·18

6·13

Fig. 6·19

6·14

Fig. 6·20

6·15

Fig. 6·21

6·16

Fig. 6·22

6·17

Fig. 6·23

6·18

Fig. 6·24

6·19

Fig. 6·25

6·20

6·21

6·22

6·23

6·24

6·25

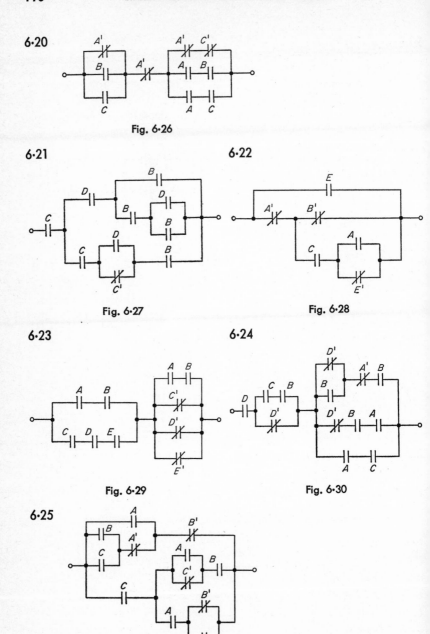

Fig. 6·26

Fig. 6·27

Fig. 6·28

Fig. 6·29

Fig. 6·30

Fig. 6·31

In Probs. 6·26 to 6·45:

1. Draw the circuit and logical diagrams represented by the original Boolean function.
2. Simplify the Boolean function.
3. Draw the circuit and logical diagram represented by the simplified function.

6·26 $AB + A(CD + EF)$

6·27 $ABC + AB(DC + EF)$

6·28 $A'B + C(A + B')$

6·29 $A + B(C + DE) + FG$

6·30 $(A + B)[CDE + (F + G)H]$

6·31 $(A + BC')(A + B' + C) + D(B' + C) + C'D$

6·32 $C'(AB + A'B')(A' + B + C')$

6·33 $A'[B(A + C') + D']$

6·34 $(ABC + DE)(DE + A' + B' + C')$

6·35 $(ABC + CD)(DE + A' + B' + C)$

6·36 $CD' + AC' + A'B'C' + B'C'D'$

6·37 $CB + AB'CD + CD' + AC'$

6·38 $ABC(A + AB + ABC)$

6·39 $ABC(A + AB' + ABC')$

6·40 $ABCD(A + AB + ABC + ABCD)$

6·41 $ABC + A'BC + AB'C + A'B'C$

6·42 $ABC + A'BC + AB'C + ABC'$

6·43 $(A + B + CD)B' + (AC')B + (B'C)A$

6·44 $(AB + CDE)(AB + C' + D' + E')$

6·45 $D(BC + D') + A'B(E'F) + D'EA + AC$

Verify the following by an expanded truth-table analysis:

6·46	Prob. 6·28	**6·47**	Prob. 6·30
6·48	Prob. 6·32	**6·49**	Prob. 6·33
6·50	Prob. 6·34	**6·51**	Prob. 6·35
6·52	Prob. 6·36	**6·53**	Prob. 6·37
6·54	Prob. 6·38	**6·55**	Prob. 6·39
6·56	Prob. 6·40	**6·57**	Prob. 6·41
6·58	Prob. 6·42	**6·59**	Prob. 6·43
6·60	Prob. 6·44		

CHAPTER 7

Analysis and Simplification of Switching Circuits with Boolean Matrices

Introduction

This chapter deals with several techniques which, when applied with the laws and rules of Boolean algebra, provide efficient methods of analyzing and simplifying certain switching circuits. All three methods are for noncombinational (i.e., non-series-parallel) circuits. The first two methods can be used for the relatively simple non-series-parallel circuits.

The Boolean matrix technique is a very useful approach to the more complex non-series-parallel switching circuits. The greatest portion of this chapter is devoted to the development of the Boolean matrix and its simplification into an equivalent circuit. Over 60 problems are included in the chapter.

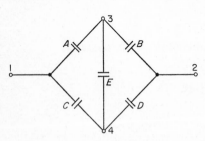

Fig. 7·1   A four-node circuit.

7·1 The Assignment of Node Numbers

A node may be defined as a junction between two or more devices. As an example, there are four nodes in Fig. 7·1. The nodes directly associated with the input and output terminals are usually assigned the lower numbers. The reason for this, and additional information about nodes as a circuit analysis technique, is given in a following section.

7·2 The Closed-path Tracing Technique (Closure Analysis)

The closed-path tracing technique for the determination of the Boolean function of a circuit is satisfactory for the analysis of many simple non-series-parallel circuits. This method consists of the following procedure:

1. All possible transmission paths are determined.
2. The Boolean function of each transmission path is determined.
3. The Boolean function of the circuit is the sum of all the possible transmission paths.

Example 1. Determine the function of Fig. 7·2 by use of the closed-path tracing technique.

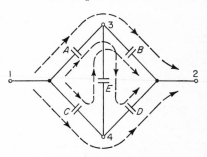

Solution

Fig. 7·2   A bridge circuit.

Step 1. All possible transmission paths are determined. Note the use of broken lines, which facilitate the analysis. Possible paths are:

1. AB
2. CD
3. CEB
4. AED

Step 2. The circuit's Boolean function is

$$f_{12} = AB + CD + CEB + AED$$

This function may be reduced by the application of the appropriate Boolean law. Rearranging the function, the first distributive law may be applied:

$$f_{12} = AB + AED + CD + CEB$$
$$f_{12} = A(B + ED) + C(D + EB)$$

The equivalent circuit of the final function is illustrated in Fig. 7·3. It should be noted that the original circuit was simplified to a series-parallel arrangement but that the number of switch contacts required was not reduced.

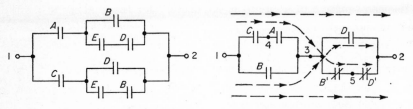

Fig. 7·3   Equivalent circuit of Fig. 7·2.   Fig. 7·4   Circuit for Example 2.

Example 2. Determine the function of Fig. 7·4 by use of the closed-path tracing technique.

Solution

Step 1. All possible transmission paths are determined.

> **1.** CAD
> **2.** $BB'D'$
> **3.** BD
> **4.** $CAB'D'$

Step 2. The circuit's Boolean function is

$$f_{12} = CAD + BB'D' + BD + CAB'D'$$

The function is then simplified by the application of the appropriate laws. Since $BB' = 0$, then $BB'D = 0$, and

$$f_{12} = CAD + BD + ACB'D'$$

Rearranging,

$$f_{12} = CAD + CAD'B' + BD$$
$$= CA(D + D'B') + BD$$
$$= CA(D + B') + BD$$
$$= CAD + BD$$

and

$$f_{12} = D(CA + B)$$

The circuit represented by the reduced function of step 2 is illustrated in Fig. 7·5. Notice that the closed-path tracing technique resulted in a simplification of the original circuit when considering nodes 1 and 2 as the transmission terminals.

This technique may also be used for circuits having three or more terminals (Fig. 7·6), but becomes a much more complex procedure.

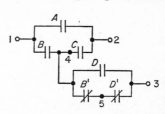

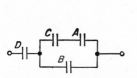

Fig. 7·5 Simplified equivalent of Fig. 7·4.

Fig. 7·6 A three-terminal circuit.

Example 3. Determine f_{12}, f_{13}, and f_{32} by the closed-path tracing technique.

Solution

Step 1. The possible closed paths for f_{12} are:

1. A
2. BC

and

$$f_{12} = A + BC$$

Step 2. The possible closed paths for f_{13} are:

1. ACD
2. $ACB'D'$
3. BD
4. $BB'D'$

Therefore,

$$f_{13} = ACD + ACB'D' + BD + BB'D'$$

Simplifying,

$$f_{13} = AC(D + B'D') + BD$$
$$= AC(D + B') + BD$$

Step 3. The possible closed paths for f_{32} are:

1. DC
2. DBA
3. $B'D'C$
4. $B'D'BA$

Therefore,

$$f_{32} = B'D'BA + B'D'C + ABD + CD$$

Simplifying,

$$f_{32} = D(C + AB) + CB'$$

7·3 The Wye-to-Delta Transformation Technique

The wye-to-delta transformation is the second method for the analysis of non-series-parallel circuits to be considered in this text. The wye circuit shall be here considered as a three-terminal circuit and may be viewed as a group of 3 two-terminal circuits. These 3 two-terminal circuits have a common point that is not a circuit terminal. From this common point, the wye circuit is formed and the circuit function can then be written.

Converting into an equivalent wye circuit. Let us apply the wye-to-delta transformation technique to the four-node bridge circuit of Fig.

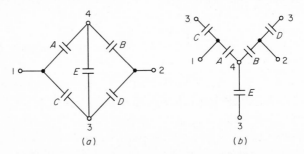

Fig. 7·7   A bridge circuit and its wye configuration.

7·7*a*. Assume that it is desired to consider node 4 the common point. The 3 two-terminal circuits required to meet at this common node are to be determined next. As shown in Fig. 7·7*b*, the 3 two-terminal circuits that have a common point at node 4 are:

1. AC
2. DB
3. E

Therefore the wye circuit has been formed. It should be noted that the manner in which a bridge circuit is made up permits the circuit analyst to select any one of the nodes for the common point of the 3 two-terminal circuits that are to make up the legs of the wye circuit. It should be emphasized, however, that the common point must be a nonterminal node. This important fact reduces the degree of choice left to the circuit analyst, since at least two of the four nodes in the original circuit must be terminal points for transmission purposes.

Converting the wye circuit into an equivalent delta circuit. The next step in this process is to convert the wye circuit of Fig. 7·7b into its equivalent delta circuit. The delta circuit is to be a three-node arrangement with the common point of the wye circuit not included. Therefore the delta circuit will have the nodes 1, 2, and 3 as its corners. This is illustrated in Fig. 7·8a.

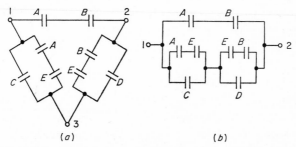

Fig. 7·8   Wye-delta series-parallel transformation: (a) wye converted to delta, (b) delta converted to terminals 1-2 series-parallel combination.

Let us examine in detail how the delta configuration is established. Once the corners of the delta circuit have been selected, the next step is to employ the closed-path tracing technique (as studied in Sec. 7·2) for transmission paths between each pair of nodes used as the corners in the delta circuit. Referring to the original bridge circuit of Fig. 7·7a, we find that the following transmission paths for the 3 two-terminal circuits of the delta configuration are readily established:

$$T_{12} = AB$$
$$T_{13} = AE + C$$
$$T_{23} = EB + D$$

The transmission functions found in this analysis are then converted into the delta switching circuit of Fig. 7·8a.

Converting the delta circuit into an equivalent series-parallel arrangement. The delta switching circuit can be converted into an equivalent series-parallel circuit. Inasmuch as a series-parallel arrangement must have two terminals for transmission purposes, the first step in this procedure is to select the two terminals that are to serve this purpose. In actual practice, these two terminals are often determined by the input and output connections to the switching circuit.

Consider the delta circuit of Fig. 7·8a for the purpose of converting it into a conventional series-parallel arrangement. Let us select nodes 1 and 2 as the output terminals for this configuration. Using the closed-path tracing technique of Sec. 7·2, we can determine all transmission paths between terminals 1 and 2:

1. $T_{12} = AB$
2. $T_{12} = AEEB$
3. $T_{12} = AED$
4. $T_{12} = CEB$
5. $T_{12} = CD$

Combining,

$$T_{12} = AB + AEEB + AED + CEB + CD$$

The circuit of Fig. 7·8b is a representation of this transmission function.

In comparing Fig. 7·8a with Fig. 7·7a, it is seen that all possible transmission paths between terminals 1 and 2 have been taken into account by the Boolean expressions and are included in the circuit of Fig. 7·8a. The ordinary methods of circuit simplification, as studied in Chaps. 5 and 6, can then be applied to this circuit with an eye toward possible reduction in hardware.

PROBLEMS

In the following problems:

1. Use the closed-path technique to determine the Boolean function of the circuit for T_{12}, T_{13} and T_{23}.
2. Draw the conventional series-parallel circuit for terminals 1 and 2, 1 and 3, and 2 and 3.
3. Simplify each circuit as far as possible.

7·1

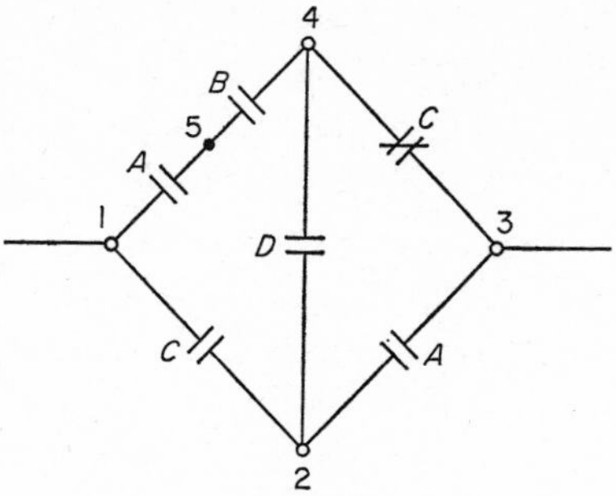

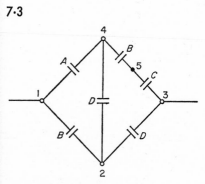

Fig. 7·9

7·2

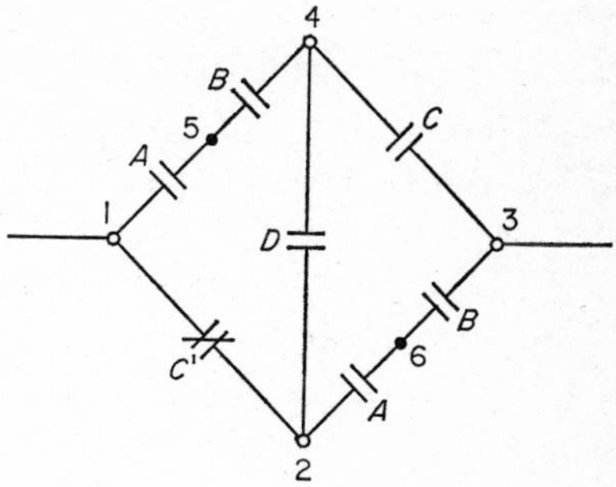

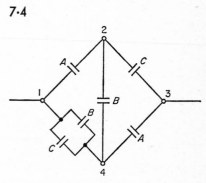

Fig. 7·10

7·3

Fig. 7·11

7·4

Fig. 7·12

7·5

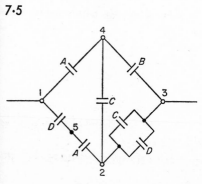

Fig. 7·13

7·6

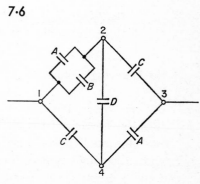

Fig. 7·14

7.7   **7.8**

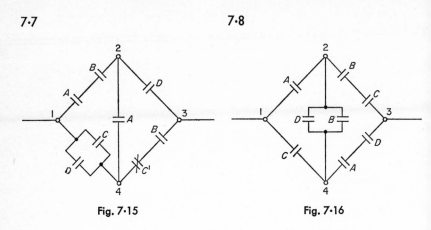

7·9   7·10

In the following problems:

1. Use the wye-to-delta transformation technique to determine the Boolean function of the circuit (f_{12}, f_{13}, f_{23}). Consider each as a three-terminal network (nodes 1, 2, and 3).
2. Draw the conventional series-parallel arrangement for terminals 1 and 2, 1 and 3, and 2 and 3.

7·11   **7·12**

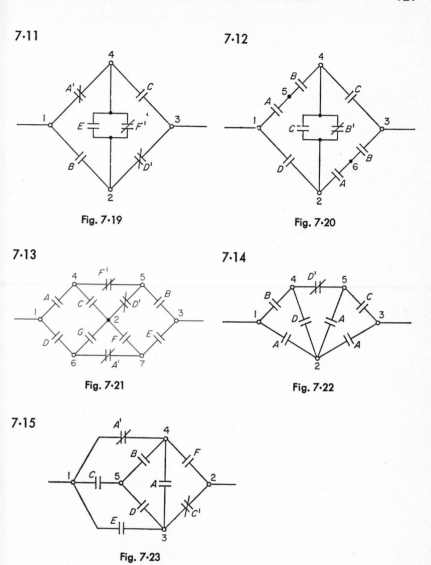

Fig. 7·19   Fig. 7·20

7·13   **7·14**

Fig. 7·21   Fig. 7·22

7·15

Fig. 7·23

7·4   The Use of Nodes in Matrix Construction

The first section of this chapter indicated a general method by which all nodes in a given circuit may be numbered. Recall that the nodes of primary interest (those associated with the input and output terminals) should be assigned the lower numbers. The elements connected between any two nodes can be called connection p_{xy}, where x and y are the numbers of the nodes under consideration. The node connection can be expressed in terms of the Boolean function between the two nodes.

When the node connections of a circuit are analyzed, the following four rules are adopted:

1. The connection p_{xy} is zero when no elements are directly connected between the two nodes.
2. The connection between a node and itself (p_{xx} or p_{yy}, etc.) is assigned the value of 1.
3. A connection in both directions is the same ($p_{xy} = p_{yx}$).
4. The number of connections in the circuit is determined by

$$P = \frac{n(n-1)}{2}$$

where P = number of possible connections
n = number of nodes

Many of the possible connections may be equal to zero.

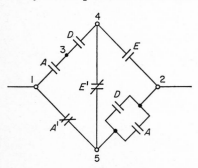

Fig. 7·24

Refer to Fig. 7·24, which illustrates a five-node circuit. The number of possible connections is found to be

$$P = \frac{5(5-1)}{2}$$

$$= 10 \text{ possible connections}$$

Some of the 10 connections may be zero, since no elements are directly connected between them. A matrix may be set up which lists all the possible connections. Table 7·1 illustrates the manner in which such a matrix is set up. The columns are labeled A through E, and the rows are numbered 1 through 5. The first step is to eliminate all the duplications. For example, $p_{12} = p_{21}$; therefore, p_{21} may be crossed out. The same is true for p_{31}, p_{32}, p_{41}, p_{42}, p_{43}, p_{51}, p_{52}, p_{53}, and p_{54}. This results in the simplified matrix of Table 7·2. Note that this simplification step is the application of rule 3.

Table 7·1   Unsimplified Five-array Matrix
for a Five-node Circuit

Row	Column				
	A	B	C	D	E
1	p_{11}	p_{12}	p_{13}	p_{14}	p_{15}
2	p_{21}	p_{22}	p_{23}	p_{24}	p_{25}
3	p_{31}	p_{32}	p_{33}	p_{34}	p_{35}
4	p_{41}	p_{42}	p_{43}	p_{44}	p_{45}
5	p_{51}	p_{52}	p_{53}	p_{54}	p_{55}

Table 7·2   First Simplification of the
Five-array Matrix

Row	Column				
	A	B	C	D	E
1	p_{11}	p_{12}	p_{13}	p_{14}	p_{15}
2		p_{22}	p_{23}	p_{24}	p_{25}
3			p_{33}	p_{34}	p_{35}
4				p_{44}	p_{45}
5					p_{55}

The next simplification step is the application of rule 2:

$$p_{11} = p_{22} = p_{33} = p_{44} = p_{55} = 1$$

The second simplification of the five-array matrix is shown in Table 7·3. In studying this table, it is seen that 10 possible connections remain, in accordance with rule 4. Keeping rule 1 in mind, one can state the Boolean function of each node connection. (Refer to the circuit of Fig. 7·24.)

Table 7·3   Second Simplification of the
Five-array Matrix

Row	Column				
	A	B	C	D	E
1	1	p_{12}	p_{13}	p_{14}	p_{15}
2		1	p_{23}	p_{24}	p_{25}
3			1	p_{34}	p_{35}
4				1	p_{45}
5					1

$p_{12} = 0$ (These two nodes are not directly connected.)

$p_{13} = A$

$p_{14} = 0$ (no direct connection)

$p_{15} = A'$

$p_{23} = 0$ (no direct connection)

$p_{24} = E$

$p_{25} = D + A$

$p_{34} = D$

$p_{35} = 0$ (no direct connection)

$p_{45} = E'$

These values can now be substituted into the matrix, as shown in Table 7·4.

Table 7·4   Substitution of Node Connection Values
into the Matrix

Row	Column				
	A	B	C	D	E
1	1	0	A	0	A'
2		1	0	E	$D + A$
3			1	D	0
4				1	E'
5					1

With each possible node connection expressed in its Boolean function, a third method of analyzing non-series circuits can be developed. The following sections deal with this technique.

7·5   The Boolean Matrix Technique

The Boolean function of a circuit determines the transmission function between the terminals of interest. Recall that it was stated earlier that the terminal nodes are to be numbered first. In Fig. 7·24, for example, nodes 1 and 2 are the two external terminals of that circuit. When a two-terminal network is being analyzed and this type of notation is followed, the large matrix is reduced to a 2×2 matrix which contains only the two terminal nodes.

The large matrix is reduced by eliminating the nonterminal nodes one at a time. In Table 7·4, for example, column E specifies the Boolean function of each possible connection for node 5.

$$p_{15} = A'$$
$$p_{25} = D + A$$
$$p_{35} = 0$$
$$p_{45} = E'$$
$$p_{55} = 1$$

It is most systematic to eliminate all the node 5 connections, then the node 4 connections (shown in column D of Table 7·4), and finally the node 3 connections (column C). Only the node 1 and node 2 connections will be left, and they will have the transmission function of the circuit in row 1 of column B.

The procedure for nodal elimination is as follows:

1. Select the last column of the matrix, which lists all possible connections for the highest-numbered node.
2. Multiply row 1 and row 2 entries in the last column. Add this product to the first row in the second column.
3. Multiply row 1 and row 3 entries in the last column. Add this product to the first row in the third column.
4. Repeat steps 2 and 3 for rows 1 and 4, rows 1 and 5, etc.
5. Repeat steps 2 and 3 with rows 2 and 4, rows 2 and 5, etc., of the last column. Then repeat with rows 3 and 4, rows 3 and 5. *Continue until a product has been added to every entry in the remaining portion of the matrix.*

Many of the products to be added to an entry may be zero, which will not affect the entry to which they are added. Also, adding any product to those entries which are 1 will not change that entry, since 1 plus anything still equals 1.

6. Repeat the entire process for the last column now remaining in the matrix. (For example, if column E was eliminated in steps 1 to 5, then the process is repeated for column D.)

7. Repeat the process for each remaining last column until the 2×2 array has been achieved. The remaining entry in row 1 of column B is the Boolean function of the two-terminal circuit being examined.

Example 1. Assume a 5×5 matrix as in Table 7·5. Column E is first eliminated.

Table 7·5 The Original Matrix

Row	Column				
	A	B	C	D	E
1	1	p_{12}	p_{13}	p_{14}	p_{15}
2		1	p_{23}	p_{24}	p_{25}
3			1	p_{34}	p_{35}
4				1	p_{45}
5					1

New entries for row 1:

$$p_{15}p_{25} + p_{12} = \text{new } p_{12}$$
$$p_{15}p_{35} + p_{13} = \text{new } p_{13}$$
$$p_{15}p_{45} + p_{14} = \text{new } p_{14}$$

New entries for row 2:

$$p_{25}p_{35} + p_{23} = \text{new } p_{23}$$
$$p_{25}p_{45} + p_{24} = \text{new } p_{24}$$

New entries for row 3:

$$p_{35}p_{45} + p_{34} = \text{new } p_{34}$$

Thus column E and row 5 are eliminated. This process is repeated for the elimination of column D, row 4, etc., until only a 2×2 matrix remains. The function for the remaining p_{12} is the transmission function T_{12} of the switching circuit.

Example 2. Determine the Boolean function for the circuit of Fig. 7·24 by use of the Boolean matrix technique.

Solution. The final simplification of the original matrix for this circuit is seen in Table 7·4. Proceeding with the stated rules, column E is first eliminated as shown in Table 7·6. The original entries are in the upper half of each box, and the sum of the appropriate product and original entry is in the lower portion of each box. In column E, the points marked with an encircled X indicate what entry was used as a factor, with the other entry marked with an arrow.

The next step is to eliminate column D in the same manner, as shown in Table 7·7. Then eliminate column C in the same manner, as shown in Table 7·8. The final 2×2 array matrix is shown in Table 7·9.

Table 7·6   Elimination of Column E

Row	Column				
---	A	B	C	D	E
1	1	0 $A'(D + A) + 0$ $A'D$	A $A'0 + A$ A	0 $A'E' + 0$ $A'E'$	A'
2		1	0 $(A + D)(0) + 0$ 0	E $(A + D)E' + E$ $E + D + A$	$A + D$
3			1	D $OE' + D$ D	0
4				1	E'
5					1

Table 7·7   Elimination of Column D

Row	Column			
	A	B	C	D
1	1	$A'D$ $A'E'(E + D + A) + A'D$ $A'D$	A $A'E'(D) + A$ $A + E'D$	$A'E'$
2		1	0 $(E + D + A)(D) + 0$ D	$E + D + A$
3			1	D
4				1

Table 7·8   Elimination of Column C

Row	Column		
	A	B	C
1	1	$A'D$ $D(A + E'D) + A'D$ D	$A + E'D$
2		1	D
3			1

Table 7·9   Reduction to the 2 × 2 Array Matrix

1	D
	1

The simplified equivalent circuit of Fig. 7·24 for nodes 1 and 2 as terminals is shown in Fig. 7·25.

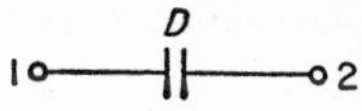

Fig. 7·25

7·6   Analysis of Multiterminal Circuits with Boolean Matrices

In many cases, transmission between three or more nodes is required in a given circuit. The transmission between two nodes can be determined by the Boolean matrix technique analyzed in the preceding section. If the transmission function between the original node 1 and some other node (other than node 2) is desired, the following procedure may be used. It should be noted that this technique avoids the necessity of renumbering the circuit nodes.

1. Set up the complete matrix, including the lower-left portion.
2. Interchange the node columns and rows to be involved in the process. For example, assume that the transmission function for nodes 1 and 5 is to be determined. The node 2 column is interchanged with the node 5 column. The second and fifth rows are then interchanged.
3. Eliminate each column in accordance with the procedure of Sec. 7·5.

Example 1. Assume that the circuit of Fig. 7·24 is to be analyzed for a transmission function between nodes 1 and 5 (as well as nodes 1 and 2).

Solution. The complete matrix for the circuit of Fig. 7·24 is shown in Table 7·10. Now column B (node 2) and column E (node 5) are interchanged as shown in Table 7·11. Then row 2 and row 5 are interchanged as shown in Table 7·12.

The next step is to reduce the matrix since there are duplicate entries. Redrawing the matrix of Table 7·12 with the node connections indicated, we can proceed to eliminate the duplicate entries in Table 7·13. By referring to this table, it can be seen that the following nodes are eliminated: p_{51}, p_{35}, p_{41}, p_{54}, p_{43}, p_{21}, p_{25}, p_{23}, and p_{24}. Notice that the lower-left portion of the rearranged matrix is eliminated, simplifying it to that shown in Table 7·14.

In Table 7·15 we eliminate column B.   Column D is then eliminated in Table 7·16. Column C is eliminated in Table 7·17.

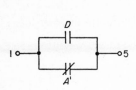

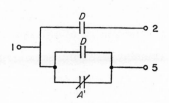

Fig. 7·26   Equivalent circuit for nodes 1 and 5.

Fig. 7·27   Equivalent circuit for nodes 1, 2, and 5.

The reduced equivalent circuit for nodes 1 and 5 is shown in Fig. 7·26. When terminals 1, 2, and 5 are considered as transmission terminals for Fig. 7·24, the equivalent circuit would appear as shown in Fig. 7·27.

Table 7·10   Matrix for Fig. 7·24

Row	Column				
	A	B	C	D	E
1	1	0	A	0	A'
2	0	1	0	E	$D + A$
3	A	0	1	D	0
4	0	E	D	1	E'
5	A'	$D + A$	0	E'	1

Table 7·11   Interchange of Nodes 2 and 5

Row	Column				
	A	E	C	D	B
1	1	A'	A	0	0
2	0	$D + A$	0	E	1
3	A	0	1	D	0
4	0	E'	D	1	E
5	A'	1	0	E'	$D + A$

Table 7·12   Interchange of Rows 2 and 5

Row	Column				
	A	E	C	D	B
1	1	A'	A	0	0
5	A'	1	0	E'	$D + A$
3	A	0	1	D	0
4	0	E'	D	1	E
2	0	$D + A$	0	E	1

Table 7·13   Elimination of Duplicate Entries

Row	Column				
	A	E	C	D	B
1	1	A'	A	0	0
5	$A'\otimes$	1	0	E'	$D + A$
3	$A\otimes$	$0\otimes$	1	D	0
4	$0\otimes$	$E'\otimes$	$D\otimes$	1	E
2	$0\otimes$	$D + A\otimes$	$0\otimes$	$E\otimes$	1

Table 7·14   Final Matrix for the Interchange of
Nodes 2 and 5

Row	Column				
	A	E	C	D	B
1	1	A'	A	0	0
5		1	0	E'	$D + A$
3			1	D	0
4				1	E
2					1

Table 7·15   Elimination of Column B

Row	Column				
	A	E	C	D	B
1	1	A' $A'+0 = A'$	$0 \cdot 0 + A = A$	0 $0 \cdot E + 0$ 0	0
5		1	0 $(D+A)(0) + 0$ 0	E' $(D+A)E + E'$ $E(D+A) + E'$	$D + A$
3			1	D $0 \cdot E + D = D$	0
4				1	E
2					1

Table 7·16   Elimination of Column D

Row	Column			
	A	E	C	D
1	1	A'	A	0
5		1	0 $[E(D+A) + E']D$ D	$E(D+A) + E'$
3			1	D
4				1

Table 7·17   Elimination of Column C

Row	Column		
	A	E	C
1	1	A' $A \cdot D + A'$ $A' + D$	A
5		1	D
3			1

132

PROBLEMS

Using the Boolean matrix technique, find the transmission function between nodes 1 and 2 for the following circuits. Draw the simplified equivalent circuit obtained for each:

7·16 Circuit of Fig. 7·14   **7·17** Circuit of Fig. 7·15
7·18 Circuit of Fig. 7·16   **7·19** Circuit of Fig. 7·17
7·20 Circuit of Fig. 7·18   **7·21** Circuit of Fig. 7·19
7·22 Circuit of Fig. 7·20   **7·23** Circuit of Fig. 7·21
7·24 Circuit of Fig. 7·22   **7·25** Circuit of Fig. 7·23
7·26 Circuit of Fig. 7·28   **7·27** Circuit of Fig. 7·29
7·28 Circuit of Fig. 7·30
7·29 Find T_{12}, T_{13}, and T_{14} of Fig. 7·31. Draw the simplified equivalent circuit obtained for each transmission.

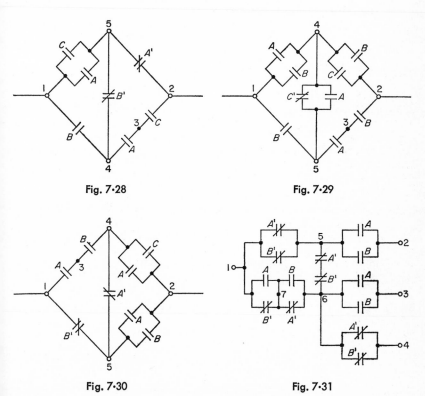

Fig. 7·28   Fig. 7·29

Fig. 7·30   Fig. 7·31

Find T_{13} for the following circuits and draw the simplified equivalent circuit obtained by use of a Boolean matrix:

7·30	Fig. 7·14	7·31	Fig. 7·15
7·32	Fig. 7·16	7·33	Fig. 7·17
7·34	Fig. 7·18	7·35	Fig. 7·19
7·36	Fig. 7·20	7·37	Fig. 7·21
7·38	Fig. 7·22	7·39	Fig. 7·23
7·40	Fig. 7·28	7·41	Fig. 7·29
7·42	Fig. 7·30		

Find T_{14} of the following circuits by use of a Boolean matrix and draw the simplified circuit obtained:

7·43	Fig. 7·14	7·44	Fig. 7·15
7·45	Fig. 7·16	7·46	Fig. 7·17
7·47	Fig. 7·18	7·48	Fig. 7·19
7·49	Fig. 7·20	7·50	Fig. 7·21
7·51	Fig. 7·22	7·52	Fig. 7·23
7·53	Fig. 7·28	7·54	Fig. 7·29
7·55	Fig. 7·30		

Find T_{15} of the following circuits by use of a Boolean matrix and draw the simplified equivalent circuit:

7·56	Fig. 7·20	7·57	Fig. 7·21
7·58	Fig. 7·22	7·59	Fig. 7·23
7·60	Fig. 7·24	7·61	Fig. 7·28
7·62	Fig. 7·29	7·63	Fig. 7·30

Find T_{16} of the following circuits by use of a Boolean matrix and draw the simplified equivalent circuit:

7·64	Fig. 7·20	7·65	Fig. 7·21

CHAPTER 8

Analysis and Simplification
of Switching Circuits
with Karnaugh Maps

Introduction

This chapter is concerned primarily with a special technique for the simplification and analysis of switching circuits, i.e., the Karnaugh map. The mechanics of constructing Karnaugh maps are developed step by step. The method by which the entries are made into the map is analyzed first. Once the technique for making entries is carefully established, the read-out method is analyzed.

Starting with the two-variable type, the concept of simplification by use of Karnaugh maps is developed. The three-, four-, five-, and six-variable Karnaugh maps are then studied. In all cases, both the read-in and read-out techniques are analyzed in detail.

The last section of the chapter indicates how logic addition and multiplication can be performed with Karnaugh maps. A total of 60 problems are included for practice in the techniques developed in the chapter.

8·1 The Two-variable Karnaugh Map

The utilization of Karnaugh maps is another technique for the simplification of Boolean functions. It provides a method by which the function can be visualized, thereby making it easier to identify and extract unnecessary terms.

The *first step* in the preparation of a Karnaugh map is to completely expand the function so that no parenthesis remains and so that it is a series-parallel circuit.

The *second step* is to eliminate those terms which are obviously unnecessary, particularly by use of the following three identities:

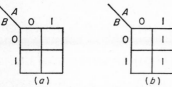

1. $A \cdot A = A$
2. $A + AB = A$
3. $AB + AB' = A$

Fig. 8·1   The two-variable Karnaugh map.

The *third step* is the construction of the map, which actually applies the last two identities listed above to the remaining function.

Karnaugh map construction. The form of the two-variable map is shown in Fig. 8·1.

Example 1. Assume that the following function is to be simplified by use of the Karnaugh map:

$$A + AB + A'B'$$

The possible combinations of states described by the universe table for two variables are shown in Table 8·1.

Table 8·1   Universe Table for Two Variables

A	B
0	0
0	1
1	0
1	1

Solution. Each term (or AND gate) within the function is analyzed, and the condition for transmission is determined.

Step 1. Analyze the first term (A). The transmission is 1 when A is 1 and B is 0 or 1. Therefore the second column is completely filled in (see Fig. 8·1b).

Step 2. Analyze the second term, which is the AND gate AB. The transmission is 1 when $AB = 1$, that is, when A is 1 and B is 1. This is the entry at the bottom of column 2 (see Fig. 8·2), which is already filled. The fact that it is filled by the previous entry indicates that the term AB did not alter the function represented by A alone, which means that

$$A + AB = A$$

This is one of the identities examined in preceding sections. Notice that circuit reduction by this identity was automatically accomplished by this map technique. It is important to note that the filling in of an entry box more than once indicates a redundancy in that portion of the original Boolean function. In our example, since both boxes in the $A = 1$ and $B = 1$ or 0 column were filled by the first term A, and the second term AB simply filled in the lower box in this column again, the term AB is redundant.

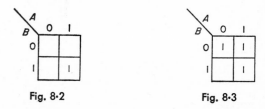

Fig. 8·2   Fig. 8·3

Step 3. Analyze the third term, which is the AND gate $A'B'$. The transmission is 1 when $A'B' = 1$ (that is, when A is 0 and B is 0). This is the upper box in the left column, as shown in Fig. 8·3.

Step 4. Analyze the final map for determination of the simplified function.

The following procedure should be followed in the determination of the final function:

The variable which changes from 1 to 0 across a horizontal or vertical adjacency will disappear in the corresponding portion of the function.

In the example being considered, the top horizontal row indicates that if $B = 0$ (which is the condition when $B' = 1$), the circuit will transmit for both conditions of A. That is,

$T_{12} = 1$ when $B' = 1$ (regardless of the condition of A)

Examination of the completed second column reveals that the circuit will transmit when A is 1, regardless of the condition of B. Combining the analysis of the top row and the second column, it is seen that the circuit will transmit when $B' = 1$ or when $A = 1$. Combining to form a simplified function,

$$A + B'$$

Notice that $A = 1$ is a vertical adjacency and that $B = 0$ $(B' = 1)$ is a horizontal adjacency. $B = 1$ crosses the vertical adjacency and therefore disappears. $A = 0$ crosses the horizontal adjacency and therefore disappears.

Because it has only two variables, this result can be readily verified by the application of Boolean laws:

$$A + AB + A'B' = A + B'$$

Example 2. Simplify the following function by use of the Karnaugh map:

$$f_x = A + AB + B + A'B + AB'$$

Solution. Analyze one term at a time.

Step 1. When $A = 1$, transmission occurs, no matter what the condition of B is. This fills in column 2 in Fig. 8·4.

Fig. 8·4

Step 2. Only when $AB = 1$—that is, only when A is 1 and B is 1—does transmission occur. This fills the lower-right box, which is already filled. Therefore AB is redundant and may be dropped.

Step 3. When $B = 1$, transmission occurs no matter what the condition of A is. This completes the bottom-row adjacency.

Step 4. When $A'B = 1$, transmission occurs. That is, $A = 0$ and $B = 1$. This fills the lower-left box, which is already filled, indicating that $A'B$ is a redundancy and may be dropped.

Step 5. When $AB' = 1$, transmission occurs. That is, $A = 1$, $B = 0$. This fills the upper right-hand box, which is already filled. Since it is a redundancy, AB' is dropped.

Step 6. Combine the remaining entries for the final function. The vertical adjacency is A and the horizontal adjacency is B, that is,

$$T_{12} = A + B$$

8·2 Construction of Three-variable Karnaugh Maps

A function with three variables has eight possible states, as shown by the three-variable universe table (Table 8·2). The map for a three-variable function should have eight entries and can be drawn as shown in Fig. 8·5.

Table 8·2 Three-variable
Universe Table

	A	B	C
1	0	0	0
2	0	0	1
3	0	1	0
4	1	0	0
5	0	1	1
6	1	0	1
7	1	1	0
8	1	1	1

Example 1. Consider the function

$$f_{(x)} = A'B + AB'C + ABC'$$

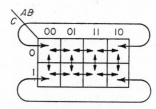

Fig. 8·5 Three-variable Karnaugh map with the 12 possible adjacencies.

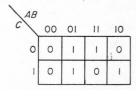

Fig. 8·6 Karnaugh map for $A'B + AB'C + ABC'$.

Solution. The map form is drawn as shown in Fig. 8·6.

Filling in the Karnaugh map (read-in). After construction of the Karnaugh map form, the next step is to examine each term in the Boolean equation in terms of its transmission requirements.

Step 1. The term $A'B = 1$ when $A' = 1$, $B = 1$, and when $C = 0$ or 1. Since the unspecified variable C can be in either of two conditions and still enable this term to transmit, it fills two entries in the Karnaugh map. These two entries are:

1. $A = 0$, $B = 1$, $C = 0$
2. $A = 0$, $B = 1$, $C = 1$

It should be noted that these two entries establish a vertical adjacency in the 01 column.

Step 2. The term $AB'C = 1$ when $A = 1$, $B' = 1$, $C = 1$. This term fills only one entry in the Karnaugh map since each of the three variables has its condition specified:

$$A = 1 \qquad B = 0 \qquad C = 1$$

This entry is in the lower box in the 10 column as shown by the placement of 1 in that box in Fig. 8·6.

Step 3. The term $ABC' = 1$ when $A = 1$, $B = 1$, $C' = 1$. As in step 2, the existence of the three variables in the expression indicates only one entry into the Karnaugh map for its representation:

$$A = 1 \qquad B = 1 \qquad C = 0$$

Step 4. After entries for all the terms of the original Boolean expression have been made, the unfilled boxes of the Karnaugh map are filled with zeros, as shown in Fig. 8·6. The presence of these zeros indicates that the terms represented by each of the boxes is not a part of the original Boolean equation.

Reading out of the Karnaugh map. Once all the entries have been made, they are to be read out of the map. When doing this, it is suggested that the adjacencies be read out first. After the adjacencies have been properly read out, then the nonadjacent entries can be read out. All the read-out entries are ored together, resulting in the complete Boolean expression for the map read-out.

Let us read out the entries of the Karnaugh map just constructed (Fig. 8·6).

Step 1. There are two overlapping adjacencies. Let us consider the vertical adjacency first.

$$A = 0 \qquad B = 1 \qquad \text{and} \qquad C = 0 \text{ or } 1$$

If these two entries are taken out separately, we obtain

$$A'BC' + A'BC$$

Then simplifying,

$$A'B(C' + C) = A'B(1) = A'B$$

It is important to notice that the variables C and C' were eliminated in the simplification process. Therefore it is seen that adjacencies of the same variable (which result in values of both 1 and 0) mean that this variable is left out of the read-out. Hence, this adjacency could have been immediately read out as $A'B$.

Step 2. Let us read out the horizontal adjacency. Notice that A has values of both 1 and 0. Therefore it is omitted from the read-out, which becomes BC'. It should be noticed that this horizontal adjacency overlaps the vertical adjacency analyzed in the preceding step. This overlap is permissible.

Step 3. There is one remaining nonadjacent entry, which is read out as $AB'C$.

Step 4. Combining all the read-out entries results in the following Boolean expression:

$$f_{(x)} = A'B + BC' + AB'C$$

It should be stated that one of the chief uses of the Karnaugh map is in the reduction of Boolean expressions that are difficult to simplify by the direct application of the Boolean laws. Sometimes it is necessary to apply the Boolean matrix technique to the read-out equation for further reduction. Another important use of Karnaugh maps is in checking the specification of a logic problem in terms of completeness and possible contradictions. This application of the Karnaugh map is analyzed in Chap. 9.

Note. The two- and three-variable Karnaugh maps have little practical application in themselves because of the relative simplicity of Boolean functions having two or three variables. Therefore the four-variable Karnaugh map is often considered the *basic* Karnaugh map, and this is studied in the following section. Examining the read-in and read-out procedures of the two- and three-variable Karnaugh maps will familiarize the student with the basic techniques of these important processes before becoming involved with the more complicated maps. It is suggested that the student become thoroughly acquainted with the read-in and read-out techniques before going on to the four-variable map.

8·3   Construction of a Four-variable Karnaugh Map

The four-variable Karnaugh map takes the form illustrated in Fig. 8·7. Two of the four variables are placed on the horizontal axis (AB in Fig. 8·7) and the remaining two variables are placed on the

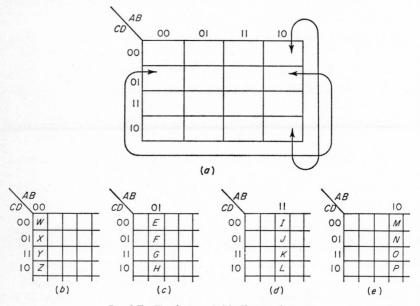

Fig. 8·7   The four-variable Karnaugh map.

vertical axis (CD in Fig. 8·7). Adjacencies are formed by any two entries that are horizontally or vertically next to each other. Adjacencies also occur over the top and around the sides (as indicated by the arrows in Fig. 8·7). Furthermore, adjacencies can consist of 4, 8, and 16 squares. The four corners also make up an adjacency.

The manner in which the columns and rows are read is as follows:

1. First column on the left, as shown in Fig. 8·7b.
   Entry $W = A'B'C'D'$; Entry $X = A'B'C'D$; Entry $Y = A'B'CD$; Entry $Z = A'B'CD'$.

Therefore it is seen that the first column on the left includes all the possible conditions of $A'B'$ in relation with the variables C and D. The two variables C and D have four possible combinations for each condition of the other two variables A and B. These four possible combinations are indicated by the four rows (00, 01, 01, 10) in Fig. 8·7b.

2. Second column from the left, as shown in Fig. 8·7c:
    Entry $E = A'BC'D'$; Entry $F = A'BC'D$; Entry $G = A'BCD$; Entry $H = A'BCD'$
    In this column, the four conditions of $A'B$ in association with C and D are listed.

3. The third column from the left, as shown in Fig. 8·7d includes the four possible conditions of AB in association with C and D:
    Entry $I = ABC'D'$; Entry $J = ABC'D$; Entry $K = ABCD$; Entry $L = ABCD'$.

4. The fourth column from the left as shown in Fig. 8·7e includes the four possible conditions of AB' in association with C and D.
    Entry $M = AB'C'D'$; Entry $N = AB'C'D$; Entry $O = AB'CD$; Entry $P = AB'CD'$.

The manner in which the map is actually filled in from a Boolean equation is best analyzed by solving a problem.

Example 1. Construct a four-variable Karnaugh map for the function

$$f_{(x)} = B' + CD + A'D'C'B$$

Solution

Step 1. Construct the four-variable Karnaugh map form, as shown in Fig. 8·8a.

Step 2. Determine the entries for the term $B' = 1$. Since this term only specifies the normal condition of the variable B, the other three possible variables $(A, C, \text{ and } D)$ can be in any state and will not in any way affect the transmission of $B' = 1$. The three unrelated variables have 2^n possible combinations, where n is the number of variables involved in the complete original Boolean equation. Therefore there are $2^3 = 8$ possible combinations, which will result in the use of eight

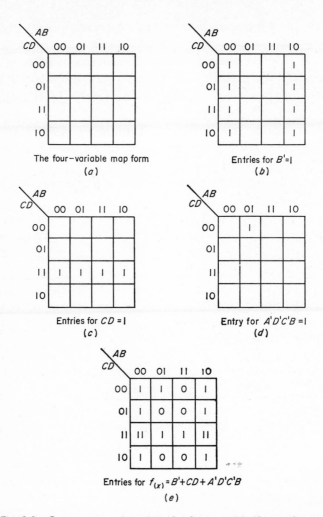

Fig. 8·8 Construction and read-in of a four-variable Karnaugh map.

entries in the Karnaugh map to designate all the possible conditions for $B' = 1$.

Note that B' occurs in the 00 and 10 columns. Therefore these eight entries are filled in with 1, as shown in Fig. 8·8b.

Step 3. Determine the entries for $CD = 1$. The condition of two of the four possible variables are specified in this term. The states of the other two variables (A and B) have no effect on the transmission characteristic of this term. Therefore, a total of $2^n = 2^2 = 4$ possible combinations exist; they occupy the horizontal row labeled 11. These entries are shown in Fig. 8·8c.

Step 4. Determine the entry for $A'D'C'B$. In this term the condition of each of the four variables is specified. Therefore only one entry is made to designate this term. Figure 8·8d illustrates the placement of this entry.

Note. Actually, the entries for each of these terms would be made into the same map, as shown in Fig. 8·8e. Notice that two of the entries for $B' = 1$ are also entries for $CD = 1$. This indicates the use of literals in the original Boolean expression which are not necessary in terms of maintaining the transmission characteristics of the original equation. These extra literals result in *redundancies* in the map and will be eliminated upon read-out of the entries. The redundancies are indicated by the double entries in Fig. 8·8e. One of the advantages of using the Karnaugh map is that many redundancies are readily identified. This results in a final read-out equation with the most economical use of literals.

The last action to be taken in the construction of the map is to fill all unused boxes with zeros (see Fig. 8·8e).

Map read-out. After constructing the map for a given function, the transmissions are read out of the map and simplified. The read-out procedure is:

1. Locate the largest groups of adjacencies. (These groups may consist of two, four, or eight boxes, etc.)
2. If the variable legend is 1 for that group, the variable appears unprimed.
3. If the variable legend is 0 for that group, the variable will be primed.
4. If a variable has both values of 0 and 1, it is dropped out.

Example 2. Perform the read-out of the Karnaugh map of Fig. 8·8 and simplify as much as possible.

Solution. Redrawing the map so that the adjacencies can be pointed out, we obtain Fig. 8·9.

Notice that there are four adjacencies in the map of Fig. 8·9. There are 2 four-entry vertical adjacencies (vertical columns 00 and 10). There is 1 four-entry horizontal adjacency (horizontal row 11) and a double-entry horizontal adjacency (horizontal row 00). Let us proceed to read out these adjacencies in accordance with the read-out rules just stated.

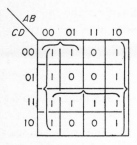

Fig. 8·9 Selection of adjacencies.

Adjacency 1 (vertical column 00)

In this column, $A = 0$ and $B = 0$ in their normal state and therefore are primed (A' and B'). In glancing down the column it is seen that both values of C (0 and 1) and both values of D (0 and 1) are included. Therefore the variables C and D are dropped out. The resulting read-out for this adjacency is simply $A'B'$.

Adjacency 2 (vertical column 10)

The same reasoning used for adjacency applies here for the variables C and D. Therefore, the read-out for this adjacency is AB'.

Adjacency 3 (horizontal row 11)

$C = 1, D = 1$ in this adjacency. Both values of A and B are encountered and are consequently dropped out. Hence, the read-out for this adjacency is CD.

Adjacency 4 (first two entries in horizontal row 00)

$C = 0, D = 0, A = 0$ for both entries. Variable B changes value from 0 to 1 and is therefore dropped out. The resultant read-out is $A'C'D'$. Combining all read-outs and simplifying, all the read-outs are ORed together, and the read-out equation is

$$f_{(x)} = A'B' + AB' + CD + A'C'D'$$

.d simplifying,

$$f_{(x)} = B'(A' + A) + CD + A'C'D'$$
$$= B' + CD + A'C'D'$$

Note that adjacencies can overlap, and that the entries in a row or column can be used more than once. Note that the four-entry adjacencies reduce to two terms, while the two-entry adjacency reduces to three terms.

Typically the Karnaugh map technique is used with the other simplification methods previously analyzed. For example, an n-terminal network can be simplified by the Boolean matrix method for T_{12}, T_{13}, etc. Upon determining the transmission function of interest, the Karnaugh map method may be utilized to further simplify the function.

Note. If separate entries not associated with adjacencies exist in the map, they are read out and ORed with the remainder of the map read-out. This is shown in the illustrated example for the three-variable Karnaugh map in Sec. 8·2 (see step 3 in the read-out portion of the example).

PROBLEMS

Construct a two-variable Karnaugh map for the following functions:

8·1 $X + Y' + Y'X$
8·2 $X + Y' + XY'$
8·3 $X' + Y + Y'X$
8·4 $Y + X' + XY'$
8·5 $X + Y + X'Y'$

Construct a three-variable Karnaugh map for the following functions. First expand the function when necessary.

8·6 $X + Y' + X'Y + Z'$
8·7 $X + Y' + X'YZ$
8·8 $XY'Z + X'Y' + Z'Z$
8·9 $X' + Y + XY' + Z$
8·10 $(X + Y' + X'Y)Z'$
8·11 $A + AB + BC$
8·12 $AC + BC + ABC$
8·13 $AB + BC + AC$
8·14 $(A + B)C + A(BC)$
8·15 $(X + Y' + X'Y)(X + Y') + X'Z$

Construct a four-variable Karnaugh map for the following functions:

8·16 $ABCD + A'BCD + AB'CD + A'BCD$

8·17 $A'B'C'D' + A'B'C'D + A'B'CD + A'BCD + ABCD$

8·18 $WXY'Z + WX'Y'Z' + W'X'Y'Z' + W'XYZ' + WX'Y'Z$

8·19 $(A + B' + C)(A'B + D)$

8·20 $A(CD + EA) + C(D + A)$

8·21 $A'B' + C'D' + A'CD' + ABD'$

8·22 $WX(Y + Z) + WZ$

8·23 $WX + W'Z + XYZ$

8·24 $WX + W'Z + X'YZ$

8·25 $GH + G'I + H'J + IJ$

8·26 $WX + Z(W' + Q)$

8·27 $MN + M'O + N'OP$

8·28 $EF + E'F + F'G$

8·29 $BC''D' + BC''D'E + D'B$

8·30 $ABC + B'DC' + C'B'$

Read out the functions from the following Karnaugh maps. Simplify and draw the final reduced circuit.

8·31

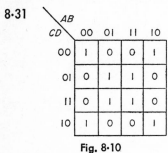

Fig. 8·10

8·32

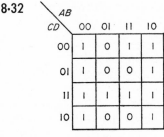

Fig. 8·11

8·33

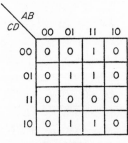

Fig. 8·12

8·34

Fig. 8·13

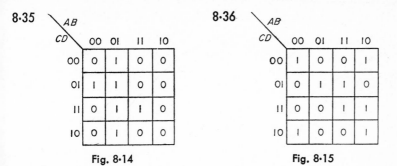

8·35

CD \ AB	00	01	11	10
00	0	1	0	0
01	1	1	0	0
11	0	1	1	0
10	0	1	0	0

Fig. 8·14

8·36

CD \ AB	00	01	11	10
00	1	0	0	1
01	0	1	1	0
11	0	0	1	1
10	1	0	0	1

Fig. 8·15

In the following circuits:

1. Determine transmissions T_{12} and T_{13} by Boolean matrices.
2. Draw a Karnaugh map for each transmission.
3. Write the simplified transmissions from the map.
4. Draw the final simplified equivalent circuit.

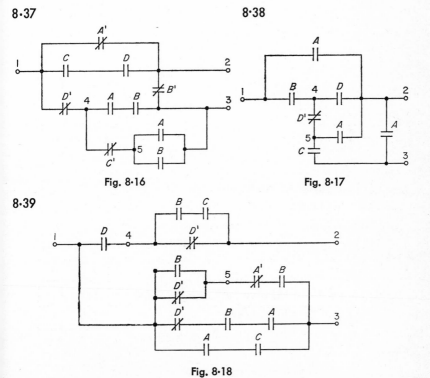

8·37

Fig. 8·16

8·38

Fig. 8·17

8·39

Fig. 8·18

8·40

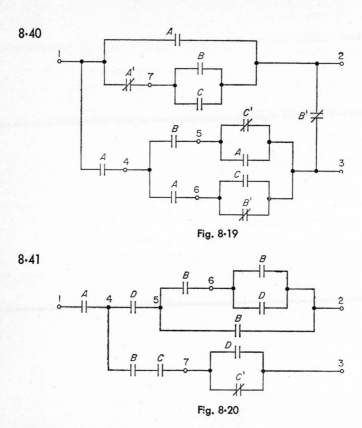

Fig. 8·19

8·41

Fig. 8·20

8·4 The Five-variable Karnaugh Map

A Karnaugh map designed to accommodate Boolean equations containing five variables is constructed with two basic four-variable Karnaugh maps. Figure 8·21 illustrates the five-variable Karnaugh map. Note that in Fig. 8·21 one of the four-variable maps takes into account four of the variables (such as $ABCD$) and the zero state of the fifth variable (such as $E = 0$). The $E = 1$ state with all conditions of the other four variables is provided for in the second basic map.

Therefore the five-variable map has provisions for 32 entries. This is in accordance with the relationship

$$2^n = 2^5 = 32 \text{ possibilities}$$

where

$$n = \text{the number of variables}$$

Reading into the five-variable map. The read-in of the five-variable map is somewhat similar to reading in entries in the four-variable map. Let us illustrate this fact by listing several sample read-ins in Fig. 8·21.

1. term $E'A'B'C'D'$ = entry GF
2. term $E'A'BCD$ = entry GL
3. term $E'AB'C'D$ = entry GS
4. term $EA'B'C'D$ = entry HG
5. term $EABCD'$ = entry HQ
6. term $EAB'C'D'$ = entry HR

Notice that the state of E is 0 in the map on the left and 1 in the basic map on the right.

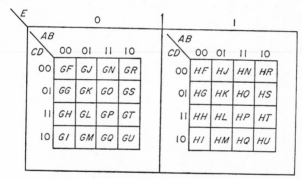

Fig. 8·21   The five-variable Karnaugh map.

Read-out. Read-out is performed in accordance with the rules governing the basic four-variable map (Sect. 8·3). Following is the read-out for several of the entries in Fig. 8·21:

1. Entry GI = term $E'A'B'CD'$
2. Entry GN = term $E'ABC'D'$
3. Entry GT = term $E'AB'CD$
4. Entry HH = term $EA'B'CD$
5. Entry HK = term $EA'BC''D$
6. Entry HP = term $EABCD$

Adjacencies exist in each basic map of the five-variable map as analyzed in the preceding section. In addition to these, adjacencies also exist between corresponding boxes of each basic map.

Example 1. Entries GK and HK make up an adjacency of this type.

Entry GK = term $E'A'BC'D$
Entry HK = term $EA'BC'D$

Solution. Note that the variable E has a value of 0 in the GK entry and a value of 1 in the HK entry. Therefore E' and E drop out when the two terms are oʀed together. Furthermore, only one of the remaining four-variable terms is retained since they are identical. Following is a Boolean law justification for this reduction:

$$\text{Entry } GK + \text{Entry } HK = E'A'BC'D + EA'BC'D$$
$$= A'BC'D(E' + E)$$
$$= A'BC'D$$

The same type of reduction occurs between any of the corresponding box adjacencies between the two basic maps of the five-variable Karnaugh map.

Example 2. Read the following Boolean function into a five-variable Karnaugh map:

$$f_{(x)} = UW + XY'(W' + U'Z)$$

Solution

Step 1. Expand tne original Boolean equation, which results in

$$f_{(x)} = UW + XY'W' + XY'U'Z$$

The next several steps determine the transmission characteristics of each term within the equation.

Step 2. Determine the transmission characteristic of UW.

$UW = 1$ when $U = 1$, $W = 1$, $X = 0, 1$; $Y = 0, 1$; and $Z = 0, 1$

$Z = 0$ is the map on the left, and $Z = 1$ is the map on the right (see Fig. 8·22). Since X and Y can be in either state, $2^2 = 4$ possible combinations exist in each basic map. These entries are made in the vertical 11 column of each basic map in Fig. 8·22.

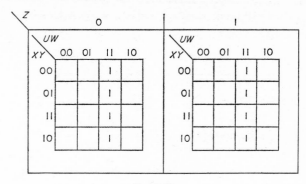

Fig. 8·22

Step 3. Determine the transmission function of $W'XY'$.

$W'XY' = 1$ when $U = 0, 1$; $W = 0$; $X = 1$; $Y = 0$; $Z = 0, 1$

Since $Z = 0$ and 1, entries will again be made in both basic maps. Of the remaining four variables (U, W, X, Y), only U can assume either condition of 0 or 1. The two entries made into each basic map are the two lower corner boxes as shown in Fig. 8·23.

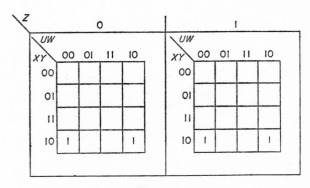

Fig. 8·23

Step 4. Determine the transmission function of $U'XY'Z$.

$U'XY'Z = 1$ when $U = 0$; $W = 0, 1$; $X = 1$; $Y = 0$; $Z = 1$

The W is the only variable that can be in both states of 0 and 1. Therefore two entries will be made. $Z = 1$ specifies that the entries are to be made in the basic map on the right-hand side (as shown in Fig. 8·24).

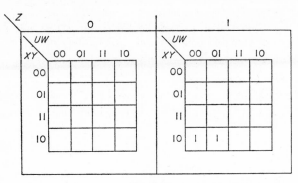

Fig. 8·24

Note. The entries for each term were made in separate maps in this example so that the student could more readily follow the read-in technique. In actual practice all the entries are made into one map. The composite read-in of this example is shown in Fig. 8·25.

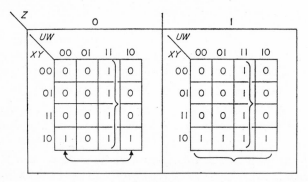

Fig. 8·25

Example 3. Read out the Boolean function from the five-variable Karnaugh map of Fig. 8·25, and simplify as much as possible.

Solution

Step 1. The vertical 11 columns in each map are adjacencies. Note that X and Y have values of both 0 and 1. Also notice that Z has values of both 0 and 1. Therefore, in keeping with the read-out rule for adjacencies, X, Y, and Z drop out, and the final term for both columns is UW.

Step 2. The horizontal row 10 in the $Z = 1$ basic map is an adjacency. The variables U and W have values of 0 and 1 and therefore drop out. The final read-out for this adjacency is $XY'Z$.

Step 3. The last adjacency exists in the lower corners of the $Z = 0$ map. Note that U has both values of 1 and 0. The read-out is $W'XY'Z'$.

Step 4. Combine the read-out terms and simplify.

$$\begin{aligned} f_{(x)} &= UW + XY'Z + W'XY'Z' \\ &= UW + XY'(Z + Z'W') \\ &= UW + XY'(Z + W') \end{aligned}$$

Therefore it is seen that the original Boolean equation

$$f_{(x)} = UW + XY'(W + U'Z)$$

which has seven literals, is reduced to an expression containing six literals.

8·5 The Six-variable Karnaugh Map

Recall that a six-variable Boolean equation has $2^n = 2^6 = 64$ possible terms. A Karnaugh map that can account for any or all of these 64 terms consists of an array of four basic maps. Figure 8·26 illustrates the six-variable Karnaugh map.

Assume, for the sake of analysis, that the six variables are A, B, C, D, E, and F. Four of the variables could be taken care of by a single basic map. The addition of a fifth variable (such as E) requires a second basic map. In this way, (as shown in Sec. 8·4), one of the basic maps accounts for the $2^4 = 16$ possibilities of the first four variables when the fifth variable is *zero*. The second basic map has 16 possibilities for the original four variables when the fifth variable is *one*. Notice that the possible combinations doubled in Fig. 8·22 from 16 to 32 by the introduction of a fifth variable. When a sixth variable is added, its two possible states (0, 1) in conjunction with the other five variables result in a total of 64 combinational possibilities. Note that the four basic maps in Fig. 8·26 are combined so that the 0 and 1 states of both E and F are taken into account.

Read-in. The read-in technique for the six-variable map is essentially the same as for earlier Karnaugh maps, with the special provision for the sixth variable. Following are several illustrated entry read-ins in Fig. 8·26:

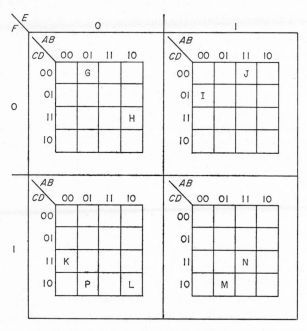

Fig. 8·26   The six-variable Karnaugh map.

1. Term $E'F'A'BC'D'$ = entry G. Notice that the variable E' indicates that one of the two basic maps on the left side of the Karnaugh map is involved. The second variable F' indicates that this entry will be made in the upper-left basic map. The remaining four variables locate the specific entry in that basic four-variable map. Therefore, $E'F'A'BC'D'$ = entry G

2. Term $E'F'AB'CD$ = entry H. Note that $E'F'$ places the entry in the upper left-hand corner basic map.

3. Term $EF'A'B'C'D$ = entry I. The selection of the upper right-hand corner map is made by the variables EF'.

4. Term $EF'ABC'D'$ = entry J

5. Term $E'FA'B'CD$ = entry K

6. Term $E'FAB'CD' = $ entry L

7. Term $EFA'BCD' = $ entry M

8. Term $EFABCD = $ entry N

The preceding examples indicate the combination of the fifth and sixth variables that is handled by each of the basic maps (refer to Fig. 8·26):

1. Upper-left map is for $E'F'$ with all combinations of A, B, C, D.

2. Upper-right map is for EF' with all combinations of A, B, C, D.

3. Lower-left map is for $E'F$ with all combinations of A, B, C, D.

4. Lower-right map is for EF with all combinations of A, B, C, D.

Read-out. The process of reading out is identical to that of the earlier Karnaugh maps. The only significant difference is that six variables are involved.

Example 1

$$\text{Entry } P = E'FA'BCD'$$

Solution. Notice that $E'F$ is read out as soon as the entry was found to be in the lower left-hand corner basic map. The remaining four variables are read out in the usual manner.

Adjacencies occur in the six-variable map in the same way they appear in the five-variable map. Therefore corresponding entries also form adjacencies.

Example 2. Consider entries P and M, which are adjacencies.

Solution. Both entries have the same values within their respective basic maps, i.e.,

$$A'BCD'$$

$F = 1$ for both entries, while E has both values of 0 and 1. Therefore E is dropped out and the read-out is $FA'BCD'$.

Justifying this outcome by conventional Boolean algebra,

$$
\begin{aligned}
\text{Entry } P + \text{entry } M &= E'FA'BCD' + EFA'BCD' \\
&= FA'BCD'(E' + E) \\
&= FA'BCD'
\end{aligned}
$$

Example 3. Read in the entries for the following equation into a six-variable Karnaugh map:

$$f_{(z)} = X(YW + X') + U'V(Y'Z) + XYU + UW$$

Solution

Step 1. Expand the initial equation to

$$f_{(z)} = XYW + U'VY'Z + XUY + UW$$

The next four steps determine the entries for each term of the equation above. The entries are to be made in Fig. 8·27.

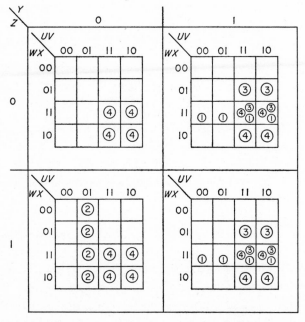

Fig. 8·27 Six-variable map for $f_{(z)} = XYW + U'VY'Z + XYU + UW$.

Step 2

$$XYW = 1 \text{ when } U = 0, 1; V = 0, 1; W = 1; X = 1; Y = 1; Z = 0, 1$$

The combination of $Y = 1$, $Z = 0$ and 1 indicates that entries for this term are to be made in the two basic maps on the right-hand side.

Entries are to be made in these two maps for the given states of the four variables U, V, W, and X. Notice that W and X must be in the '1' state while U and V can assume both values of 0 and 1. A truth table will indicate the $2^2 = 4$ entries that are required to designate this term (XYW).

W	X	U	V
1	1	0	0
1	1	0	1
1	1	1	0
1	1	1	0

Fig. 8·28 Entries for term XYW in the YZ' and YZ basic maps.

The four entries listed in the truth table of Fig. 8·28 are to be made in both the YZ' and YZ basic maps of Fig. 8·27. These entries form the four entry adjacencies in the horizontal 11 rows in the two basic maps on the right (in Fig. 8·27) and are labeled with an encircled number 1.

Step 3

$$U'VY'Z = 1 \text{ when } U = 0; V = 1; W = 0, 1; X = 0, 1; Y = 0; Z = 1$$

The combination of $Y = 0$ and $Z = 1$ indicates the entries for this term are to be made in the lower left-hand corner basic map. Since U and V values are specified while W and X can assume both values of 0 and 1, four entries are to be made. These entries form the four-entry adjacency in the 01 vertical column in this map (see Fig. 8·27) and are labeled with the encircled number 2.

Step 4

$$X'YU = 1 \text{ when } U = 1; V = 0, 1; W = 0, 1; X = 0; Y = 1; Z = 0, 1$$

U	V	W	X
1	0	0	1
1	0	1	1
1	1	0	1
1	1	1	1

Fig. 8·29 Truth table for term $X'YU$.

The combination of $Y = 1$ and $Z = 0$ and 1 indicates that entries will be made in the two basic maps on the right-hand side of Fig. 8·27. Two of the four remaining variables can assume only one state ($U = 1$, $X = 0$). The remaining two variables can have values of 0 and 1. Therefore $2^2 = 4$ combinational possibilities exist in each basic map. These possibilities are listed in the truth table of Fig. 8·29.

The encircled number 3 indicates that these entries will be placed in the two basic maps on the right-hand side of Fig. 8·27. Notice that two of these entries occur in boxes that were previously filled. As analyzed in an earlier section, this indicates a redundancy of literals in the original equation which will be simplified upon read-out.

Step 5

$$UW = 1 \text{ when } U = 1; V = 0, 1; W = 1; X = 0, 1; Y = 0, 1; Z = 0, 1$$

The combination of $Y = 0$, 1 and $Z = 0$ and 1 indicates that entries will be made in each of the four basic maps. Of the four variables within each basic map, $U = 1$ and $W = 1$. Since V and X can have values of 0 and 1, $2^2 = 4$ combinational possibilities exist in each map. These entries are labeled with the encircled number 4 in Fig. 8·27. The read-in process is now complete.

Note. The entries in Fig. 8·27 were made with the numbers 1 to 4 to enable the reader to better follow the read-in process described here. In actual practice, all entries are made with 1 and the unfilled boxes are assigned 0. Figure 8·30 illustrates this.

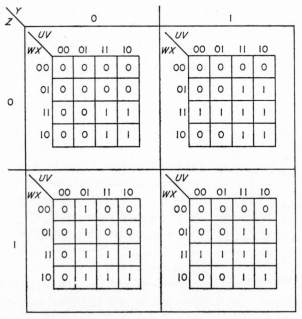

Fig. 8·30   Final Karnaugh map for $f_{(x)} = XYW + U'VY'Z + XYU + UW$.

Example 4. Read out the completed Karnaugh map of Fig. 8·30 and simplify as much as possible.

Solution. A systematic approach of some sort is suggested. Let us clear one basic map at a time and then OR all read-outs.

Step 1. $Y'Z'$ basic map

Two double adjacencies are found here and are read out as

$$Y'Z'WXU + Y'Z'WX'U$$

and simplifying,

$$= Y'Z'WU(X + X') = Y'Z'WU$$

Step 2. YZ' basic map

Three horizontal adjacencies are in this map, and their read-out is

$$YZ'(WX + W'XU + WX'U) = YZ'(XW + UX + UW)$$

Simplifying,

$$YZ'W(X'U + X + X'U) = YZ'W(X + U)$$

Step 3. YZ basic map

The same three horizontal adjacencies as found in the YZ' map are found:

$$YZWX + YZW'XU + YZ'WX'U$$

Simplifying,

$$YZ'W(X'U + X + X'U) = YZW(X + U)$$

Step 4. $Y'Z$ basic map

Three vertical adjacencies, which read out as

$$Y'ZU'V + Y'ZUVW + Y'ZUV'W$$

Simplifying,

$$Y'ZV(U' + UW) + Y'ZUV'W$$
$$Y'ZVU' + Y'ZVW + Y'ZUV'W = Y'ZVU' + Y'ZW(V + V'U)$$
$$= Y'ZVU' + Y'ZWV + Y'ZWU = Y'Z(VU' + WV + WU)$$

Step 5. Combine all the read-outs.

$$f_{(x)} = Y'Z'WU + YZ'W(X + U) + YZ'(XW + UX + UW)$$
$$+ Y'Z(VU' + WV + WU)$$

and simplifying,

$$= Y'Z'WU + YZ'W(X + U) + Y'Z(VU' + WV + WU)$$
$$+ Y'ZVU' + Y'ZWV + Y'ZWU$$
$$= Y'ZWU + YZ'WX + YZ'WU + Y'ZVU' + YZ'WV + Y'ZWU$$
$$+ Y'ZWV + Y'ZWU + Y'ZVU'$$
$$= YZ'(XW + UX + UW)$$

The original Boolean equation of 12 literals has been reduced to an equivalent Boolean equation having 8 literals.

8·6 Karnaugh Map Techniques for Series and Parallel Connections

The Karnaugh map approach may be utilized in the solution of several terminal circuits that are in series or in parallel with each other. The map for 2 two-terminal circuits that are in series is equal to the product of the two maps. The multiplication is done term by term in accordance with Boolean laws ($1 \times 0 = 0; 1 \times 1 = 1$). Figure 8·31 illustrates Karnaugh map multiplication.

Refer to Fig. 8·31. The item in row 1, column 3 of map 2 is multiplied by the corresponding entry in map 1, which is 0; this results in a

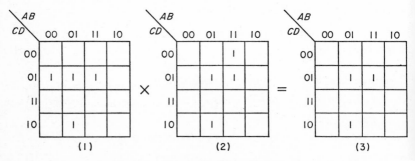

Fig. 8·31 Karnaugh map multiplication.

product of 0. The item in row 2, column 3 of map 2 is 1 and is multiplied by the corresponding entry in map 1 which is also 1, resulting in a product of 1. This appears in the product map (3). The remainder of the entries in map 2 are treated in the same manner, resulting in the completed product map 3.

When 2 two-terminal circuits are connected in parallel, their maps can be added entry by entry, resulting in a sum map. This technique is illustrated in Fig. 8·32.

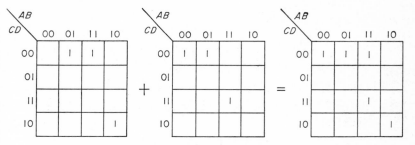

Fig. 8·32 Karnaugh map addition.

As in the case of multiplication, the Boolean laws must be observed $(1 + 0 = 1; 1 + 1 = 1)$. Examination of Fig. 8·32 reveals the process of Karnaugh map addition.

PROBLEMS

In each of the following problems, perform the following:

1. Draw the circuit represented by the original Boolean function.
2. Reduce the original function as far as possible by use of the Karnaugh map technique.
3. Upon read-out from the constructed Karnaugh map, simplify as far as possible by the application of Boolean laws and other techniques.
4. Draw the circuit of the final simplified function.

8·42 $ABC + BCDE + ADE + B'DE$
8·43 $UVW + UV(WX + YZ)$
8·44 $ACE + CF + BC + BCAD$
8·45 $Y'Z + Z(X' + Y) + UWX + XYZ$
8·46 $UVABC + A'UV + B'UV + DUV$
8·47 $(F' + E)BA' + FD'A + CA$

8·48 $AB + C'D + D'E + E'A$

8·49 $A'B + ABC' + AB'C + A'B'C'D + D'$

8·50 $CD(W + A) + (A + W)ZC$

8·51 $B'CD' + A'CD'E + AB$

8·52 $UWX'Y + WX'Z' + UZ$

8·53 $U'WX + XZ + WXY + Y'Z'$

8·54 $G'M' + L'M + K'L + HKM$

8·55 $B'GC + BC'F + BEC' + D'C'B'$

8·56 $C'D'B' + B'DA + A'BE + AF'B$

8·57 $UX + W'U' + Y'X'W' + Z'XW + WXM$

8·58 $ABE + E'B + B'DE' + ECB' + FE'B$

8·59 Solve the following by Karnaugh map addition of the two functions:

$$f(1) = X'Y'Z + W'XY' + WY'$$
$$f(2) = WX'YZ + YZ' + XY$$

8·60 Solve the following by Karnaugh map multiplication of the two functions:

$$f(1) = BC + AB'CD + CD$$
$$f(2) = B'C'D' + A'BC' + AC'$$

CHAPTER 9

Conversion of Original Circuit Requirements into a Simplified Switching Circuit

Introduction

Putting together various components to form a circuit which performs a predetermined function may be called *synthesis*, which is the opposite of analysis. The construction of switching circuits is actually a synthesis from cause to effect. In most instances, the cause is the specifications or verbal requirements. The effect is the schematic design of the switching circuit which will perform the functions that were dictated by the cause (specifications).

It is not unusual to have original specifications or verbal requirements which are not entirely complete. One of the earliest steps is to rewrite or amend the specifications so that they are more concrete and definite. Upon completion of this important step, each statement within the specifications is converted into a Boolean function. Each of these functions can then be classified with the help of an input-output table into one of three categories, namely, "yes," "no," or "don't care or impossible." The functions within the input-output table can then be used to construct a synthesis map.

Analysis of the synthesis map quickly locates its contradictions and ambiguities so that these flaws in the original specifications can be rectified. The completed synthesis map is then used to set up the Boolean function for the final circuit, and the job is essentially completed. This chapter devotes considerable attention to the techniques of this desirable procedure.

9·1 Phrasing the Logic into a Set of Statements and Assignment of Symbols

The initial requirements of the problem may have already been carefully converted into verbal statements—thereby reducing the task of arriving at the final circuit. Whether or not the specifications have been converted, they should be carefully analyzed for contradictions and ambiguities. The majority of the statements in the specifications should take an if-then form. Carefully phrased specification statements frequently incorporate the use of "if" for controls and "then" for outputs. An example of this follows:

"If any one or more of the doorbell buttons are pressed, then the doorbell chimes will ring."

In this example, the controls are the doorbell buttons, and the output is the doorbell chime. Block diagraming is often an effective technique in the analysis or determination of specifications. A suitable block diagram for the preceding example could be drawn as shown in Fig. 9·1.

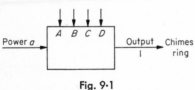

Fig. 9·1

By use of the block diagram, the specifications can be reexamined with an eye toward clarity and completeness. In Fig. 9·1, for example, it is evident that none of the controls (A, B, C, or D or any combination of them) can cause the chimes to ring unless the power is on. Therefore the specifications can be made clearer by the addition of the statement: "The power is always on."

Notice that symbols have been assigned to the input, output, and controls. In Fig. 9·1, the input is the power supply and is always on. Therefore it functions purely as an input. Inputs which do not have control characteristics can be assigned small letters (a in Fig. 9·1). Controls and or control inputs serve as the independent variables. They determine the condition of the output and can be assigned capital letters (A, B, etc. in Fig. 9·1). The output, which is the terminal from which the information is obtained, may be assigned a number (1 in Fig. 9·1).

Adopting a consistent procedure for notation, such as outlined in the preceding paragraphs, results in more effective analysis of the specifications. Referring back to Fig. 9·1 and its specifications, we see that "if" is associated with the controls and "then" is affiliated with the output.

9·2 Determination of the Number of States

Recall that each control has two possible states—ON or OFF. Therefore the number of possible states that are theoretically possible is predicted by the following relationship:

$$S = 2^n$$

where S = number of possible states
n = number of controls

Some of the theoretically possible states fortunately fall within one of the following categories in actual practice:

1. Impossible
2. Uninteresting

The impossible and/or uninteresting states should be identified as early as possible, thereby simplifying the circuit synthesis. Several methods by which the impossible or uninteresting states can be effectively used are examined in the following sections. State coding, another technique which uses impossible states for synthesis simplification, is studied in the following chapter.

9·3 Specifications Analysis with an Input-Output Table

After the assignment of a symbol to each control, input, and output, each input-output combination is analyzed. After the analysis of each individual combination, they are combined.

Consider the preceding example (Fig. 9·1), whose specifications are:

1. The power is always ON.
2. If any one or more of the doorbell buttons are pressed, then the doorbell chimes will ring.

Statement 1 is not directly concerned with the circuit logic. It simply indicates that the circuit must always be connected to the power supply regardless of the state(s) of the controls.

Statement 2 deals with four controls (A, B, C, and D), each of which has two possible states. If any one or more of these controls are ON the output is 1. In accordance with the previous equation, the number of theoretically possible states can be determined.

$$S = 2^n = 2^4 = 16$$

Let us list the possible combinations in a universe table (Table 9·1) and add a fifth column to denote the output (0 or 1).

Table 9·1   Output Possibilities for the Various Combinations

Possibility	A	B	C	D	T_{a1}
1	0	0	0	0	0
2	0	0	0	1	1
3	0	0	1	0	1
4	0	1	0	0	1
5	1	0	0	0	1
6	0	0	1	1	1
7	0	1	0	1	1
8	1	0	0	1	1
9	0	1	1	0	1
10	1	0	1	0	1
11	1	1	0	0	1
12	0	1	1	1	1
13	1	1	1	0	1
14	1	1	0	1	1
15	1	0	1	1	1
16	1	1	1	1	1

All the combinations except the first will result in a transmission of 1. Table 9·1 shows that statement 2 actually includes all the possibilities except one. Let us assume that all the possibilities in Table 9·1 are to be taken into account in the synthesis, resulting in no uninteresting states in the problem.

It should be noted that each row in Table 9·1 is a specific substatement of statement 2 of the original specifications. Since there are four controls (A, B, C, D), 16 substatements must be made to consider every possible control combination. Therefore each of the rows in Table 9·1 can be converted into a verbal statement and into a Boolean equation. Let us make the verbal statement and then convert that statement into a Boolean equation for rows 1 to 4 of Table 9·1.

1. If A and B and C and D are open with the presence of a signal, then the chimes will not ring.

$$A'B'C'D', T_{a1} = 0$$

2. If A and B and C are open and D is closed, then the chimes will ring.

$$A'B'C'D, T_{a1} = 1$$

3. If A and B and D are open and C is closed, then the chimes will ring.

$$A'B'CD', T_{a1} = 1$$

4. If A and C and D are open and B is closed, then the chimes will ring.

$$A'BC'D', T_{a1} = 1$$

Stating the remaining rows in Boolean form,

5. $AB'C'D', T = 1$
6. $A'B'CD, T = 1$
7. $A'BC'D, T = 1$
8. $AB'C'D, T = 1$
9. $A'BCD', T = 1$
10. $AB'CD', T = 1$
11. $ABC'D', T = 1$
12. $A'BCD, T = 1$
13. $ABCD', T = 1$
14. $ABC'D, T = 1$
15. $AB'CD, T = 1$
16. $ABCD, T = 1$

All the functions hold for $T = 1$, except the possibility of number 1, which is to be included in the $T = 0$ portion of the input-output table. In this example, there are no uninteresting states.

9·4   Construction of a Synthesis Map

After completing the input-output table, these entries are placed into a synthesis map, which is somewhat similar to the Karnaugh map analyzed in Chap. 9.

Since four controls are involved, a four-variable (basic) map is needed, as shown in Fig. 9·2.

Since only one Boolean function is involved for the $T = 0$ condition, this entry can be made first. $A'B'C'D' = 1$ ($T = 0$ condition), when $A' = 1$, $B' = 1$, $C' = 1$, and $D' = 1$. This is the box in the first column, first row, as shown in Fig. 9·2. Notice that 0 was used in this map entry since it is a $T = 0$ condition. By inspection of the Boolean functions for the $T = 1$ condition, it is seen that 15 possibilities exist which are the 15 remaining entries in the synthesis map. (The reader can verify this by inserting the entry for each of the 15 Boolean functions into the synthesis map of Fig. 9·2.)

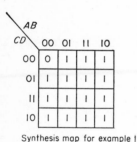

Synthesis map for example I

Fig. 9·2

Notice that all boxes in the synthesis map are filled. An unfilled box would indicate an ambiguity—a condition not accounted for in the specifications. The appearance of an unfilled box at this state of the circuit synthesis would indicate a need to revise the specifications to account for these possibilities as yes (1) or no (0) or don't care (∅) or impossible (∅). Any box containing more than one type of entry indicates a contradiction. For example, 0 and 1 in the same box indicates transmission and no-transmission for the exact same condition—a serious contradiction. 0, ∅ or 1, ∅ in the same box may not be a serious contradiction. If ∅ indicates "don't care," the designer can make it 1 or 0, as he sees fit. On the other hand, if ∅ indicates "impossible" and the second entry in the box is 1, this is a serious contradiction, and the specifications must be revised.

9·5 Conversion of the Synthesis Map into the Boolean Function of the Final Circuit

The read-out of the synthesis map is identical to the read-out of any Karnaugh map. In Fig. 9·2, taking the largest adjacencies first:

$$T_{a1} = A'B + AB + AB' + C'D + CD + CD'$$

and simplifying,

$$T_{a1} = A + B + C + D$$

The circuit for this function is shown in Fig. 9·3. Note that the preceding example could have been synthesized without the use of the synthesis map. This simple problem was selected to enable the reader to better understand the procedure which utilizes this particular synthesis technique.

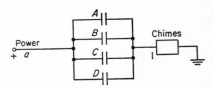

Fig. 9·3 Circuit for $T_{a1} = A + B + C + D$.

9·6 Design of an Interlock System for a Power Supply

Some logic problems dealing with combinational circuits do not readily lend themselves to the map synthesis technique because of the large number of variables. Following are several illustrated problems which can be placed within this category.

Problem. A power supply is to be furnished with an interlock system which will safeguard both operators and equipment. This interlock system should perform the following functions:

1. A main power switch is to control all power.
2. A filament switch is to control filament power and activation of a time delay unit, which will close after the required time following the closure of the filament switch.
3. Upon closure of the time delay switch, door interlock switch, temperature control switch, current release, voltage release, blower control switch, and panic control switch, then the plate-voltage switch will close.

4. If the plate-voltage switch, the master plate switch, and the main power switch are closed, the plate voltage for the mercury vapor rectifiers is to be available.
5. The filament voltage should remain ON if the main power is ON and the plate voltage is OFF or ON.
6. If the filament power should turn OFF, the time delay switch opens. (If the filament power is turned OFF, the time delay unit must be reactivated before plate voltage will be available.)
7. The output of the power supply is shorted if the power supply is turned OFF.

Solution. This problem may be solved by one of several approaches. Let us consider the following plan of attack:

1. Design of the filament power circuit
2. Design of the plate-voltage switch circuit
3. Design of the plate-voltage circuit
4. Combination of the three circuits
5. Incorporation of statement 7 into the combined circuit

Step 1. Design the filament power circuit. Statements 1 and 2 deal with the filament control circuit. Assigning symbols,

$$A = \text{main power switch}$$
$$B = \text{filament power switch}$$
$$C = \text{time delay switch}$$

The filament power will be ON if the main power switch and filament power switch are ON. The time delay switch is closed in a predetermined amount of time after the filament power is ON.

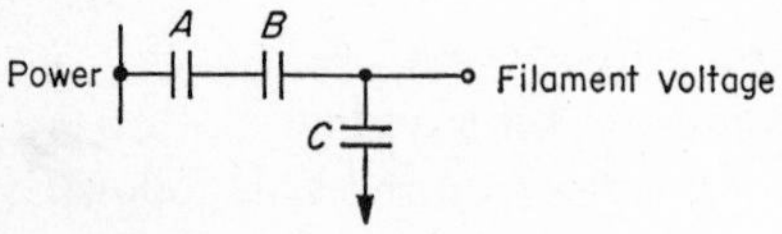

Fig. 9·4   Filament power circuit.

$$AB = \text{filament power}$$
$$C = \text{time delay switch}$$

Convert into circuitry.

Step 2. Design the plate-voltage switch circuit. After the time delay switch is closed, the plate-voltage switch will close if the following switches are closed: door interlock, temperature control, current release, voltage release, blower control, panic control. Assigning symbols,

D = door interlock
E = temperature control
F = current release
G = voltage release
H = blower control
I = panic control

Since the main power switch and the filament control switch must be ON before the time delay switch can close, they must also be considered in the plate-voltage switch circuit:

$$ABCDEFGHI = \text{plate control switch}$$

Converting into circuitry,

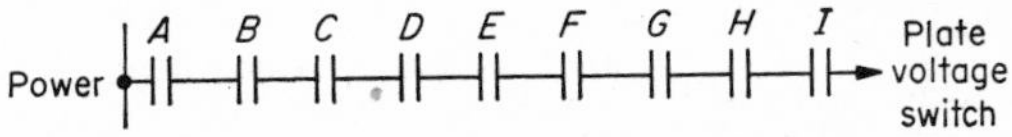

Fig. 9·5   Plate-voltage switch circuit.

Step 3.   Design the plate-voltage circuit. Statement 4 of the original specifications indicates that the plate-voltage switch, the master plate switch, and the main power switch are closed when plate voltage is available.
Assigning symbols,

J = plate-voltage switch
K = master plate switch

and

AJK = plate voltage

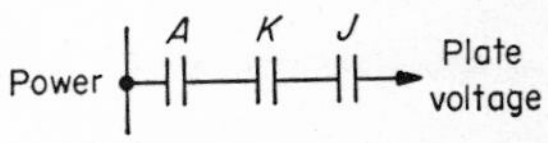

Fig. 9·6   Plate-voltage circuit.

Convert into circuitry.

Step 4.   Combine the circuits. In step 2, it was seen that activation of switches A, B, C, D, E, F, G, H, and I was required to close switch K. Therefore switch K can be a pair of contacts not electrically connected to the energizing circuit (as shown in Fig. 9·7).

Switches K and A also control the plate voltage, of course. The filament circuit, since it utilizes the same switches A and B required of the plate supply circuit, can be tapped off as shown in Fig. 9·7.

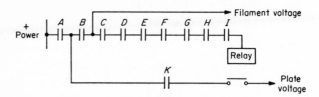

Fig. 9·7   Plate- and filament voltage circuit.

Step 5. Incorporate statement 7 into the combined circuit. Statement 7 demands that the output be shorted when the power supply is OFF. Notice that the pair of contacts of relay J are closed when the power supply is ON and open when the power supply is OFF. Another set of contacts of relay J, which are closed when the power supply is OFF and open when the power supply is ON, can be connected across the output. This is shown in the final circuit of Fig. 9·8.

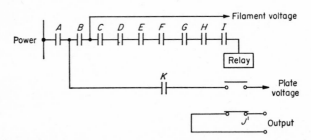

Fig. 9·8   Final combined circuit.

9·7   Design of the Logic Circuit for an "In-line Numerical Read-out Display"

Problem. To design the circuit for an "in-line numerical read-out display" for a twenty-four-hour clock with a minimum number of relays and contacts. The lights of the read-out display are in the formation shown in Fig. 9·9. All digits 0 to 9 can be displayed in the manner indicated in Table 9·2.

Table 9·2   Lights for Numerical Displays

Number	Lights ON
0	E, D, B, A, G, F
1	F, G ·
2	E, F, C, B, A
3	E, F, C, G, A
4	D, C, F, G
5	E, D, C, G, A
6	D, C, B, A, G
7	E, F, G
8	E, D, B, C, A, F, G
9	E, D, C, F, G

The twenty-four-hour clock will have four banks, reading up to 2,359. The pulse following 2,359 will cause the read-out to return to

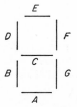

Fig. 9·9   **Light arrangement.**

Fig. 9·10   **Numbering of banks.**

0000. The banks will be numbered as shown in Fig. 9·10. Bank 1 should read out all digits from 0 to 9 on command from the input pulses. Bank 2 will read out digits 0 to 5, bank 3 from 0 to 3, and bank 4 from 0 to 2.

Step 1. Design the bank 1 circuit. Bank 1 is to read all digits from

Table 9·3   Truth Table for Bank 1

Digit	Lights							No. OFF active	No. ON active
	A	*B*	*C*	*D*	*E*	*F*	*G*		
0	1	1	0	1	1	1	1	1	6
1	0	0	0	0	0	1	1	5	2
2	1	1	1	0	1	1	0	2	5
3	1	0	1	0	1	1	1	2	5
4	0	0	1	1	0	1	1	3	4
5	1	0	1	1	1	0	1	2	5
6	1	1	1	1	0	0	1	2	5
7	0	0	0	0	1	1	1	4	3
8	1	1	1	1	1	1	1	0	7
9	0	0	1	1	1	1	1	2	5
								23	47

0 to 9. Table 9·3 indicates the condition of each lamp at the time a particular digit is being read out. This table shows that 47 contact

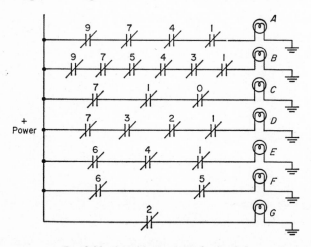

Fig. 9·11   Initial lamp circuit for bank 1

pairs are required by use of switches in the active ON condition (switches that are normally OFF). Notice that only 23 contact pairs are initially required if the switches are used in the active OFF condition (switches that are normally ON). In the interest of using the minimum number of switches, let us select switches that are normally ON (as shown in Fig. 9·11).

Since the design is to be with the ON condition, there will be a circuit in series with each lamp. The switches in series with each lamp are those that are normally ON. Since the truth table lists the condition of each switch (0 to 9) for signal condition, those switches labeled 0 are normally ON. The series circuit for each lamp is readily determined by going up the column for each lamp (Fig. 9·11).

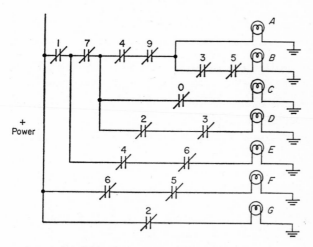

Fig. 9·12   Final lamp circuit for bank 1.

The next logical step is to simplify the initial circuit to as great an extent as possible. Look for those switches that appear in more than one lamp circuit. Switch 1 appears in circuits A, B, C, D, and E; switch 7 appears in circuits A, B, C, and D; switch 4 appears in circuits A, B, and E; switch 9 appears in circuits A and B. Redrawing the circuit results in the circuit shown in Fig. 9·12.

The simplification could have been at least partially accomplished directly from the bank 1 truth table by noting the 0 horizontal adjacencies. Note that the circuit has been simplified from 23 switches to 14 switches (8 relays and 14 contact pairs).

Step 2. Design the bank 2 circuit. Bank 2 should read out from 0 to 5. The truth table for these possibilities is shown in Table 9·4. It should be noticed that truth Table 9·4 is identical to the upper por-

Table 9·4   Truth Table for Bank 2

Digit	Lights							No. ON (for read-out) active	No. OFF active	Reduction
	A	*B*	*C*	*D*	*E*	*F*	*G*			
0	1	1	0	1	1	1	1	6	1	
1	0	0	0	0	0	1	1	2	5	1
2	1	1	1	0	1	1	0	5	2	
3	1	0	1	0	1	1	1	5	2	
4	0	0	1	1	0	1	1	4	3	1
5	1	0	1	1	1	0	1	5	2	
								27	15	

tion of the truth table for bank 1. Notice that the smallest number of contacts occur when relays that are normally closed are used (15 versus 27 for normally open). Therefore the normally closed condition is again selected, which means the contacts will be in series with the lights.

The largest horizontal adjacency again occurs for digit 1. Therefore replacement of contacts *A*, *B*, *C*, *D*, and *E* with one pair of contacts which will be called relay 1 is the first step in the simplification procedure. This is illustrated in Fig. 9·13.

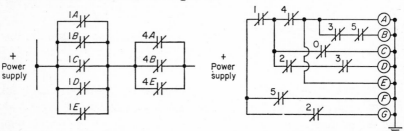

Fig. 9·13   Bank 2 circuit construction diagram A.   **Fig. 9·14   Final bank 2 circuit.**

A second horizontal adjacency which can be simplified is seen in digit 4, where contacts *A*, *B*, and *E* can be simplified to what will be called relay 4. This reduction may be placed in series with relay 1 since the three contacts simplified into relay 4 were also contained in the original five contacts of relay 1.

The remainder of the circuit for bank 2 can be constructed by analyzing each column in order to determine the series path from the power supply to each light. This results in the circuit of Fig. 9·14.

Figure 9·14 shows that six relays and nine contacts are required for the bank 2 circuit.

Step 3. Design of bank 3 circuit. The bank 3 read-out must be from 0 to 9 during two successive runs and from 0 to 3 on the third run, after which the chain of events is repeated. Therefore it would be the same circuit as bank 1.

Step 4. Design the bank 4 circuit. This read-out is from 0 to 2 only. Following the procedures used in steps 1 to 3, the truth table is set up. The circuit is then determined by combining as many contacts as possible and tracing the series path by traveling up each column to its corresponding light.

Table 9·5   Truth Table for Bank 4

Digit	Lights							No. ON active	No. OFF active	Reduction
	A	*B*	*C*	*D*	*E*	*F*	*G*			
0	1	1	0	1	1	1	1	6	1	
1	0	0	0	0	0	1	1	2	5	1
2	1	1	1	0	1	1	0	5	2	

From Fig. 9·15 it is seen that three relays and four contacts are required for bank 4.

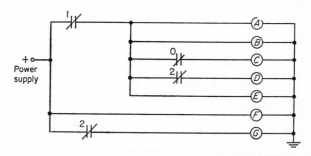

Fig. 9·15   Bank 4 circuit.

Step 5. Combine the individual bank circuits. The entire circuit for the four-bank read-out is shown in Fig. 9·16, which requires a total of 9 relays and 41 contacts.

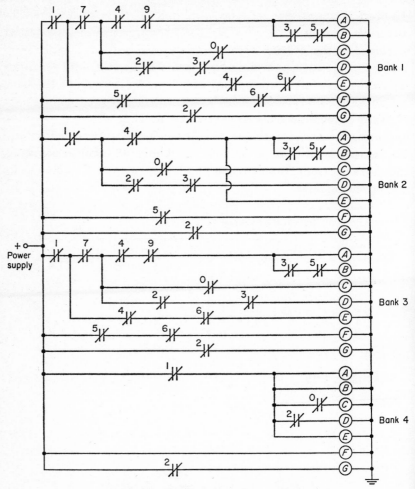

Fig. 9·16   The four-bank read-out circuit.

Although each bank of the read-out circuit just considered is combinational in nature, its control circuit is sequential and is not examined in this chapter.

9·8   Design of a Switching Circuit by the Synthesis Map Technique

Let us design a switching circuit for a hypothetical manufacturing process.

Problem. A motor-driven device receives its raw material on a conveyor system. The finished product is fed from the device into another conveyor system, which delivers it to the next state of manufacture. A blower unit and a water-supply unit are to be turned ON when the device is ON and vice versa.

The conveyor systems can both move when the input conveyor is full and the motor, the blower, and the water supply are ON. Only the output conveyor system will move if the motor, the water supply, and the blower are OFF and the output conveyor is full. Neither conveyor can move under any other condition.

A green lamp is to light when the output conveyor system is moving; and a yellow lamp is to light when the output conveyor is not moving.

Solution

Step 1. Assign control symbols. Let

A = input conveyor ON (full); A' = input conveyor OFF
B = output conveyor ON; B' = output conveyor OFF
C = motor ON; C' = motor OFF
D = blower ON; D' = blower OFF
E = water supply ON; E' = water supply OFF.

Step 2. Analyze transmission for the green lamp. The green lamp is ON when

$$ABCDE + A'BC'D'E'$$

and the synthesis map for the green lamp is shown in Fig. 9·17. The specified hindrance transmission function for the green lamp is next

AB $E=0$	00	01	11	10
CD				
00	0	1	0	0
01	0	0	0	0
11	0	0	0	0
10	0	0	0	0

AB $E=1$	00	01	11	10
CD				
00	0	0	0	0
01	0	0	0	0
11	0	0	1	0
10	0	0	0	0

Fig. 9·17 Synthesis map for the green lamp.

determined. Upon examination of the original specifications we can reason that the green lamp is OFF for all those conditions that would result in the output conveyor being OFF. In other words, the green lamp is OFF for the remaining 14 conditions (see Fig. 9·17).

Reading out of the synthesis map and simplifying, the Boolean function of the green lamp circuit is

$$B(ACDE + A'C'D'E')$$

Notice the ease with which all the possible combinations can be checked by examination of the synthesis map.

Step 3. Analyze transmission for the yellow lamp circuit. The yellow lamp is ON when the output conveyor is not moving. Since the output

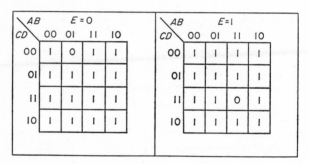

Fig. 9·18   Synthesis map for the yellow lamp.

conveyor is moving in 2 of the 16 possible conditions, it is obvious that it will not be moving for the remaining 14 possibilities. Expressing this in a synthesis map results in Fig. 9·18, and reading out,

$$A'B'E' + ABE' + AB'E' + A'BE'(C'D + CD + CD')$$
$$+ A'B'E + ABE(C'D' + C'D + CD') + AB'E + A'BE$$

Simplifying,

$$E'(A + C + D) + E(A' + C' + D') + B'$$

Step 4. Construct the lamp circuits. Restating the Boolean function for the two lamps,

$$\text{Green lamp} = B(ACDE + A'C'D'E')$$

and

$$\text{Yellow lamp} = E'(A + C + D) + E(A' + C' + D') + B'$$

which results in the circuit illustrated in Fig. 9·19.

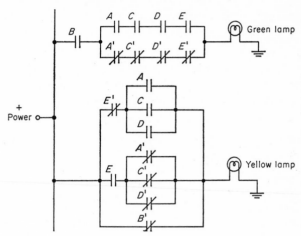

Fig. 9·19   Lamp circuit.

In the green lamp circuit:

Contact pairs can be used for A and A', E and E', assuming the use of relays.

In the yellow lamp circuit:

Contact pairs can be used for E and E', A and A', C and C', D and D'.

9·9   The Design of a Dispensing Machine

Following is a problem and its complete solution.

Problem. A coin-operated dispensing machine is to furnish the following drinks: black coffee, coffee with sugar, coffee with cream, regular coffee, plain tea, tea with sugar, tea with cream, regular tea, and soup. A predetermined amount of hot water and a cup are required for each drink. The machine is to be made ready to operate by pushing the button associated with the desired drink after a dime, two nickels, or a quarter is inserted into the coin slot. When a quarter is inserted, three nickels are to be returned. If less than three nickels are available, a green light is to go on, which illuminates a sign that reads "Use correct change only." Design the switching circuit for this dispensing machine.

Solution

Step 1. Assign symbols. Let us use the following symbols:

A = coffee (black)
B = sugar
C = cream
D = tea (plain)
E = soup
F = water (hot)
G = dime contact
H = nickel contact
I = quarter contact
J = cup release
K = nickel sensing
L = nickel release

Step 2. Analyze transmission of the coin circuit. To operate the machine first insert a coin (or coins). The insertion of a dime, two nickels, or a quarter places all the selection buttons in the "ready to operate" condition. Upon receipt of a quarter, the machine must perform one of two possible operations:

1. Return three nickels and place all the selection buttons in the "ready to operate" condition.
2. Return the quarter if less than three nickels are available in the nickel release (at which time a green lamp is to be turned on).

The transmission function of the coin circuit is

$$T_{12} = G + H + IK'$$
$$T_{13} = IK'$$
$$T_{14} = K$$

where Node 1 is the power terminal.

Node 2 is the terminal to which all selection buttons are connected.

Node 3 is the terminal to which the nickel release is connected.

Node 4 is the green lamp connection.

The diagram of the coin circuit is shown in Fig. 9·20. The nickel-sensing switch is to have a NO(K) and two NC(K') positions. The NO (normally open) position is connected to the green lamp whose NC (normally closed) contacts are associated with the nickel release and all selections circuits. The circuit of Fig. 9·20 indicates the condition of the switches prior to the insertion of any coin. Switch G is closed by the insertion of a dime; H is closed by the insertion of two nickels; I is closed by the insertion of a quarter. If K' is closed (more than three nickels in the nickel return) when I is closed, three nickels will be released and the

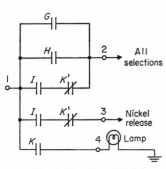

Fig. 9·20 Coin circuit.

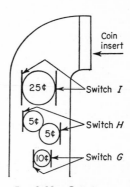

Fig. 9·21 Coin input.

circuit to all the selection buttons is complete. If K' is open (which occurs when less than three nickels are in the nickel return), the green lamp is ON (since K is now closed) and the quarter passes through the coin mechanism to the return receptacle.

A mechanism which would function in accordance with the preceding description is illustrated in Fig. 9·21.

Refer to Fig. 9·21. The dime can make a continuous electrical path only between the two bottom contacts. In order to establish continuity with nickels, notice that two nickels are required. The continuity made by the quarter is similar to that of the dime.

Step 3. Analyze transmission of the vending circuit. A first approach to analyzing the transmission possibilities of the vending circuit is to set up a transmission table. This table will consist of nine rows, one for each possible output, and seven columns (one for each relay). See

Table 9·6, which indicates the state of each relay when the particular output is required.

Table 9·6   Vending Machine Transmissions

Output	Relays							Normally open	Normally closed
	A	B	C	D	E	F	J		
1	1	0	0	0	0	1	1	3	4
2	1	1	0	0	0	1	1	4	3
3	1	0	1	0	0	1	1	4	3
4	1	1	1	0	0	1	1	5	2
5	0	0	0	1	0	1	1	3	4
6	0	1	0	1	0	1	1	4	3
7	0	0	1	1	0	1	1	4	3
8	0	1	1	1	0	1	1	5	2
9	0	0	0	0	1	1	1	3	4
								35	28

Notice that the circuitries associated with relays F and J are short circuits, regardless of the required output. In other words, a cup (J) and hot water (F) must be furnished for every output. The series circuit of each relay (A to J) consists of those contacts which are normally closed (0's in Table 9·6) in their associated column.

The initial circuit for each output can be drawn directly from the transmission table, as shown in Fig. 9·22.

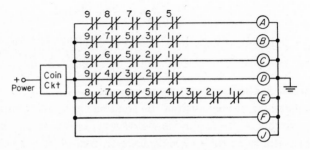

Fig. 9·22   Initial vending circuit.

This circuit is then reduced to its simplest arrangement, as shown in Fig. 9·23.

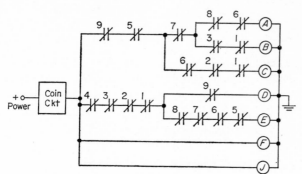

Fig. 9·23   Simplified vending circuit.

Step 4. Synthesize the entire circuit. The designed coin circuit of Fig. 9·20 in series with the simplified vending circuit of Fig. 9·23 makes up the entire circuit and is shown in Fig. 9·24.

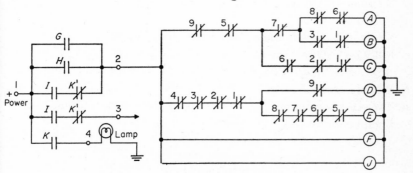

Fig. 9·24   The complete dispenser circuit.

Step 5. Analyze the designed circuit. As a check for the operation of the circuit, let us perform the duties of the dispensing machine.

Coin circuit operation. If a dime is inserted, switch G is closed. When two nickels are inserted, switch H is closed. When a quarter is inserted, switch I is closed if K' is closed (three or more nickels in the change return), and three nickels are released. When a quarter is inserted and K is open (less than three nickels in the change return), the quarter is returned; K is closed and the green lamp is ON when there are less than three nickels in the change return.

Upon the insertion of the correct coin(s), the circuit has continuity through the coin circuit via one of the paths described in the preceding paragraph.

Vending circuit operation. Notice that the selection relays (1 to 9) are closed when in a normal state. When one of the selector buttons is pressed, its associated relay is *opened*. Keeping this relationship in mind, we can examine the circuit action for each selection and compare it to the output predicted in transmission Table 9·6.

Selection 1. Relay 1 is opened by pressing button 1. Only the circuits to A, F, and J have continuity (see Fig. 9·24). In Boolean form:

Selection 1: AFJ (coffee, hot water, cup)

Continuing this analysis for each selection button,

Selection 2: $ABFJ$ (coffee, sugar, hot water, cup)

Selection 3: $ACFJ$ (coffee, cream, hot water, cup)

Selection 4: $ABCFJ$ (coffee, sugar, cream, hot water, cup)

Selection 5: DFJ (tea, hot water, cup)

Selection 6: $BDFJ$ (sugar, tea, hot water, cup)

Selection 7: $CDFJ$ (cream, tea, hot water, cup)

Selection 8: $BCDFJ$ (sugar, cream, tea, hot water, cup)

Selection 9: EFJ (soup, hot water, cup)

Therefore the designed circuit performs the logic as required by the original specifications.

PROBLEMS

9·1 A two-terminal switching network consists of three switches. The circuit will transmit if any one of the switches is energized. Design the circuit.

9·2 A two-terminal switching network consists of three switches. The circuit will transmit if any two of the switches are energized. Design the circuit.

9·3 A two-terminal switching network consists of three switches. The circuit will transmit if all three of the switches are energized. Design the circuit.

9·4 A switching network consists of three switches. The red lamp is ON when both A and C are closed. The green lamp is ON when both B and C are closed. Design the circuit.

9·5 A switching network consists of three switches. The red lamp is ON only when all switches are open. The green lamp is ON only when B is closed. Design the circuit.

9·6 A switching network consists of three switches. The red lamp is ON only when all switches are closed. The green lamp is OFF only when B is open. Design the circuit.

9·7 A switching network consists of three switches. The red lamp is ON only when A is closed. The green lamp is ON only when C is closed.   Design the circuit.

9·8 A switching network consists of three switches. The red lamp is ON only when all three switches are open. The green lamp is ON only when all three switches are closed. Design the circuit.

9·9 Three switches can operate in any combination. Only the red lamp is ON when A, B, and C are closed. Only the green lamp is ON when A and B are open and C is closed. Both lamps are ON for all other combinations except when A, B, and C are all open. Design the circuit.

9·10 Three switches (A, B, C) can operate in any combination. Only the red lamp is ON when A, B, C are closed. Only the green lamp is ON when A, B are open and C is closed. Both lamps are OFF for all other combinations. Design the circuit.

9·11 Three switches (A, B, C) can operate in any combination. Only the red lamp is ON when A, B, C are open. Only the green lamp is ON when A and C are closed. Both lamps are OFF for all other combinations. Design the circuit.

9·12 Three switches (A, B, C) can operate in any combination. Only the green lamp is ON for the following combinations:

a. B, C OFF; A ON
b. A, C OFF; B ON
c. A, C ON; B OFF
d. B, C ON; A OFF

Only the red lamp is ON for the following combinations:

e. A, B, C (ON)
f. A, B, C (OFF)
Neither lamp is ON for other combinations.

9·13   A system has four controls. The system transmits only when A and B are closed. Design the circuit.

9·14   A system has four controls. The system transmits only when A, B, and D are closed. Design the circuit.

9·15   A system has four controls. The system transmits only when A and D are closed. Design the circuit.

9·16   A system has four controls. The system transmits only when A, B, and C are open. Design the circuit.

9·17   A system has four controls. The system transmits when any one and only one of the controls is closed. Design the circuit.

9·18   A system has four controls. The system transmits when any two and only two of the controls are closed at any one time. Design the circuit.

9·19   A system has four controls. The system transmits when any three and only three of the controls are closed. Design the circuit.

9·20   A system has four controls. The system transmits when all four of the controls are closed at any one time. Design the circuit.

9·21   Four switches (A, B, C, D) can operate in any combination. Only the red lamp is ON when A, B, C, D are ON. Only the green lamp is ON when any two of the switches are ON and the remaining two are open. Both lamps are ON for all other combinations except when A, B, C, D are open, at which time both lamps are OFF. Design the circuit.

9·22   Four switches (A, B, C, D) can operate in any combination. Only the red lamp is ON when any one of the switches is closed. Only the green lamp is ON when any three of the switches are closed. Both lamps are OFF for all other combinations. Design the circuit.

9·23   Four switches (A, B, C, D) can operate in any combination. Only the red lamp is ON when any one or two of the switches are closed. Only the green lamp is ON when any three of the switches are closed. Both lamps are ON when all switches are closed. Both lamps are OFF when all switches are open. Design the circuit.

9·24   Four switches can operate in any combination. Only the red lamp is ON when the four switches are OFF. Only the green lamp is ON when only switch C is closed. Both lamps are ON when only switch D is closed or when switch only B is closed. Both lamps are OFF for all other combinations. Design the circuit.

9·25   Four switches can operate in any combination. Only the red lamp is ON when any three switches are OFF. Only the green lamp is ON when only switch B is open. Both lamps are ON when only switch A is open or when switch only D is closed. Both lamps are OFF for all other combinations. Design the circuit.

9·26   Four switches can operate in any combination. Only the red lamp is ON when only B and C are closed. Only the green lamp is ON when only A and B are closed. Both lamps are ON when all switches are closed. Both lamps are OFF for all other combinations. Design the circuit.

9·27   Four switches can operate in any combination. Only the red lamp is ON when only switches B and D are open. Only the green lamp is ON when only A is closed. Both lamps are ON for all other combinations. Design the circuit.

9·28   Four switches can operate in any combination. Only the red lamp is ON when only B and C are open. Only the green lamp is ON when all switches are open. Both lamps are ON for all other combinations. Design the circuit.

9·29   The spaceship (see Fig. 9·25) is at atmospheric pressure at all times. The inside door can be opened only when the external

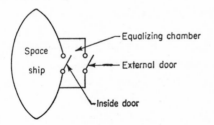

Fig. 9·25

door is closed and the equalization chamber is at atmospheric pressure. The external door can be opened only when the inside door is closed and the equalizing chamber is at vacuum. The surrounding space is a vacuum. The doors can be operated only by a person inside the spaceship. One signal light must indicate when the inside door can be safely opened. One signal light must indicate when the outside door can be safely opened. Design the circuit.

9·30 A hall light is to have three switches: an office switch, a front door switch, and a rear door switch. A circuit is required that permits the closure of any one of these three switches to turn the hall light ON. Design the circuit.

9·31 An office telephone is to have five lines. When line 1 is busy, the next call is to be routed to line 2. This system is to be designed so that five calls can be handled at any one time. Provisions are to be made so that any busy line will not be interrupted by another telephone call. Design the circuit.

9·32 Five switches can operate in any combination. Only the red lamp is ON when only one switch is closed. Only the green lamp is ON when only two switches are closed. Only the yellow lamp is ON when only three switches are closed. All three lamps are ON when all switches are closed. All lamps are OFF for all other conditions. Design the circuit.

9·33 In a process refrigeration system the compressor is to start when the temperature rises to 32°F, if there is pressure in the water supply and the sewer valve is open. The solenoid controls the sewer valve, and the solenoid is normally deenergized. No power to the solenoid is the normal condition with the sewer valve closed. After the compressor is started, the circulating fan must go ON.

Defrosting action: If the frost detector indicates ice on the coil, the bypass valve around the receiver (storage tank) is opened (this allows hot compressed gas to pass through the cooling coil). When this condition exists, then

1. The timer must start.
2. The timer must run for 5 minutes.
3. The timer must shut off in 5 minutes.
4. Then the bypass valve must be closed.

When the temperature reaches 20°F:

1. The compressor must shut off.
2. The fan must stop.
3. The sewer valve must close.

Safety specifications: No contact which handles power can be used to handle the signal. Design the circuit.

9·34 A coin changer is to be designed in accordance with the following specifications:

1. Any coin other than a dime or a quarter will not activate the circuit.
2. When a dime is inserted, two nickels will be released, if two nickels are available, or the dime will be returned.
3. When a quarter is inserted, the following outputs are possible:

   a. Five nickels if less than one dime and at least five nickels are available.
   b. Two dimes and one nickel if two or more dimes and one nickel are available.
   c. One dime and three nickels if only one dime and three or more nickels are available.
   d. The quarter is returned if none of the three combinations listed above are possible.

CHAPTER 10

Circuit Synthesis by Use of Boolean Matrices and Minimization of Switches

Introduction

Chapter 9 introduced a method by which a set of specifications is converted into a synthesis map. From the correct interpretation of the synthesis map, all contradictions and ambiguities are identified and then resolved. The next logical step is to convert the derived function into the simplest circuit. The following sections analyze several methods for circuit simplification.

10·1 Circuit Design by Expansion of a Boolean Matrix

The expansion of a Boolean matrix is essentially the reverse of the Boolean matrix technique used in an earlier chapter. In the case of circuit synthesis, the transmission function is dictated by the specifications. The technique here is to find a simple circuit which will perform the function stated by the specifications. This expands the matrix into the desired number of terminals.

Recall that any transmission function may be converted into a circuit by simply connecting the switches in series and/or parallel as dictated by the Boolean function. Notice that a series, parallel, or series-parallel circuit must always result. Non-series-parallel forms can be obtained by the matrix-expansion technique, a decided advantage in many instances. Let us proceed to determine how to expand a matrix.

Assume the read-out from the synthesis map of a particular problem resulted in the following transmission function:

$$T_{12} = A + BC$$

Placing this into a 2×2 matrix,

$$\begin{array}{cc} 1 & A + BC \\ & 1 \end{array}$$

The 2×2 matrix may be expanded to a 3×3 array by converting p_{12},

$$\begin{array}{ccc} 1 & p_{12} & p_{13} \\ & 1 & p_{23} \\ & & 1 \end{array}$$

From the 3×3 matrix, it is seen that in contracting the matrix,

$$p_{12}(2 \times 2) = p_{12}(3 \times 3) + p_{13}p_{23}$$

Now, expanding the 2×2 array into a 3×3 matrix (which is the reverse of the preceding action),

$$\begin{array}{ccc} 1 & A & B \\ & 1 & C \\ & & 1 \end{array}$$

The p_{12} entry in the 3×3 array is the OR portion of the original transmission function and the AND portion is used for p_{13} and p_{23}. In effect, the p_{12} entry of the 2×2 array is converted to the general form $(A + BC)$, where A becomes p_{12} in the 3×3 matrix, B becomes p_{13}, and C becomes p_{23}.

By expanding the original two-terminal matrix into a 3×3 array, the original two-terminal circuit has been converted into a three-terminal arrangement, as shown in Fig. 10·1.

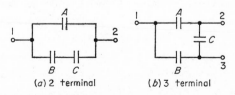

(a) 2 terminal   (b) 3 terminal

Fig. 10·1 **Conversion of a two-terminal circuit into a three-terminal equivalent circuit.**

Example 1. The following transmission function was determined from the read-out of a synthesis map:

$$T_{12} = ABC + A'B'C + AB'C'$$

Convert this to a four-terminal equivalent circuit.

Solution

Step 1. The 2 × 2 matrix for this function is

$$1 \qquad ABC + A'B'C + AB'C'$$
$$1$$

Step 2.   Expand to a 3 × 3 matrix. To expand into a 3 × 3 matrix, the p_{12} function must be reexpressed in the general form of $(A + BC)$, i.e.,

$$ABC + A'B'C + AB'C' = AB'C' + C(AB + A'B')$$

where

$$AB'C' = p_{12}$$
$$C = p_{13}$$
$$(AB + A'B') = p_{23}$$

Placing these entries into the 3 × 3 matrix, we obtain

$$1 \qquad AB'C' \qquad C$$
$$1 \qquad (AB + A'B')$$
$$1$$

Step 3. Expand to a 4 × 4 matrix. To expand into a 4 × 4 matrix, each individual entry in the 3 × 3 matrix must be converted into the general form $(A + BC)$.

$$p_{14}p_{24} + p_{12}{}^{(4×4)} = p_{12} \text{ of the } 3 \times 3 \text{ array} = AB'C'$$

Let

$$p_{14} \qquad = AC'$$
$$p_{24} \qquad = B'$$
$$p_{12}{}^{(4×4)} = 0$$
$$p_{14}p_{34} + p_{13}{}^{(4×4)} = p_{13} \text{ of the } 3 \times 3 \text{ array} = C$$

where $p_{14} = AC'$ from the preceding step.

$$AC'[?] + ? = C$$

Let

$$p_{34} = A'$$
$$p_{13}{}^{(4\times4)} = C$$

Then,

$$AC'(A') + C = C$$

$$p_{24}p_{34} + p_{23}{}^{(4\times4)} = p_{23} \text{ of the } 3 \times 3 \text{ array } = AB + A'B'$$

Since

$$p_{24} = B'$$
$$p_{34} = A'$$

Then

$$A'B' + p_{23}{}^{(4\times4)} = AB + A'B'$$

Therefore, let

$$p_{23}{}^{(4\times4)} = AB$$

The completed 4×4 matrix is

$$
\begin{array}{cccc}
1 & 0 & C & AC' \\
 & 1 & AB & B' \\
 & & 1 & A' \\
 & & & 1
\end{array}
$$

It will be noticed that other matrix results can sometimes be obtained. In the preceding example, the original T_{12} function could have been converted into two other possibilities:

$$ABC + A'B'C + AB'C' = A'B'C + A(BC + B'C')$$

or

$$ABC + A'B'C + AB'C' = ABC + B'(A'C + AC')$$

These two possibilities would, when expanded, result in other equivalent circuits, which would perform the same logical operation as the converted expression used in the example. The circuit for the preceding example is shown in Fig. 10·2.

As an illustration of how an alternate circuit which would perform the same logical operation could be

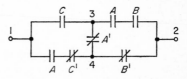

Fig. 10·2 Circuit for Example 1.

developed, let us expand the matrix for the same transmission function of Example 1 using one of the other possible converted functions.

Example 2. Determine the four-terminal circuit for the following transmission function:

$$T_{12} = ABC + A'B'C + AB'C' = A'B'C + A(BC + B'C')$$

Solution

Step 1. The 2 × 2 array follows.

$$1 \quad A'B'C' + A(BC + B'C')$$
$$1$$

Step 2. Convert to a 3 × 3 matrix.

$$p_{13}p_{23} + p_{12}{}^{(3\times3)} = p_{12} \text{ of the 2 × 2 array}$$

Let

$$p_{13} \quad = (BC + B'C')$$
$$p_{23} \quad = A$$
$$p_{12}{}^{(3\times3)} = A'B'C$$

and the 3 × 3 array is

$$1 \quad A'B'C \quad BC + B'C'$$
$$1 \quad\quad A$$
$$1$$

Step 3. Convert to a 4 × 4 matrix.

$$p_{14}p_{24} + p_{12}{}^{(4\times4)} = p_{12} \text{ of the 3 × 3 array} = A'B'C$$

Let

$$p_{12}{}^{(4\times4)} = 0$$
$$p_{14} \quad = B'C$$
$$p_{24} \quad = A'$$

These values are now placed in the 4 × 4 array:

$$1 \quad 0 \quad BC + B'C' \quad B'C$$
$$1 \quad\quad A \quad\quad A'$$
$$1 \quad\quad 0$$
$$1$$

$$p_{14}p_{34} + p_{13}{}^{(4\times4)} = p_{13} \text{ of the 3 × 3 array} = BC + B'C'$$

where $p_{14} = B'C$ from the previous step.

Let

$$p_{13}{}^{(4\times4)} = BC + B'C'$$
$$p_{34} \quad = 0$$

Then the entry is made into the matrix,

$$p_{24}p_{34} + p_{23}{}^{(4\times4)} = p_{23} \text{ of the } 3 \times 3 \text{ array} = A$$

From previous steps,

$$p_{24} = A$$
$$p_{34} = 0$$

Since

$$A0 + p_{23}{}^{(4\times4)} = A$$

Then

$$p_{23}{}^{(4\times4)} = A$$

The circuit for Example 2, which is equivalent to Example 1, is illustrated in Fig. 10·3.

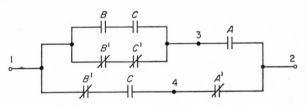

Fig. 10·3   Circuit for Example 2.

10·2   Spurious Terms

In the process of expanding a matrix, new terms are formed. When the new terms do not cancel, the unwanted term is called a *spurious term*. If not removed from the expression, it will change the transmission function of the circuit. This is not permissible. When such spurious terms do appear, a different method of factoring must be found. Each step in the expansion process should be carefully checked for this. The possibility of spurious terms makes the matrix-expansion technique an essentially trial and error process. With increased experience, spurious terms are more readily detected and utilized to full advantage.

An illustration of the utilization of spurious terms to advantage is the manner in which p_{34} was determined in Example 1. In that case

$$p_{14}p_{34} + p_{13}{}^{(4\times4)} = p_{13} \text{ of the } 3 \times 3 \text{ array} = C$$

where p_{14} was predetermined in an earlier step as AC'.
Let

$$p_{34} = A'$$

Then

$$p_{14}p_{34} = A'(AC') = 0$$

Therefore it is not a spurious term and

$$p_{13}{}^{(4\times4)} = C$$

10·3 Minimization in Relay Circuits

It should be noted that each group of relay contacts is actually a three-terminal network with the functions of A and A'. One of the chief minimization possibilities with relay circuits is to reduce the number of transfer contact sets. In many cases, it is more economical to use more literals so that the number of transfer contact sets can be reduced. Commercial relays can have up to four or six sets of transfer contacts.

A transfer contact pair can be recognized in a Boolean matrix in the following manner: When a variable and its prime (such as A and A') appear in the same row or column, a transfer contact pair can be made since they possess a common node.

Consider the 4×4 matrix for Example 2 of Sec. 10·1: In row 1, a transfer contact pair can be formed by B and B' of item p_{13} and by C and C' of p_{13}. B' of p_{14} will be one of the other normally closed contacts of the relay B; C of p_{14} will be one of the other normally open contacts of the same relay C. In row 2, A of p_{23} and A' of p_{24} will form a transfer contact. Therefore only three actual relays are required for the circuit of Fig. 10·3.

10·4 Minimization of Diode Matrix Circuits

Refer to Fig. 10·4, which is a matrix that utilizes a total of 24 diodes. Notice the $FF2$ stage: the left terminal of $FF2$ is consecutively used for 000, 001 ($D2$ and $D5$), then 100, 101 ($D14$, $D17$). Since $D2$ and $D5$ are

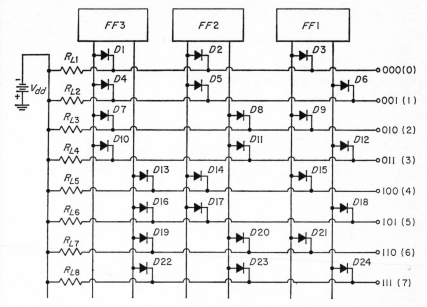

Fig. 10·4   A diode matrix for detection of binary numbers from 000 to 111 inclusive.

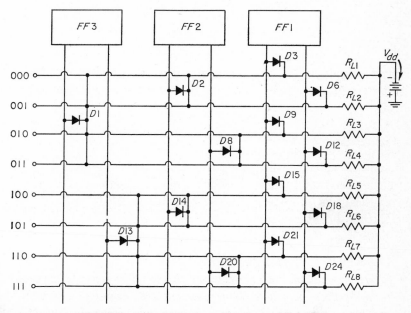

Fig. 10·5   Reduced diode matrix circuit of Fig. 10·4.

functioning simultaneously, they can be replaced with one diode ($D2$ in Fig. 10·5). Notice how the output of $D2$ in Fig. 10·5 is divided into two branches. The same situation exists for $D14$ and $D17$ of Fig. 10·4 and can be replaced with $D14$ of Fig. 10·5. A reduction is possible whenever the same output of a flip-flop is used more than once in succession. Table 10-1 indicates the original diodes and what diodes can be

Table 10·1

Fig. 10·4	Fig. 10·5	Diodes saved
$D1, D4, D7, D10$	$D1$	3
$D13, D16, D19, D22$	$D13$	3
$D2, D5$	$D2$	1
$D14, D17$	$D14$	1
$D8, D11$	$D8$	1
$D20, D23$	$D20$	1
		10: Total saved

eliminated and the overall savings in diodes. Therefore this arrangement (Fig. 10·5) enables 14 diodes to perform the same logic as the original 24 diodes (shown in Fig. 10·4). Notice in Fig. 10·5 that the diode load resistors and supply potential V_{dd} are shown on the right side and the number outputs on the left.

10·5   Minimization in Diode Circuits by the Logic Tree Technique

The preceding section pointed out the technique of matrix-circuit simplification which can result in a reduction in the number of diodes required. Besides simplifying the matrix circuit in this manner, there is another method of arranging the matrix which can also result in reducing the total number of required diodes. This technique utilizes what is called a *logic tree* or *pyramid*. You will see a logic tree developed in setting up the switching circuit of the control circuit in Sec. 11·7. Following are the rules for developing a pyramid.

1. Divide the flip-flop circuits into pairs.
2. Determine the four possible output combinations for each pair of flip-flops. AND each possible output from each pair of flip-flops. This results in 00, 01, 10, and 11 outputs for each pair of flip-flops.

3. Take the corresponding AND pairs from each set of flip-flops and AND them together. The output will be the desired binary numbers.

Let us illustrate these rules by using them in the following problems.

Example. A four-stage flip-flop counter is to have diode detect circuits for each number possibility. Design the diode matrix by use of the tree technique.

Step 1. Divide the flip-flop circuits into pairs as shown in Fig. 10·6.

Step 2. Determine all the possible outputs for each pair of flip-flops. Since a pair of flip-flops has four output terminals, and each terminal can be 0 or 1, four possible outputs exist for each flip-flop pair. These are illustrated in Fig. 10·7.

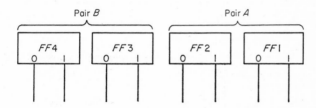

Fig. 10·6   Division of the four flip-flops into pairs.

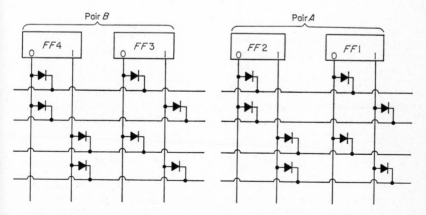

Fig. 10·7   Determination of the four possible outputs for each flip-flop pair.

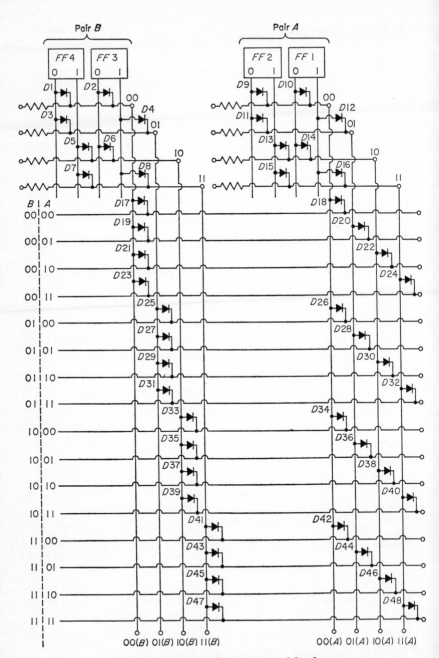

Fig. 10·8   Logic tree for two pairs of flip-flops.

Step 3. Construct an AND circuit between each output of pair B and the four outputs of flip-flop pair A. Figure 10·8 illustrates this process for all the output possibilities.

Notice how 00 output of pair B is coupled to 00 output of pair A by means of $D17$ and $D18$. This results in a final binary output of 0000. $D19$ and $D20$ couple the 00 output of pair B to the 01 output of pair A, which results in the final binary output of 0001. $D21$ and $D22$ couple $00(B)$ to $10(A)$, with a final binary output of 0010. $D23$ and $D24$ couple $00(B)$ to $11(A)$ with a final binary output of 0011.

Notice that $D17$, $D19$, $D21$, and $D23$ are connected to the $00(B)$ terminal, indicating their common origin. Also notice how $D18$, $D20$, $D22$, and $D24$ are progressively to the right of each other, which indicates the systematic manner in which 0000, 0001, 0010, and 0011 are connected. The two right-hand positional values are determined by the pair A output while the two left-hand positional values are determined by the pair B output. Therefore, the fact that $D17$, $D19$, $D21$, and $D23$ are tied to $00(B)$ indicates the first four outputs will have 00 as their first two left-hand positional values.

Diodes $D25$, $D27$, $D29$ and $D31$ are all tied to $01(B)$. Therefore the next four binary outputs will have 01 as their first two left-hand positions. The arrangement of $D26$, $D28$, $D30$, and $D32$ is similar to that of $D18$, $D20$, $D22$, and $D24$. Therefore the composite outputs for this next four combination are 0100, 0101, 0110, and 0111.

Notice that the same system is utilized in the establishment of outputs for the remaining four-position binary numbers. Note the relationship,

$$D = f2^f$$

where D = the number of diodes required in the matrix

f = the number of flip-flop stages involved

Therefore, in the preceding example

$$D = 4(2)^4 = 64$$

That is, a total of 64 diodes would have been necessary if the conventional matrix was used in the circuit of Fig. 10·8. The preceding example has shown that using the tree technique resulted in a savings of 16 diodes.

PROBLEMS

Convert the two-terminal Boolean functions of Probs. 10·1 to 10·10 into four-terminal circuits by the use of the Boolean matrix-expansion technique:

10·1 $T_{12} = UVW + UV(WX + YZ)$

10·2 $T_{12} = X'Y'Z' + W'XY' + WY'$

10·3 $T_{12} = WX'YZ + YZ + XY$

10·4 $T_{12} = B'C'D' + A'BC' + AC'$

10·5 $T_{12} = BC + AB'CD + CD$

10·6 $T_{12} = BA'(F' + E) + FD'A + CA$

10·7 $T_{12} = ABC' + AB'C + A'B'C'D$

10·8 $T_{12} = A'B' + C'D' + A'CD$

10·9 $T_{12} = AB + A(CD + EF)$

10·10 $T_{12} = ABC + AB(DC + EF)$

10·11   A four-control system is to be activated when any one and only one of the controls is turned ON.

    a. Using the synthesis map technique, design the two-terminal circuit.

    b. Using the Boolean matrix-expansion technique, convert this into a four-terminal circuit.

10·12   A four-control system is to be activated when any two and only two of the controls are turned ON at the same time.

    a. Design the two-terminal circuit by use of a synthesis map.

    b. Convert the two-terminal circuit into a three-terminal circuit by the Boolean matrix-expansion technique.

10·13   A four-control system is to be activated when any three and only three of the controls are turned ON at the same time.

    a. Design the two-terminal circuit by use of the synthesis map.

    b. Convert the two-terminal circuit into a three-terminal circuit by the Boolean matrix-expansion technique.

10·14   A four-control system is to be activated when all four of the controls are turned ON at the same time.

    a. Design the two-terminal circuit by use of the synthesis map.

    b. Convert the two-terminal circuit into a three-terminal circuit by the Boolean matrix-expansion technique.

10·15 A four-control system is to be activated when A and B or B and C are turned ON at the same time.

    a. Design the two-terminal circuit by use of the synthesis map.

    b. Convert the two-terminal circuit into a three-terminal circuit by the Boolean matrix-expansion technique.

10·16 Refer to the diode matrix of Fig. 10·9. Simplify as much as possible.

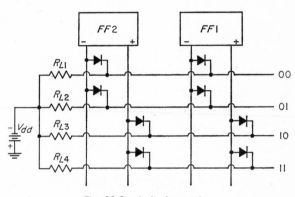

Fig. 10·9   A diode matrix.

10·17 Refer to the diode matrix of Fig. 10·10. Simplify as much as possible.

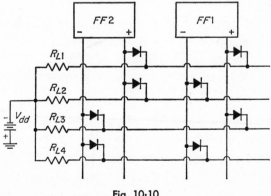

Fig. 10·10

CHAPTER 11

Circuit Synthesis by
Use of Coding Systems
and the Odd Parity Check

Introduction

This chapter analyzes several coding systems and how they can be utilized in switching circuits. The method by which map entries can be made in numbers is dealt with first. The next five sections deal with state coding and its uses. The chapter also deals with the Gray code whose mathematical analysis was developed in Secs. 2·12, 2·13, and 2·14. The concluding section is concerned with the odd parity check including an illustrated example of how it can be used in control circuit design.

11·1 Identification of Map Entries by Numbers

In Chap. 9 the technique of circuit synthesis by use of the Karnaugh synthesis map was studied. This section considers a technique for the synthesis of a system (a combination of circuits). State coding is a technique to study an entire system; it incorporates the following procedures:

1. Determination of a desirable group of control variables
2. Derivation of the required circuitry by the synthesis map technique

In the Karnaugh maps analyzed in previous chapters, each entry specified a certain combination of states of the variables involved (each variable is either 0 or 1). These states may be expressed in binary numbers, or in the decimal equivalents of the binary numbers.

In Fig. 11·1a, each entry is specified in the binary code, and the decimal equivalent of each entry is shown in Fig. 11·1b. With the use

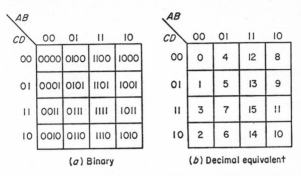

(a) Binary   (b) Decimal equivalent

Fig. 11·1   Expressing a Karnaugh map in numbers.

of this type of entry, a given Boolean expression may be also stated in binary or decimal equivalent form.

Example 1. Express $ABC'D' + A'B'C'D + ABCD' + A'B'CD$ in its binary and decimal equivalent forms.

Solution

Step 1. The entries are first made in the usual manner, as shown in Fig. 11·2.

Step 2. Converting the entries of Fig. 11·2 into binary notation, we obtain Fig. 11·3.

AB\\CD	00	01	11	10
00			X	
01	X			
11	X			
10			X	

Fig. 11·2

Step 3. Now converting the binary notations of Fig. 11·3 into their decimal equivalents, we obtain Fig. 11·4.

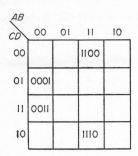

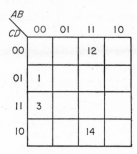

Fig. 11·3   Binary notation for Fig. 11·2.   Fig. 11·4   Decimal equivalents of Fig. 11·3.

Step 4. The binary notation, in the order dictated by the original function is (1100, 0001, 1110, 0011).

Step 5. The decimal equivalent is (12,1, 14,3).

11·2   System States and State Diagrams

A state of a system is defined as a possible combination of outputs. A state diagram is composed of those states which make up the useful output combinations and also those malfunction states that must be considered for safety reasons. All other possible output combinations which fall within the general category of "don't care" or "uninteresting" do not appear in the state diagram. A state diagram carefully defines the states of the system and how the system can change from one state to another.

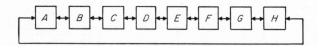

Fig. 11·5   A state diagram of an eight-state system.

In Fig. 11·5, each box illustrates a state (*A* to *H*). Notice the use of arrows in the state diagram which indicate how the state of the system can be changed. Consider state *B* for illustrative purposes: If the system is in state *B*, it can change to state *A* or state *C* as its first change but cannot directly change to states D, E, F, G, or H. The diagram further illustrates the states through which the system must pass in order to change from one state to another. In order to change from state D to G, for example, the system must pass first through state E, then state F, and finally to state G. Not all state diagrams are as simple as Fig. 11·5 however.

11·3 Determination of the Required Number of Controls

For combinational circuits, the number of controls can be determined from the following equation:

$$\text{Con} = \text{Int } (\log_2 S)$$

where Con = number of controls required
      Int = next larger integer (whole number), if $\log_2 S$ is not an integer
      S = number of states

The preceding equation provides the designer with a suitable check. If the number of anticipated controls is less than required by the equation, the designer should look for one of the following conditions:

1. A hidden control has not been spotted.
2. The nature of the system is sequential rather than combinational.

If the number of anticipated controls is greater than indicated by the checking equation, the designer should search for a redundancy. This redundancy should either be eliminated or utilized for some useful purpose (such as self-checks).

Another important relationship found in state diagrams for combinational circuits is that every path is bidirectional.

11·4 State Coding and Uses

The coordination of the states of a system with the desired control combinations is called state coding. Inasmuch as the controls are of a binary nature (0, 1), the combination of desired controls can be expressed in binary notation. The states of the system are available from the prepared state diagram, and the condition of each control can be assigned in a tabular method.

Example 1. A control unit is to have eight states (to be labeled 1 to 8). Only one state can be the output at any one instant. A remote control unit is to select the desired state.

  1. Draw the state diagram.
  2. Determine the required number of controls.
  3. Code the state diagram.

Solution

Step 1. Draw the state diagram.
Since this is a combinational circuit (any one of the outputs has nothing to do with any other output), the eight states may be represented in the manner shown in Fig. 11·6.

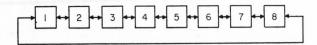

Fig. 11·6 **A state diagram for the eight-state problem.**

Step 2. Determine the number of required controls.

$$\text{Con} = \text{Int} \ (\log_2 S)$$

where $S = 8$
Substituting,

$$\text{Con} = \log_2 8 = 3$$

Therefore three controls are required and will be assigned the terms A, B, and C.

Step 3. Assign the controls for each state. Since each control is binary in nature (0 or 1), the universe table may be used in this assignment. They may be assigned in the order shown in Table 11·1 which indicates the condition (0 or 1) of each control for every possible state (1 to 8). By utilization of this technique, it should be noted that the change from one state to the next requires the opening or closing of only one contact (if relays are used).

Table 11·1 Control
Assignment for Each
State

State	Controls		
	A	B	C
1	0	0	0
2	1	0	0
3	1	0	1
4	1	1	1
5	1	1	0
6	0	1	0
7	0	1	1
8	0	0	1

Step 4. Code the state diagram. The state diagram may now be redrawn with the settings of each control indicated for each box representing the individual states, as shown in Figs. 11·7 and 11·8. The

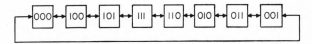

Fig. 11·7 Coding the state diagram of Fig. 11·6, step 1.

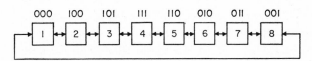

Fig. 11·8 Coding the state diagram of Fig. 11·6, step 2.

control conditions are listed in alphabetical order (*ABC*). This is known as coding the state diagram.

11·5 Translation of a Coded State Diagram into Control Circuitry

Let us translate the state diagram of the preceding example into a cam circuit. Rearranging the control assignment table, we obtain Table 11·2. In this table, the arrows indicate that one control is changed when moving from one state to the next. To move from state 2 to state 3, for example, control C is changed from 0 to 1. In order to move from state 2 to state 1, control A is changed from 1 to 0. As specified in the original problem, a change from any given state can only be made to the next lower or next higher state. If a change is to be made to any other state, it must be made in a number of successive steps, as indicated in an earlier paragraph.

Table 11·2   Rearranged Control
Assignment for Each State

Controls	States							
	1	2	3	4	5	6	7	8
A	0↔1	1	1	1↔0	0	0		
B	0	0	0↔1	1	1	1↔0		
C	→0	0↔1	1↔0	0↔1	1←			

Upon examination of Table 11·2, we can readily determine the condition of each control (1 or 0) for each state. One possible control circuit for these requirements can be designed by the utilization of three cams, each of which is associated with a microswitch that is normally open. Since there are eight states, each cam can be divided into eight segments. For those states where the control is to be open, a notch will be provided on the cam, thereby permitting its associated microswitch to spring open. For those states where the control is to be closed, the cams will not have a notch which will close its associated microswitch. By mounting the three cams on a common shaft, all three cams can be activated simultaneously when switching from one state to the next. Figure 11·9 illustrates the arrangement of the cams and microswitches.

Simplification of the cam circuit. Close examination of Fig. 11·9 reveals that cams A and B both have four consecutive cutaway sections. For cam A, sections 2 to 5 are cut away. For cam B, sections 4 to 7 are cut away. When the cams are rotated in a clockwise direction, section 8 of cam B is the first of four consecutive sections which are not cut away. Section 6 of cam A is the first of four consecutive non-cutaway sections (still assuming a clockwise direction). Therefore

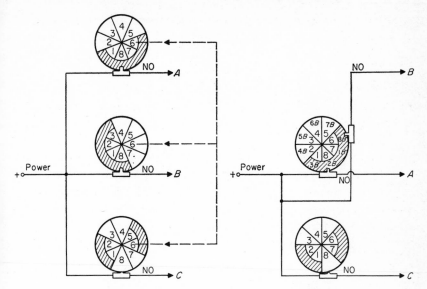

Fig. 11·9 Cam arrangement.   **Fig. 11·10 Simplified cam arrangement.**

cam A can double as cam B by mounting microswitch B at the section 6 position of cam A. See Fig. 11·10.

Example 2. A read-out display is to have numerical read-outs of 0 to 9 by utilization of a Nixie tube. A given number can be directly changed to the number preceding or following it in this problem. A remote control unit is to select the desired number.

1. Draw the state diagram.
2. Determine the required number of controls.
3. Code the state diagram.
4. Translate the coded state diagram into control circuitry.

Solution

Step 1. Draw the state diagram. Each possible digit read-out is a state, and the state diagram can be drawn as illustrated in Fig. 11·11.

Fig. 11·11 State diagram for Example 2.

Step 2. Determine the number of required controls.

$$\text{Con} = \text{Int } (\log_2 S)$$

where $S = 10$
Substituting,

$$\text{Con} = \text{Int } \log_2 10 = 4$$

Since the $\log_2$ of 10 is greater than 3 but less than 4, the number of required controls is 4.

Step 3. Assign controls for each state. Since each control is binary in nature, the universe table may be used in this assignment. If possible, the change from one state to the preceding or next one is to be accomplished by the change of only one of the controls. Table 11.3 illustrates one possibility for the assignment of controls for each state where only one control is changed when switching to either the preceding or following state.

Table 11·3   Control
Assignment for Each
State

State	\multicolumn{4}{c}{Controls}
	W	X	Y	Z
1	0	0	0	0
2	0	0	0	1
3	0	0	1	1
4	0	1	1	1
5	1	1	1	1
6	1	1	1	0
7	1	1	0	0
8	1	0	0	0
9	1	0	0	1
0	1	0	1	1

Step 4. Code the state diagram. The state diagram may now be redrawn, and each state may be identified as a four-bit entry, as shown in Fig. 11·12.

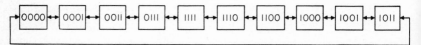

Fig. 11·12   Coding the state diagram of Fig. 11·11.

Step 5. Translate the coded state diagram into control circuitry. Rearranging the control assignment table of Table 11·3 for convenience, we obtain Table 11·4. As in the preceding example, cams in association with microswitches can be utilized. In this case, four cams (each divided into 10 segments) can be used. The four cams are mounted on the same shaft as they will rotate from one state to another (either the preceding or succeeding one) in step. The cam arrangement is illustrated in Fig. 11·13.

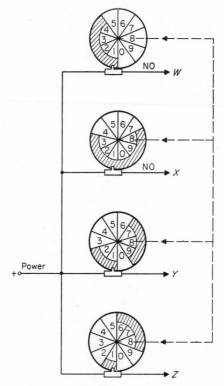

Fig. 11·13   Initial cam arrangement for Example 2.

11·6   The Gray Codes and Uses for Control Circuit Design

One of the most popular coding systems is the Gray code. (Its arithmetical aspects are analyzed in Chap. 2.) In this type of code, successive numbers are one unit apart. The *conventional Gray code* follows this order:

$$000, 001, 011, 010, 110, 101, 100$$

It should be noted that the code used in Example 1 of Sec. 11·5 was actually the reverse order of the conventional gray code. The code incorporated in Example 2 (Table 11·3) is another version of the Gray code. *The transition from one state to another involves the change of only one in any Gray code system.*

There are cases where it is not possible to utilize a Gray code. The following criteria may be used in ascertaining whether a Gray code can be used: *Any loop in a state diagram that involves an even number of states can be Gray-coded; loops which have an odd number of states cannot be Gray-coded.*

If it is found that a state diagram cannot be Gray-coded because it involves an odd number of states, *a dummy state can sometimes be added.* Figure 11·14 illustrates the change required in a state diagram

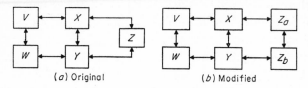

(*a*) Original   (*b*) Modified

Fig. 11·14   Introduction of a dummy state to permit Gray coding.

to perform this adjustment. Provisions must be made to insure that state Z_a and Z_b both perform the same logic. The following example illustrates this technique.

Example 1. A motor has four speeds and a stop position. Design a control circuit with Gray coding such that the motor states can be switched in the following ways:

   1. stop $- F1 - F2 - F3 - F4 -$ stop
   2. stop $- F4 - F3 - F2 - F1 -$ stop
   3. $F1 - F4 - F1$

Solution

Step 1. Draw the original diagram. There are five states, which can be drawn as shown in Fig. 11·15.

As seen in Fig. 11·15, all the requirements indicated in the specifications with regard to state switching are accounted for. Based on the criteria which determine whether the state diagram can be Gray-coded, it is apparent that a dummy state must be introduced so that an even number of states (six in this case) is obtained.

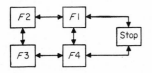

Fig. 11·15   Original state diagram.

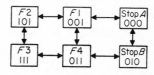

Fig. 11·16   Modified and Gray-coded state diagram.

Step 2. Modify and Gray code the state diagram. Let the dummy state be a duplicate of the stop-state, resulting in the state diagram of Fig. 11·15. Since six states are involved, the required number of controls is three, which will be called A, B, and C. The diagram is coded so that the switching from one state to another requires the change of only one control.

Step 3. Convert the Gray-coded state diagram into a relay circuit. Table 11·4 designates the condition of each control for every state.

Table 11·4   Conditions of Controls for Each State

State	Controls		
	A	B	C
Stop B	0	1	0
Stop A	0	0	0
$F1$	0	0	1
$F2$	1	0	1
$F3$	1	1	1
$F4$	0	1	1

Let us design a relay type control circuit in this problem. In Table 11·4, the 1s are normally open switches and the 0s are normally closed switches. Using the normally closed switches, the series circuit for each control is determined from its associated column, as illustrated in Fig. 11·17.

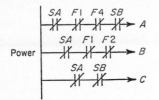 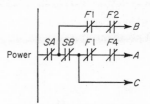

Fig. 11·17   Initial control circuit.   Fig. 11·18   Simplified control circuit.

Inspection of Fig. 11·17 indicates that simplification is possible, resulting in the circuit of Fig. 11·18. The control circuit could have been designed for cams, as in several earlier examples, or for diodes.

11·7   The Odd Parity Check and Uses for Control Circuit Design

In the interest of system reliability, a method of self-checking is frequently desirable. The deliberate introduction of redundancy will result in self-checking but at a relatively large expense. The *parity check* is a common approach to the self-checking problem. In this system a code denoting each state is set up so that the total number of bits in the binary number is an odd number (when added horizontally).

For example, consider an eight-state (three-control) system which was originally Gray-coded, as shown in columns 1 and 2 of Table 11·5.

Table 11·5   Parity Check for an 8-state System

State	Gray code	Parity-check code	Total no. of bits
1	000	1000	1
2	001	0001	1
3	011	1011	3
4	010	0010	1
5	110	1110	3
6	111	0111	3
7	101	1101	3
8	100	0100	1

The principle behind the parity-check code is to detect single failures. The Gray code is itself not self-checking since each state is one unit from the preceding and following states. The inclusion of one additional control will permit the system to detect malfunctions at one unit distance from the correct binary numbers. Column 3 of Table 11·5 illustrates how a parity check can be inaugurated for the eight-state, three-control system which was originally Gray-coded.

The even-number parity-check code is customarily not desirable because it cannot detect a total system failure (00000 . . .).

Problem. Design the control circuit for an eight-state system, using the conventional Gray code. Also design an odd parity-check code for the system such that a green lamp is ON when each state is operating normally.

Solution

Step 1. Draw and Gray code a state diagram for the circuit.

Step 2. Draw the Gray-coded state diagram with an odd parity check.

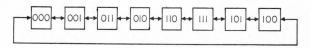

Fig. 11·19   Gray-coded state diagram.

Step 3. Convert the odd parity-check state diagram into a circuit.

(*A*) *Odd parity-check circuit for switch* A

Figure 11·20 indicates the eight states during which the green light must be ON, thereby indicating normal operation. Listing the combinations in table form such as Table 11·6 often facilitates the analysis. Notice that each control is 1 for four states and 0 for the other four states. Let us analyze the condition of each variable one at a time in alphabetical order.

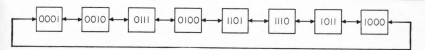

Fig. 11·20   Odd parity-check state diagram for Fig. 11·19.

Table 11·6 Control
Conditions for Each
State

State	A	B	C	D
1	0	0	0	1
2	0	0	1	0
3	0	1	1	1
4	0	1	0	0
5	1	1	0	1
6	1	1	1	0
7	1	0	1	1
8	1	0	0	0

Control A is 0 for states 1 to 4 and 1 for states 5 to 8, as indicated in the block diagram of Fig. 11·21. The lamp circuit path must have electrical continuity for each state. Therefore the lamp path is from the

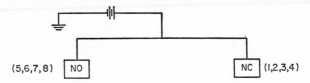

Fig. 11·21   Control A lamp connections.

NC (normally closed) terminal of switch A for states 1 to 4 inclusive and from the NO (normally open) terminal for states 5 to 8.

(B) Odd parity-check lamp circuit for switches A *and* B

Control B is 0 for states 1, 2, 7, and 8. Therefore the lamp circuit path will be the NC terminal of switch B for these states. The lamp circuit path will be through NO terminal of switch B for states 3 to 6 inclusive since control B is then closed. Since the lamp circuit comes from the NC terminal of control A for states 3 and 4 and from the NO terminal of control A for states 5 and 6, two single-pole double-throw switches will be used for control B, as shown in the block diagram of Fig. 11·22.

In states 1 and 2, switch A is 0 and B is 0. Therefore the lamp line for these two states would pass through the NC connection of both A

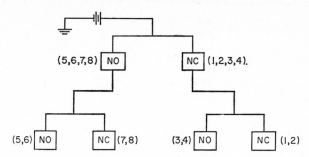

Fig. 11·22 Lamp circuit for controls A and B.

and B. In states 3 and 4, A is 0 and B is 1. Therefore the lamp connection must be through NC for A and NO for B. In states 5 and 6, A is 1 and B is 1 and the lamp circuit must be through NO of both A and B. In states 7 and 8, A is 1 and B is 0, and the lamp circuit is through the NO connection of control A and the NC connection of control B.

(C) Odd parity-check lamp circuit for switches A, B, *and* C.

Let us examine Table 11·6 for the relationship of control C to controls A and B. In states 1 and 2, A is 0, B is 0, and C is 0 (state 1) and 1 (state 2). Therefore the lamp circuit would be through NC of both control A and control B. For state 1, the lamp circuit would be to NC of control C and NO of switch C for state 2. Therefore let us place a single-pole double-throw switch for the leads that come off NC of switch B (see Fig. 11·23).

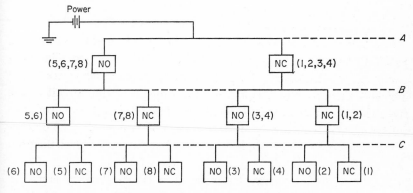

Fig. 11·23 Lamp circuit for controls A, B, and C.

Continuing with states 3 and 4:

State 3: A(NC) to B(NO) to C(NO)
State 4: A(NC) to B(NO) to C(NC)

A second single-pole double-throw switch is placed underneath B(NO), and the lamp circuit connections are made (see Fig. 11·23).

State 5: A(NO) to B(NO) to C(NC)
State 6: A(NO) to B(NO) to C(NO)

A third single-pole double-throw switch is placed underneath B(NO), and these lamp circuit connections are made.

State 7: A(NO) to B(NC) to C(NO)
State 8: A(NO) to B(NC) to C(NC)

And a fourth single-pole double-throw switch is placed underneath B(NC), and these lamp connections are made.

The lamp circuit connections for controls A, B, and C are now complete.

(*D*) *Complete odd parity-check lamp circuit for controls* A, B, C, *and* D.

The condition of switch D for each state is found in the last column of Table 11·6. Switch D in its indicated state is connected in series

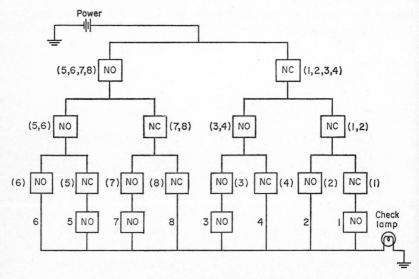

Fig. 11·24 Complete odd parity-check lamp circuit.

with the correct series combinations of A, B, and C for each state, as shown in Fig. 11·25.

Step 4. Simplify the odd parity-check lamp circuit. In order to facilitate the simplification of the circuit illustrated in Fig. 11·24, let us

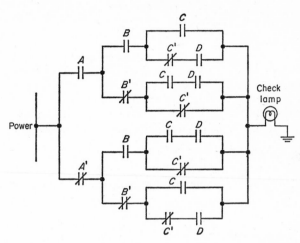

Fig. 11·25 Circuit of Fig. 11·24 in conventional switch notation.

redraw the circuit with the conventional switch notation. See Fig. 11·25. The Boolean function for the lamp circuit of Fig. 11·25 is

$$f_x = A[B(C + C'D) + B'(CD + C')]$$
$$+ A'[B(CD + C') + B'(C + C'D)]$$

By the application of several Boolean rules, the function is simplified:

$$f_x = A[BC + BD + B'C' + B'D] + A'[BC' + BD + B'C + B'D]$$
$$= A[D + BC + B'C'] + A'[D + BC' + B'C]$$
$$= AD + ABC + AB'C' + A'D + A'BC' + A'B'C$$

and

$$f_x = D + B(AC + A'C') + B'(AC' + A'C)$$

And the simplified lamp circuit has 11 switches instead of the original 18 switches. See Fig. 11·26 for the circuit. In the interest of minimiza-

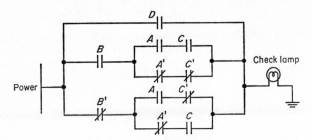

Fig. 11·26   Simplified lamp circuit for the odd parity check.

tion, note that A and A' can be two sets of transfer contacts since they share a common terminal; C and C' can be two sets of transfer contacts for the same reason; and one set of transfer contacts can serve for B and B'.

Step 5.   Convert the control circuit with the odd parity-check system into a cam circuit. (See Table 11·6 for control conditions of each state.)

Figure 11·27 illustrates a cam circuit for the eight-state control circuit with the odd parity-check system. Notice that a normally open (NO) switch is used for each of the controls A, B, C, and D. Controls A, B, and C are required to permit the system to be switched from one state to the state before it or after it. Control switch D has been introduced for the odd parity-check circuit.

Each cam is divided into eight sections since there are eight states in the system being considered in this problem. It has been arbitrarily decided that cams, all mounted on a common shaft, are to be rotated clockwise for changing from a lower-numbered state to the next highest number state (from state 1 to 2, for example). Examination of Fig. 11·27 reveals this relationship.

The sections of each cam which designate the states in which the corresponding control switch is to be open are cut out (since the control switches are to be normally OFF). For example, Table 11·6 indicates that control switch A should be open for states 1, 2, 3, and 4. Therefore sections 1, 2, 3, and 4 of cam A are cut out, so that control switch A will remain open when cam A is in these positions. The cut-out sections of the other three cams are determined in the same manner.

The conversion of the lamp circuit for the odd parity-check system into switches within the cam setup is accomplished by simply wiring

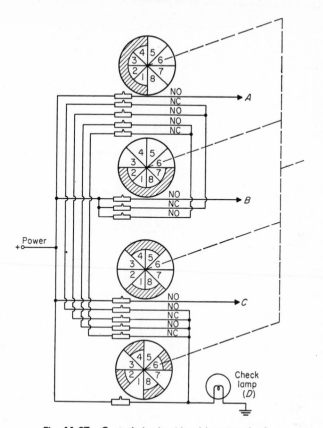

Fig. 11·27   Control circuit with odd parity check.

the switches in the manner indicated by the simplified lamp circuit of Fig. 11·26. A comparison of Fig. 11·26 with the lamp circuit switches in Fig. 11·27 indicates that the switch connections in both circuits are electrically identical.

Step 6. Simplify the cam circuit. As a final step, the cam circuit should be carefully analyzed with an eye toward reduction or simplification. Upon examination, it is noticed that cams A and B both have four consecutive sections cut out. Notice that section 1 of cam B corresponds to section 3 of cam A, thereby eliminating the need for cam B. This simplification could have been recognized from Table 11·6. The final simplified cam circuit is shown in Fig. 11·28.

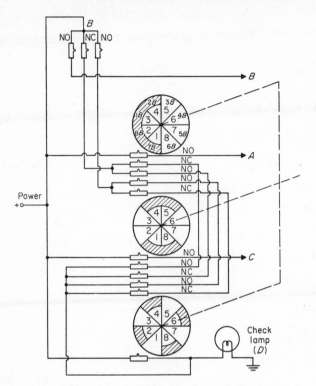

Fig. 11·28   Final cam circuit with provisions for odd parity check.

PROBLEMS

11·1   Design a relay control circuit which will perform the same functions as the cam circuit of Fig. 11·10.

11·2   Design an odd parity-check lamp circuit for Prob. 11·11.

11·3   Design a relay control circuit which will perform the same functions as the cam circuit of Fig. 11·13.

11·4   Design an odd parity-check lamp circuit for Prob. 11·3.

11·5   Design a relay control circuit which will perform the same functions as the cam control circuit of Fig. 11·28. Include provisions for the odd parity-check circuit.

11·6   Design a cam control circuit which will perform the same functions as the relay control circuit of Fig. 11·18.

Answers to Odd-numbered Problems

Chapter 1

1·1	7	**1·3**	9	**1·5**	25	**1·7**	23
1·9	33	**1·11**	0.75	**1·13**	0.625	**1·15**	0.375
1·17	0.9375	**1·19**	0.609375	**1·21**	6.75	**1·23**	4.125
1·25	11.5625	**1·27**	14.4375	**1·29**	51.75	**1·31**	10001
1·33	100011	**1·35**	110110	**1·37**	11011	**1·39**	1001100

Chapter 2

2·1	0++	**2·3**	+++	**2·5**	+−+	**2·7**	−+0
2·9	− − −	**2·11**	−13	**2·13**	−9	**2·15**	10
2·17	8	**2·19**	−5	**2·21**	1101	**2·23**	−11
2·25	1100	**2·27**	111	**2·29**	1001	**2·31**	0+−
2·33	0+0	**2·35**	00+	**2·37**	−00	**2·39**	− − −
2·41	183	**2·43**	68	**2·45**	278	**2·47**	410
2·49	123	**2·51**	300	**2·53**	1,246	**2·55**	1,520
2·57	366	**2·59**	617	**2·61**	0.86328	**2·63**	0.49218
2·65	0.6055	**2·67**	0.7149	**2·69**	0.3046	**2·71**	0.430446+
2·73	0.634530+			**2·75**	0.20000	**2·77**	0.434121+
2·79	0.657473+			**2·81**	11	**2·83**	126
2·85	115			**2·87**	0.34	**2·89**	0.72
2·91	7.66			**2·93**	7.76	**2·95**	756.734
2·97	1042.454			**2·99**	77.77	**2·101**	1110

2·103	10100101000	**2·105**	110100101111
2·107	100010000110101	**2·109**	111110101100001
2·111	1010110.0011	**2·113**	100010000.00010001
2·115	1100111100.011100001	**2·117**	1101001111.0010011

2·119	111100101010.010101100111	2·121	0010 0100 1001	
2·123	0001 0100 0000	2·125	0100 1000 0101	
2·127	0101 0111 0011	2·129	0001 0100 0001 1000	
2·131	869	2·133	484	
2·135	716	2·137	957	
2·139	879	2·141	0101 1001	
2·143	0100 1000 0100	2·145	0100 1100 0101	
2·147	0111 1100 1001	2·149	1010 0100 0101 1011	
2·151	409 2·153 965	2·155	780 2·157 267	
2·159	689	2·161	0101 1011 0001	
2·163	1100 1001 1110	2·165	0010 0000 1001	
2·167	1010 0011 1000	2·169	1100 1101 1010	
2·171	0010 1110 0100	2·173	1111 0111 1111	
2·175	0101 1000 1011	2·177	1000 0011 1011	
2·179	1100 1100 0100	2·181	0110 0100	
2·183	0010 0101 0001	2·185	0010 1010 0001	
2·187	0100 0110 1010	2·189	1010 1010 1010 0010	

2·191	879	2·193	977	2·195	810	
2·197	585	2·199	277	2·201	10	00001
					01	00100
2·203	01 00100	2·205	01 01000	2·207	01	00100
	10 10000		10 01000		01	10000
	01 01000		01 10000		01	01000
2·209	01 01000	2·211	2	2·213	9	
	10 00001					
	01 00010					
	01 10000					
2·215	7	2·217	4	2·219	3	

Chapter 3

3·1	10010	3·3	1100011	3·5	10111000010
3·7	11100100101	3·9	1000011101	3·11	10010110110
3·13	10000010	3·15	1011010110	3·17	1101.01101
3·19	11001101.01	3·21	10	3·23	1100
3·25	100	3·27	111101111	3·29	11001101
3·31	1001101000	3·33	1000100	3·35	111110010

3·37	110011.1	**3·39**	101.111	**3·41**	4,250
3·43	1,409	**3·45**	1,367	**3·47**	2,351
3·49	−1,400	**3·51**	1100	**3·53**	11110010
3·55	1011011000	**3·57**	110	**3·59**	1
3·61	110.0101	**3·63**	1001101	**3·65**	−1001
3·67	−101.111	**3·69**	−110011.100	**3·71**	10100.111
3·73	−101001101	**3·75**	11110111	**3·77**	101010110
3·79	10000110				

Chapter 4

4·1	11	**4·3**	1111	**4·5**	101
4·7	1110	**4.9**	1100	**4·11**	10010
4·13	1011	**4·15**	1000001	**4·17**	100111
4·19	1000110	**4·21**	101000	**4·23**	10010
4·25	100100	**4·27**	1010100	**4·29**	1101001
4·31	10	**4·33**	1	**4·35**	11
4·37	101	**4·39**	110	**4·41**	1 $101\frac{1}{1111}$
4·43	10 $101\frac{1}{1010}$	**4·45**	10 $111\frac{1}{1001}$	**4·47**	10
4·49	11 $100\frac{1}{1000}$	**4·51**	10 $11\frac{1}{1101}$	**4·53**	11 $10\frac{1}{1001}$
4·55	11 $110\frac{1}{1000}$	**4·57**	10 $110\frac{1}{1011}$	**4·59**	10 $\frac{1}{1111}$
4·61	10	**4·63**	8	**4·65**	9
4·67	10	**4·69**	45	**4·71**	45
4·73	44	**4·75**	47	**4·77**	49
4·79	48	**4·81**	0++	**4·83**	+00
4·85	+−−	**4·87**	−++	**4·89**	0−0
4·91	0+−	**4·93**	0+0	**4·95**	0−+
4·97	−0+	**4·99**	+−−	**4·101**	0+0
4·103	0++	**4·105**	+−+	**4·107**	+−−
4·109	+0−	**4·111**	+−−	**4·113**	0+−
4·115	++−	**4·117**	+−−	**4·119**	+−0

Chapter 5

5·1	$AA = A$	**5·3**	$ABA' = 0$
	$A = A$		$0 = 0$
5·5	$ABAB = 1$	**5·7**	$ABCAB = 1$
	$AB = 1$		$ABC = 1$

5·9 $ABCDA' = 0$
$0 = 0$

5·11 $A = A$

5·13 $AB = C$

5·15 $A'B' = C'$

5·17 $ABCDE = F$

5·19 $ABCD = E$

5·21 $A + A' = 1$
$1 = 1$

5·23 $A + B + A = 1$
$A + B = 1$

5·25 $A + B + C + B = 1$
$A + B + C = 1$

5·27 $A + B + A + B' = 1$
$1 = 1$

5·29 $A + B + A + C + D = 1$
$A + B + C + D = 1$

5·31 $A + B + B = 1$
$A + B = 1$

5·33 $A + A + B + C = 1$
$A + B + C = 1$

5·35 $A + B + B + C + B + A = 1$
$A + B + C = 1$

5·37 $A + B + C + D = 1$
No simplification

5·39 $A + A + B + B + C + D + E + B = 1$
$A + B + C + D + E + F = 1$

5·51 $AB + CDE = x$

5·53 $(AB + CD)(EF + G)(H + I) = x$

5·55 $(AB + C'D + EF')(G')(HI + J + K') = x$

5·57 $A[B(C + D') + E'G] + F = N$

5·59 $A(BC' + D)[(E + F)GH + IJ' + K'LM] = N$

Chapter 6

6·1

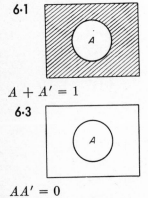

$A + A' = 1$

6·3

$AA' = 0$

6·5

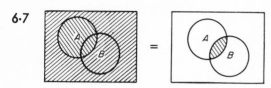

$A(B + C) = AB + AC$

6·7

$A(A' + B) = AB$

6·9

$A \times 1 = A$

6·11 $f = (ABC) + (ABD)$
$f = AB(C + D)$

6·13 $f = ABCD + BCE$
$f = BC(AD + E)$

6·15 $f = (ACE + AD)(CE + CB)$
$f = AC(E + DB)$

6·17 $f = (A + B)[(C + D)A + BCC']$
$f = A(C + D)$

6·19 $f = (A + B + C)[D'BC + (D + B)(A'A)](A + C)$
$f = (A + C)(B + D)$

6·21 $f = (C)\{D[B + B(D + B)] + (C)(D + C')B\}$
$f = BCD$

6·23 $f = (AB + CDE)(AB + C' + D' + E')$
$f = AB$

6·25 $B'[A + A'(B + C)] + C[B(A + C') + A(B' + C)] = f$
$f = AC + B'(A + C)$

6·27 $f = ABC + AB(DC + EF)$
$f = AB(C + EF)$

6·29 $f = A + BC + BDE + FG$
No simplification

6·31 $f = (A + BC')(A + B' + C) + B'D + CD + C'D$
$f = A + D$

6·33 $f = A'[B(A + C')]D'$
$f = A'(BC' + D')$

6·35 $f = (ABC + CD)(DE + A' + B' + C)$
$f = C(AB + D)$

6·37 $f = CB + AB'CD + CD' + AC'$
$f = CB + CD' + A$

6·41 $f = ABC + A'BC + AB'C + A'B'C$
$f = C$

6·43 $f = (A + B + CD)B' + ABC' + AB'C$
$f = AB'AC' + B'CD$

6·45 $f = D(BC + D') + A'B(E'F) + D'EA + AC$
$f = B(CD + A'E'F) + A(D'E + C)$

Chapter 7

7·1 $T_{12} = C + AB(C'A + D)$
$T_{12} = C + AB$
$T_{13} = AB(C' + AD) + C(DC' + A)$
$T_{13} = AB + AC = A(B + C)$
$T_{23} = A + CABC' + DC'$
$T_{23} = A + DC'$

7·5 $T_{12} = AD + AC + B(C + D)$
$T_{12} = A(C + D)$
$T_{13} = A[B + C(C + D)] + AD(CB + C + D)$
$T_{13} = A(B + C + D)$
$T_{23} = C + D + ADAB + CB$
$T_{23} = C + D$

7·11 $T_{12} = A'CD' + A'(E + F') + B$
$T_{12} = A'[CD' + (E + F')] + B$
$T_{13} = A'C + A'(E + F')D' + B(E + F')C + BD'$
$T_{13} = A'(C + D'[E + F']) + B(C[E + F'] + D')$
$T_{32} = D' + CA'B + C(E + F')$
$T_{32} = D' + C[A'B + (E + F')]$

7·15 $T_{12} = A'(F + AC' + BDC') + C[B(AC'F) + D(AF + C')]$
$$+ EF(A + BD + C')$$
$T_{12} = A'(F + BC'D) + CF(B + AD) + (A + B + C')EF$
$T_{13} = A'(BD + A + FC') + C[D(A + FC')] + E$
$T_{13} = A'(BD + FC') + C(D + AB) + E$
$T_{23} = C'F[A + B(CE + D) + A'E]$
$T_{23} = C' + AF + BCEF + BDF + A'EF$

7·17

	A	B	C	D
1	1	AB	0	C+D
2		1	D	A
3			1	C'B
4				1

	A	B	C
1	1	A(C+D)+AB	1
2		1	AC'B+D
			1

	A	B
1	1	AC'B+D+A(C+D)+AB
		1

$T_{12} = A(B + C) + D$

7·25

	A	B	C	D	E		A	B	C	D
1	1	0	E	A'	C		1	0	CD+E	CB+A'
2		1	C'	F	0			1	C'	F
3			1	A	D				1	DB+A
4			1	B						1
5				1						

	A	B	C
	1	F(CB+A')	BCD+ACB+A'DB
		1	F(DB+A)+C'

$T_{12} = [F(DB + A) + C'](BCD + ACB + A'DB) + F(CB + A')$

7·35

	A	B	C	D
1	1	B	0	A'
2		1	D'	E+F'
3	D'	1	C	
4			↑	

	A	C	B	D
1	1	0	B	A'
3		1	D'	C
2			1	E+F'
4				1

	A	C	B
1	1	A'C	A'E+A'F'
3		1	CE+CF'+D'
2			1

$$T_{13} = (A'E + A'F)(CE + CF' + D') + A'C$$
$$T_{13} = A'[D'(E + F') + C]$$

7·45

	A	B	C	D	E	F
1	1	A	0	C	0	0
2	A	1	0	B+D	0	B
3	0	0	1	0	D	C
4	C	B+D	0	1	A	0
5					↑	0
6						1

	A	D	C	B	E	F
1	1	C	0	A	0	0
4	C	1	0	B+D	A	0
3	0	0	1	0	D	C
2	A	B+D	0	1	0	B
5					1	0
6						1

	A	D	C	B	E
1	1	C	0	A	0
4		1	0	B+D	A
3			1	BC	D+BC
2				↑	0
5					1

	A	D	C	B
1	1	C	0	A
2		1	AD+ABC	B+D
3			1	BC
4				1

	A	D	C
1	1	AB+AD+C	ABC
2		1	BC+AD
3			

$$T_{14} = ABC(BC + AD) + AB + AD + C$$
$$T_{14} = A(B + D) + C$$

7·55

	A	B	C	D	E
1	1	0	A	0	B'
2	0	1	0	C+A	A+B
3	A	0	1	B	0
4	0	C+A	B	1	A'
5					1

	A	D	C	B	E
1	1	0	A	0	B'
4		1	B	C+A	A'
3			1	0	0
2				1	A+B
5					1

	A	D	C	B	E
1	1	0	A	0	B'
4		1	B	C+A	A'
3			1	0	0
2				1	A+B
5					1

	A	D	C	B
1	1	A'B'	A	A'B
4		1	B	A+B+C
3			1	0
2				1

	A	D	C
1	1	A'	A
4		1	B
3			1

$$T_{14} = A + A'B = A + B$$

7·65

	A	B	C	D	E	F	G
1	1	0	0	A	0	D	0
2		1	0	C	D'	G	F
3			1	0	B	0	E
4				1	F	0	0
5					1	0	0
6						1	A'
7							1

	A	F	C	D	E	B	G
1	1	D	0	A	0	0	0
6		1	0	0	0	G	A'
3			1	0	B	0	E
4				1	F'	C	0
5					1	D'	0
2						1	F
7							1

	A	F	C	D	E	B
1	1	D	0	A	0	0
6		1	A'E	0	0	A'F+G
3			1	0	B	EF
4				1	F'	C
5					1	D'
2						1

	A	F	C	D	E
1	1	D	0	A	0
6		1	A'E+GEF	A'CF+CG	A'D'F+D'G
3			1	CEF	EFD'+B
4				1	CD'+F'
5					1

	A	F	C	D
1	1	D	0	A
6		1	BD'(A'F+G)+E(A'+FG)	D'F'G+A'CF+CG
3			1	BCD'+BF'+CEF
4				1

	A	F	C
1	1		
6		1	
3			1

Chapter 8

8·21

$\begin{array}{c}AB\\CD\end{array}$	00	01	11	10
00	1	1	1	1
01	1	0	0	0
11	1	0	0	0
10	1	1	1	0

$= A'B' + C'D' + BCD'$

8·31 $BD + B'D'$

8·41

	A	B	C	D	E	F	G
1	1	0	0	A	0	0	0
2		1	0	0	B	$B+D$	0
3			1	0	0	0	$D+C'$
4				1	D	0	BC
5					1	B	0
6						1	0
7							1

	A	B	C	D	E	F
1	1	0	0	A	0	0
2		1	0	0	B	$B+D$
3			1	$BC(D+C')$	0	0
4				1	D	0
5					1	B
6						1

	A	B	C	D	E
1	1	0	0	A	0
2		1	0	0	B
3			1	BCD	0
4				1	D
5					1

	A	B	C	D
1	1	0	0	A
2		1	0	BD
3			1	BCD
4				1

	A	B	C
1	1	ABD	$ABCD$
2		1	BCD
3			1

$$T_{12} = ABD + ABCD + ABD(1+C) = ABD$$

$T_{12} = ABD$

$= ABD$

	A	C	B	D	E	F	G
1	1	0	0	A	0	0	0
3		1	0	0	0	0	D+C'
2			1	0	B	B+D	0
4				1	D	0	BC
5					1	B	0
6						1	0
7							1

	A	C	B	D	E	F
1	1	0	0	A	0	0
3		1	0	BC(D+C')	0	0
2			1	0	B	B+D
4				1	D	0
5					1	B
6						1

	A	C	B	D	E
1	1	0	0	A	0
3		1	0	BCD	0
2			1	0	B
4				1	D
5					1

	A	C	B	D
1	1	0	0	A
3		1	0	BCD
2			1	BD
4				1

	A	C	B
1	1	ABCD	ABD
3		1	BCD
2			1

$T_{13} = ABCD + ABCD = ABCD$

8·45 $f_x = Y'Z + ZX' + ZY + UWX + XYZ$

$f_x = V(Y'Z + YZ + WXZ') + V'(Y'Z + YZ)$
$ = UWX + Z$

8·51 $f_x = B'CD' + A'CD'E + AB$
$f_x = AB + CD'E + CD'A'B'E' + CD'AB'E'$
$\quad = AB + CD'(E + B')$

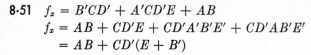
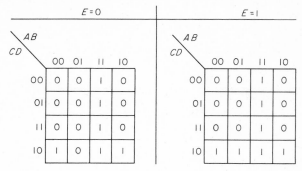

	E = 0					E = 1			
CD \ AB	00	01	11	10	CD \ AB	00	01	11	10
00	0	0	1	0	00	0	0	1	0
01	0	0	1	0	01	0	0	1	0
11	0	0	1	0	11	0	0	1	0
10	1	0	1	1	10	1	1	1	1

8·55 $f_x = B'CG + BC'F + BEC' + B'C'D'$
$f_x = F(BC' + B'C'D') + B'C'D' + BC'E + G(B'C)$
$\quad = BC'(F + E) + B'(C'D + CG)$

F = 0, G = 0:

DE \ BC	00	01	11	10
00	1	0	0	0
01	1	0	0	1
11	0	0	0	1
10	0	0	0	0

F = 1, G = 0:

DE \ BC	00	01	11	10
00	1	0	0	1
01	1	0	0	1
11	0	0	0	1
10	0	0	0	1

F = 0, G = 1:

DE \ BC	00	01	11	10
00	1	1	0	0
01	1	1	0	1
11	0	1	0	1
10	0	1	0	0

F = 1, G = 1:

DE \ BC	00	01	11	10
00	1	1	0	1
01	1	1	0	1
11	0	1	0	1
10	0	1	0	1

Chapter 9

9·1

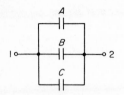

9·5

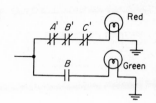

9·11

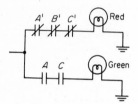

9·15

9·21

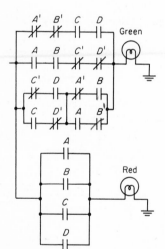

9·25

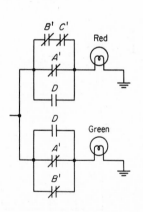

Chapter 10

10·1

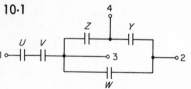

$$T_{12} = UVW + UV(WX + YZ)$$
$$= UV(W + YZ)$$
$$= UVW + UVYZ$$

1	UVW	UV	0
	1	0	Y
		1	Z
			1

10·5

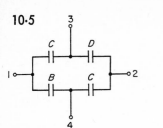

$$T_{12} = BC + AB'CD + CD = BC + CD$$

$$
\begin{array}{cccc}
1 & 0 & C & B \\
  & 1 & D & C \\
  &   & 1 & 0 \\
  &   &   & 1
\end{array}
$$

10·11

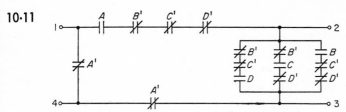

$$T_{12} = AB'C'D' + A'BC'D' + A'B'CD' + A'B'C'D$$
$$= AB'C'D' + A'(BC'D' + B'CD' + B'C'D)$$

$$
\begin{array}{ccc}
1 & AB'C'D' & A' \\
  & 1 & (BC'D + B'CD' + B'C'D) \\
  &   & 1
\end{array}
$$

$$
\begin{array}{cccc}
1 & AB'C'D' & 0 & A' \\
  & 1 & (BC'D' + B'CD' + B'C'D) & 0 \\
  &   & 1 & A' \\
  &   &   & 1
\end{array}
$$

10·15

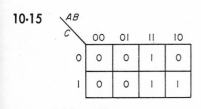 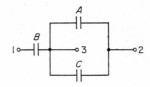

$$T_{12} = B(A + C)$$

$$
\begin{array}{ccc}
1 & AB & B \\
  & 1 & C \\
  &   & 1
\end{array}
$$

Index

Addition, binary fractions, 36
  binary integers, 33
  binary mixed numbers, 37
  excess-3 code, 64–66
  ternary code, 67
Ambiguities, 165
AND circuit, 73

Binary-coded decimal notation
  system, 25
Binary conditions, 5
Binary point, 7
Biquinary code, 29
Bistable multivibrator, 6
Bit, 7
Boolean laws and language, 85
Boolean matrix, Boolean function determination, 127–
  129
  concepts of, 125–129
  expansion of, 194–198
  multiterminal circuit analysis,
  129–132
  nodal elimination in, 125
Boolean multiplication, 73

Circuit simplification, criteria,
  98–102
  double-dual method, 103–105
Closed-path tracing technique,
  113–116
Closure analysis (see Closed-path
  tracing technique)
Complementary techniques,
  44–56
Contradictions, 165
Controls, determining number of,
  211
Conversion, binary to decimal,
  8–9
  direct method, 8–9
  double-dabble method, 9
  binary fractions to decimal
  equivalents, 10
  binary to Gray code, 27
  binary to octal, 21
  Boolean equation into logical
  diagram, 86
  decimal digits to biquinary
  code, 29
  decimal fractions to binary
  fractions, 13

Conversion, decimal fractions to
    octal, 20
  decimal integers to binary,
    11
  decimal integers to octal, 19
  delta circuit into equivalent
    series-parallel, 118
  direct method, 11–12
  Gray code to binary, 27–28
  lamp circuit for odd-parity
    check into switches, 226–
    228
  octal to binary 22
  octal to decimal, 19
  octal fractions to decimal, 20
  transmission function into
    circuit by matrix expan-
    sion, 194
  trinary to binary, 17
  two-terminal circuit into three
    terminals by matrix
    expansion, 195
  verbal statement into Boolean
    equation, 169
Cyclic code (*see* Gray code)

Decimal number, concepts of, 4
  switch representation of, 5
Division, binary, 61
Double-dual technique, 103–105
Double negation, 108
Duality, 103
Dummy state, 218

Excess-3 code, 25

First distributive law, 81–82
First-order logic circuit, 81
Flip-flop (*see* Bistable
    multivibrator)

Gray code, analog-to-digital
    conversion, 27
  concepts of, 26
  conventional type, 218

Input-output table, 167

Karnaugh maps, addition type,
    163
  adjacencies in, 137
  concepts of, 135
  expressed in binary, 209
  expressed in decimal, 209
  five-variable type, 150–155
  four-variable type, 142–147
  multiplication type, 162–163
  six-variable type, 155–162
  three-variable type, 139–142
  two-variable type, 135–139

Literals, 85
Logic, orders of, 87
  symbols of, 89
Logic tree, 202–205
Logical addition, 76
Logical multiplication, 73

Matrix, construction of, 122
  expansion of, 194–198

Matrix, simplification of, 123–124
  substitution of node connection
    values in, 124
  (*See also* Boolean matrix)
Minimization, of diodes, 200–205
  logic tree method, 202
  in relays, 200
Multiplication, binary, 58
Multivibrator, 6

Negation, of normally open
    parallel circuit, 105
  of normally open series circuit,
    105
  principles of, 72
  rules for, 106
Nixie tube, 215
Node numbers, concepts of, 112
  expressed as Boolean func-
    tions, 122
  in matrix construction, 122
Noncombinational circuits, 112
Notation procedure, 167

Odd-parity check, 221–226
1's complement, 53–54

Parallel circuit logic, 78–79
Parallel circuit notation, 76
Parity check, 220–221
Partial product, 59
Perforated tape, 8
Positional value, binary, 7
  concepts, 2

Positional value, progressions of, 3
  trinary system, 16
Pyramid (*see* Logic tree)

Radix, binary system, 6
  decimal system, 1
  trinary system, 16
Redundancy in self-checking, 220
Reflected binary (*see* Gray code)

Second distributive law, 83–84
Series circuit logic, 78
Series circuit notation, 73
7421 code, 28
Specifications, analysis of, 167
  concepts of, 165–166
Spurious terms, 199
State coding, concepts of, 208–
    210
  translation into control
    circuitry, 213–218
  uses of, 211
State diagram, 210
States of devices, 71
Subtraction, binary, 1's
    complement, 54
  2's complement, 51
  decimal, 9's complements,
    47–48
    10's complements, 44–45
    10's complements with
      negative remainders, 46
  direct binary, fractions and
    mixed numbers, 42
    integers, 39
  ternary code, 68–69

Switch notation, 71
Switch representation, 72
Synthesis, concepts of, 165
Synthesis map, ambiguity in, 170
    construction of, 170
    contradiction in, 170
    conversion into Boolean
        function, 171
    design of switch circuit with,
        180–182
    unfilled boxes in, 170

Ternary system (*see* Trinary
    system)
Toggle (*see* Bistable
    multivibrator)
Trinary system, 16
    quantities of, 17

Truth table, expanded, 102–103
2's complement, 50

Uncorrected remainder, 48
Universe table, 95–98

Variables, 85
Venn diagrams, AND possibilities,
    93
    concepts of, 92
    OR possibilities, 93
    other possibilities, 94

Wye-to-delta transformation,
    116–118

Zero, purpose of, 2